THE MAN BEHIND THE HERO:
SEARING ROMANCES,
SECRET LOVES,
AND THE SILENT GRIEF OF HEARTBREAK

Lupe Velez—A hot-blooded Mexican spitfire, her stormy affair with Coop was the scandal of Hollywood. Driven to a frenzy when he lost interest, she swore she would kill him—and tried.

Countess Dorothy di Frasso—Taking her pleasures like a man, she lured Coop to Rome and transformed the Montana cowboy into a princely lover, the rakish darling of European society.

Rocky Cooper—An Eastern deb with money, breeding and class, her marriage to Coop was painfully scarred by his flagrant infidelities—yet Rocky vowed she would never let him go.

Patricia Neal—Swept up in an ill-starred romance with Coop, she was shunned by society and ravaged by guilt. Years later, she would pay a terrible price for the sin of falling in love.

"A repository of treasures . . . the most fulfilling Cooper biography of the decade."
—*Seattle Post*

Bantam Books by Hector Arce

GARY COOPER: An Intimate Biography
THE SECRET LIFE OF TYRONE POWER

GARY COOPER

An Intimate Biography

Hector Arce

BANTAM BOOKS
TORONTO · NEW YORK · LONDON

This low-priced Bantam Book
has been completely reset in a type face
designed for easy reading, and was printed
from new plates. It contains the complete
text of the original hard-cover edition.
NOT ONE WORD HAS BEEN OMITTED.

GARY COOPER: AN INTIMATE BIOGRAPHY

A Bantam Book / published by arrangement with
William Morrow & Company, Inc.

PRINTING HISTORY

William Morrow edition published November 1979
Bantam edition / August 1980

ISBN 0-553-14130-9

Published simultaneously in the United States and Canada

PRINTED IN THE UNITED STATES OF AMERICA

0 9 8 7 6 5 4 3 2 1

Acknowledgments

In the writing of this biography, I am especially grateful to Joseph Adamson for his incisive analysis of the films of Gary Cooper.

My thanks also go to Diana Dreiman for permission to extract from *The Films of Fred Zinnemann*, her 1971 master of arts thesis at the University of California at Los Angeles.

Many others unselfishly cooperated, including the staff of the library of the Academy of Motion Picture Arts and Sciences, as well as the following who shared personal insights or offered their professional assistance: Gene Andrewski, James Bacon, De Witt Bodeen, David Bradley, Bill Chapman, Brian Marx Culhane, Robert B. Cushman, Walt Daugherty, Mrs. Delmar Daves, Fitzroy Davis, Lindsay M. Doran, Mrs. William Goetz, Henry Golas, the late Mrs. Samuel Goldwyn, Roberta Haynes, the late Stuart Heisler, Mary Welsh Hemingway, Gail Hensley, Tab Hunter, Rodney Kemerer, Richard Lamparski, June Lockhart, Rouben Mamoulian, Ted Montague, Colleen Moore, Howard Prouty, Esther Ralston, Charles (Buddy) Rogers, David E. Shepard, Richard Simonton, L. Allan Smith, Phyllis Thaxter, King Vidor, Mrs. Jack Warner, Stuart Whitman, and Teresa Wright. To them and to others who requested anonymity, my deepest thanks.

North Hollywood   HECTOR ARCE
October 1979

Prologue

Another era had passed, longtime observers of the Hollywood scene bemoaned. What kind of town was it that couldn't accommodate its most luminous event, and had to stage it out of town?

After ten years at the overcrowded Pantages Theatre at Hollywood and Vine, the annual self-glorifying rites—the Academy Awards—were being transferred some seventeen miles west to the less ornate but larger Santa Monica Civic Auditorium. Yet, the industry had survived many other periods of change, as it would this one. One thing wouldn't be changed. No matter from where they emanated, the thirty-third annual ceremonies sponsored by the Academy of Motion Picture Arts and Sciences would appear to a worldwide television audience as a spectacle filled with glamour, laughter, and even some suspense.

The high drama of the evening was expected to be the appearance of Elizabeth Taylor, a Best Actress nominee for *Butterfield Eight,* who only a month before had won a death-bout with pneumonia, healing the rift with a public that had disapproved of her stealing Eddie Fisher from her good friend Debbie Reynolds. But the scene-stealer of the evening turned out to be James Stewart, standing in for Gary Cooper, who was being awarded an honorary Oscar. Stewart choked back tears when he said, "I am very honored to accept this award tonight for Gary Cooper. I am sorry he's not here to accept it, but I know he's sitting by the television set tonight, and, Coop, I want you to know I'll get it to you right away. With it goes all the friendship, and affection, and the admiration . . . and the deep respect of all of us. We're very, very proud of you, Coop. All of us are tremendously proud."

Those in attendance, unaware of the drama being played in the Cooper home, were dumbfounded at Stewart's inexplicable display.

At the starkly contemporary Cooper residence on Baroda Drive in Holmby Hills, the actor, his wife Rocky, and their daughter Maria waited for Jimmy and Gloria Stewart to arrive with producer Jerry Wald. They had watched the TV show with Cooper's agent and friend Charles Feldman and Samuel and Frances Goldwyn.

Cooper met Stewart at the door and put his arm around him. Stewart was upset because he had publicly indulged his emotions. He had opened the floodgates and the inquisitive press would soon descend on them all. An announcement would have to be made confirming the news Cooper himself had learned only a few weeks before, his wife staunchly shouldering the burden of the impending tragedy for nearly a year. But not tonight. Gary Cooper and his friends would converse until two the following morning, when the ailing actor excused himself.

HOW ILL IS GARY COOPER? So asked a headline the next day over a United Press International story written by Rick Du Brow. The film community was coming to the realization that Gary Cooper hadn't been chosen for the honor solely because he more than any other actor typified "The New Frontier," a catchall phrase for the domestic and international reforms planned by incoming President John F. Kennedy. A sentimental Academy, aware of Cooper's grave illness, may have wanted to let him know one last time how much they appreciated what he stood for. From that point on, whenever a person was named to receive an honorary Oscar, there would be the suspicion that the honoree was gravely ill. More often than not the conjecture was well founded.

In April of 1960, the actor had undergone a prostatectomy at Massachusetts General Hospital in Boston, purportedly because of an enlarged prostate gland. No sooner had he returned to his home in California than he was admitted to Cedars of Lebanon Hospital to have part of his bowel removed.

He was sufficiently recovered to go to England to make a film that fall, although he was totally exhausted when he returned to California.

Two days before Christmas, while being examined by his physician, Dr. Rexford Kennamer, it was discovered that the cancer had spread throughout his body. The disease was terminal. Dr. Kennamer let the Coopers enjoy Christmas before revealing the tragic news to Rocky and Maria on December 27.

Gary Cooper might have wondered why he was being thrust into the spotlight again. In his own mind, he'd been coasting on past laurels for eight years, often delivering sloppy performances in badly written vehicles. Suddenly, however, he was a symbol and myth to be honored and cherished. His time, in several ways, had come. And he had come a long way in his time.

Some would have described his earliest years in California in less than admiring terms. His proficiency as a swordsman in the boudoir had been as much a hindrance as a help at the start of his career. To his detractors, he was an opportunistic stud—the subject of mild contempt—who caught on as an actor by dallying with influential women who could do him the most professional good. He'd bed-hopped from perfumed percales to satin sheets, until he'd reached the dubious apogee, playing the pampered lapdog to a criminally rich American heiress, an Italian countess by marriage. Given his appearance, which became more Grant Wood

American Gothic as he grew older, with personal attitudes evolving to match the image, Gary Cooper's had been an erratically, upwardly mobile Pilgrim's Progress.

On April 19, 1961, two days after the Academy Awards, *The Los Angeles Mirror* reported in a front-page headline: GARY COOPER HAS CANCER. Rogers & Cowan, his public relations firm, would orchestrate the death watch. In a memorandum issued to the press, the company stated, "We are presently compiling detailed and comprehensive background information on Mr. Cooper which should be completed within the next few days. Of course, this material will be made immediately available to you."

The mobilization began. Obituary writers for major newspapers were updating their material on the star. Book publishers began making discreet inquiries of Cooper's friends about the possibility of publishing an authorized biography. A film documentary on Cooper's life and career was being discussed. Meanwhile, the days dwindled.

Cooper, whom the public saw as lean, leathery, and weathered, had a surprising streak of vanity in his makeup. He'd undergone facial cosmetic surgery three years previously, and his hair had been dyed a sandy brown to complement his more youthful appearance. Now he was too ill to care, the natural grey of his hair beginning to show through where the dye had left it.

Pain was constantly with him. When it was less intense, he sat up in his easy chair, contemplating the beautiful garden view from the window and seeing guests.

He lent strength to his wife during these last days, and she returned it a thousandfold. Throughout their marriage, she had acted as his buffer, protecting him from ordinary and extraordinary demands on his time and energy, making herself the villainess to many in the process. Since he was a loner, she'd made it possible for him to periodically isolate himself, to be both removed and remote, to have the open space so vital to his well-being. Again she was protective and strong, showing him and the rest of the world the true grit of which she was made.

Gary Cooper was no longer being spared, for he was being forced to meet the catastrophe head-on. This was his final test as a man, and he wanted to appear the least perturbed by the ordeal. He and his wife would continue living as normally as possible for as long as he was able. He had recently gotten out of bed to act as best man at the wedding of Fred Zinnemann, his director in *High Noon,* and had also run a print of *The Naked Edge,* the film he'd made in England, to determine if it should be further edited.

He comforted those who bemoaned a higher being's dirty trick. "I have no regrets," he told them. "It's been full and rich . . . a wonderful life."

The choices he'd made in his personal life hadn't always been the happiest ones, but they were, in retrospect, the right ones. Throughout his career of nearly one hundred motion pictures, he'd invariably done the right thing. He was, after all, the White Knight.

Chapter 1

It was a pubescent thirteen-year-old's fantasy that captured his imagination and caused the initial stirrings in his loins. The leitmotiv would recur for the rest of his life, a clue to the aspirations of the young man who would become Gary Cooper.

In the years prior to World War I, he and his brother Arthur, six years older, had been sent from their native Montana to their parents' homeland. They were living on their paternal grandfather's farm in Bedfordshire, England, while attending Dunstable, their father's alma mater.

Grandfather Cooper's modest grounds stood next to the vast estate of the Duke of Bedfordshire. The Cooper boys would peek through a privet hedge to see formal, careful tended gardens set against a backdrop of manicured cypress trees. On many an evening, phaetons would drive up the long, graveled path. Footmen would assist the exquisitely gowned grand ladies and their well-groomed escorts as they entered the baronial mansion, where excitement and light streamed from every window. The young boy, Frank James Cooper, would look at the goings-on with great longing. He would become heady imagining the smell of the perfume the women wore, recalling the creamy shoulders of some and the décolletage that the more daring of them exposed. He yearned to be one of those dandified men, to be able to stroke the silken flesh of the women they were with. Never before had he realized how narrow and constricting were the wide-open spaces of Montana. Those close to him would be aware of his desire to become part of a sophisticated, cultivated milieu at the time that the public at large considered him little more than the tall American from the West. He would spend a lifetime straddling both worlds.

Hollywood, where he would find the fame that would make it possible for him to mingle in the most rarefied circles, was to become a macrocosm of the Duke's estate, although he may not have perceived how he would ache to belong to "The Industry" when he arrived in southern California on Thanksgiving Day of 1924. For he had no acting ambitions at first, drifting into work as a movie extra and going on to play some bit roles because he couldn't find work as an editorial cartoonist.

Prohibition notwithstanding, the town in the mid-1920s was a place where, as F. Scott Fitzgerald put it in *The Last Tycoon,* "beautiful felines were having drinks and fun." The orgies of excesses, which in the previous ten years had led to scandals still written and talked about today, were no longer those of the flesh. Or so the Hays office, created in 1921 to police the morals of the modern-day Sodom, had dictated.

Now, the most visible and famous elements of the film colony shifted gears. They were trying to pass themselves off as solid gentry, but, what with their often-excessive pretensions, they looked jerry-built. Hollywood was professing to be adopting a more circumspect way of life as the Jazz Age was being ushered in elsewhere. The hanky-panky nevertheless continued—it always does—although it wasn't as overt as in the past. Artists were subscribing to the Eleventh Commandment that thou shalt not get caught succumbing to one's favorite addiction or indulging in one's preferred aberration.

The most apparent excesses were now material ones, stars vying to determine who could flaunt the

most outlandishly expensive personal trappings. They
had all the money they wanted and the entire world in
which to spend it. For some movie queens, this entailed
casting themselves as real-life Henry James heroines
and buying husbands with European titles—some of
them even royal. Dagmar Godowsky, whose career as a
silent film vamp ended at about this time, lashed out
with a parting shot at these indulgences before the
downturn in her career forced her to tour in vaudeville:
"All those empty heads and ermine tails."

Laughing, often ingenuous cynicism and innocent
corruption combined with the deliciously clear, orange-
scented air when Frank James Cooper first arrived in
southern California. With a grubstake of $400, he
hoped to be hired by a Los Angeles newspaper. At the
moment, he was as far removed from the world of
make-believe Hollywood as he was from his native
Montana. His parents were similarly displaced. The
elder Cooper retired after one year as a Justice of the
Montana Supreme Court to administer the estates of
two relatives, who'd recently died. These cousins were
the wealthy branch of the family, their holdings including what later became the townsite of Lincoln, Nebraska.
They moved to Wyoming, selling out their holdings
there for several hundred thousand dollars before
moving on to what they thought would be The Promised Land of California. Judge Cooper, as he would always be called in the future, had made out the wills of
these cousins, who died in short order, leaving him to
supervise the disbursement of their holdings . . . to
other relatives.

Montana, in more than one way, was the end of
the trail for white men in the nineteenth century. It was
the farthest point of the Lewis and Clark expedition
which explored 1,600 miles up the Missouri River in
1805. The territory was also the setting for Custer's
vainglorious last stand at Little Big Horn in 1876,
which resulted in the Indian massacre of five companies
of the Seventh Cavalry under the American Lieutenant

Colonel's command. Over the next few years, in the 1880s and 1890s, Montana would also prove to be the pot at the end of the rainbow. Copper and gold mining flourished. Capital, railroads, and new technology made it possible for many to find their fortunes there. During that period the town of Helena had fifty millionaires (the total population was only in the tens of thousands), and they competed with each other in building absurdly ornamented mansions.

Gary Cooper's father, Charles H. Cooper, was a man set apart. He'd emigrated to Montana from Bedfordshire in 1885 at the age of nineteen, four years before Montana was admitted to the Union as the forty-first state. Although he came of farming stock, he planned to become a lawyer. He worked at the Northern Pacific Railroad roundhouse in Helena to finance his studies at the local college. His progress, predictably, was slower than that of entrepreneurs in copper and gold who became rich overnight.

He was still working on the railroad, though American citizenship was now his, when Alice Brazier came to Montana in 1893. She was of distant French stock which had settled in the English shipbuilding center of Gillingham in Kent. Her brother, Alfred, had preceded her to Montana and urged her to visit him there. He and his wife needed another feminine hand to help in the raising of their infant children. The trip was an adventure in a primitive land. She ensured her safe delivery back to England by depositing the return fare in a local bank. The silver lode in Montana had been petering out over the last few years, however, and the freezing of the bank's assets coincided with her desire to return to England. She found herself stranded in a foreign land.

Alfred introduced her to his friend, Charles Cooper, who knew a little bit about law, having studied it at night for the past eight years. He counseled her over the next few weeks on the alternatives open to her, and the one that eventually seemed the most suitable to them both was that they should marry.

Their first son, Arthur, was born in 1895, and the couple bought a two-story brick house on Eleventh Avenue shortly thereafter, which backed on Last Chance Gulch, the main street of Helena. The gold strike of 1864 had created a hell-raising boom town called Last Chance Gulch. This became the territorial capital in 1882, and the name was changed to Helena as a more sedate element colonized the town.

By the time Frank James Cooper was born on May 7, 1901, his father had been admitted to the state bar, and the family seemed permanently settled in the area. Alice Brazier Cooper, however, never gave up on her long-range plan to return to England, where her sons could be raised in a more civilized environment. This desire was the reason for her constant bickering with her husband.

"The story of the Coopers' marriage reads surprisingly like the plot of a Western," René Jordan wrote in *Gary Cooper,* "and their marital conflict between inflexible lawman and genteel lady has prophetic overtones in their son's future films, from *The Last Outlaw* to *The Virginian* to *High Noon.*"

Cooper made modest progress as a lawyer over the next few years, also getting caught up in Republican party politics. When Theodore Roosevelt made his Western campaign swing in the Presidential election of 1904, Cooper was delegated to introduce him in the various state precincts on the President's itinerary. The spoils he received for his volunteer work was an appointment as Assistant to the United States Attorney for Montana.

The family developed sufficient financial resources for the elder Cooper to purchase the Seven-Bar-Nine, a six-hundred acre railroad land-grant ranch in 1906. He now had a place to turn his boys loose in the summer. It was a dusty day's ride by horse and carriage—sixty miles in all—from the family house in Helena to the ranch, located in the bend of the Missouri River near the Big Belt Mountains. The land was uncommonly fertile, and it was adjacent to thousands of acres of free government grazing land.

When his wife became seriously ill in 1910—it could well have been a lingering case of homesickness— her doctor advised a sea voyage. She took her sons back to spend the summer in England. Arthur was fifteen and Frank was nine that year. The younger son had recently developed an interest in art, having seen the Charles Russell mural of Lewis and Clark at Ross Hole, which was displayed in the State Capitol Building. He had developed a precocious interest in girls at about the same time, he and his brother Arthur, who shared a front bedroom upstairs, yelling like banshees out their window at any who happened to pass by.

The boys were exposed to a summer of shabbily genteel culture before they returned to Montana for the fall school term. Their mother, however, was devising a plan. When her doctor urged her to take another sea voyage the following summer, she persuaded her husband to come along with her and the boys. The state legislature was not in session, and the town of Helena was virtually dead, so the elder Cooper agreed. During this trip, Alice Cooper told her husband that he should at least allow their sons to have a classic English education.

It took her a year to persuade him. Finances were tight, yet if the boys and their mother lived with their grandfather, they could afford to matriculate at Dunstable public school.

At first, the boys were regarded as barbarians by their British schoolmates, and the merciless hazing they were subjected to had them wondering who was actually the more civilized, they, the innocents abroad, or the malicious home-grown products. Within months, however, they adjusted to life there, their broad Western speech becoming clipped British and their manner of dress becoming more formal.

Arthur stayed on after he graduated from Dunstable, while Frank continued his studies there. He wasn't a distinguished student, having a short attention span. The only subject which captured his imagination was art, and he passed many idle hours drawing cartoons and caricatures.

When the United States entered the First World War in 1917, Mrs. Cooper took her two sons hurriedly back to Montana. She and her husband wanted them as far away from the European battlefields as possible.

Arthur, however, was now twenty-two, and he promptly enlisted in the service, to be shipped back to the front from which his parents had tried to extricate him. Frank, now sixteen and having reached his full height of nearly six-foot-three, returned to school in Helena. His first day there, he arrived wearing a well-cut black suit over a shirt with an Eton collar. His clothing was virtually torn from his back. The next day, he returned to school in overalls. His Western drawl returned in short order. So much, at least outwardly, for the three years expended in making him over into an English gentleman. And nothing his mother could do could turn him into a scholar.

The Seven-Bar-Nine had been turning a modest profit over the last few years, its management delegated to a foreman. With the onset of war, manpower became unavailable. The best solution, given Charles Cooper's commitments in Helena, was for Frank to drop out of school to run the ranch and tend the five hundred head of cattle. His mother decided to join him. They stayed there until the end of the war in 1918, when Arthur and their ranch hands were able to resume operations.

Frank Cooper at seventeen was of an age when his high school education might well have been completed. But, because of his three years at Dunstable, there were many gaps in his education. He may have taken some effete courses in England, but they had no application to the rough and tumble of the Montana school system. Some of his English credits, however, were accepted, and if he applied himself, he might complete the four-year high school curriculum in two-and-a-half years.

Even if he adapted to this accelerated pace, he'd be twenty when he graduated from high school.

Alice Cooper knew her son could never succeed in this goal if he stayed in Helena, noticing the cow eyes her younger son was making at several local girls. She decided to send her less than studious son to Bozeman, seventy miles southeast of Helena, to complete his schooling. The old and decorous town was the gateway to Yellowstone National Park. Local ordinances prohibited dancing in beer halls at any time and anywhere else after midnight. It was illegal to drink beer while standing. Young Frank should have no distractions from his studies. And if his high spirits threatened to get the best of him, he could always work out his frustrations while making money as a guide at Yellowstone.

A classmate of the time, Mildred Blankenship, recalled Frank Cooper as a boy who liked to draw cowboys and Indians in the margins of her notebooks. She regretted that she wasn't one of his schoolday girl friends, but she described him as "just about the best-looking fellow in school. All the girls were sweet on him. But, he was shy and never escorted the girls much."

He was long, rangy, and handsome. Because he carried himself in an apologetic manner which implied he was unaware of his attractiveness, he became even more attractive to females of all ages. He seemed tentative with girls of his own age, bringing out maternal feelings in them. Any who got close enough to him soon realized that his attitude toward them had little to do with that of the bumbling little boy. He was similarly retiring with older women, as well as polite and deferential, so they too were drawn to him . . . theoretically for different reasons.

The first mentor to take a true maternal interest in him, other than his mother, was Ida W. Davis, one of his teachers at Gallatin County High School. She taught him English and mathematics, put him on the debating team, and assigned him to join dramatics class. "She

13

was the woman partly responsible for me giving up cowboy-ing and going to college," Cooper later told Hollywood columnist Joe Hyams. "She was a wonderful person who hauled a lot of us kids out of the mire of indecision."

One of his best friends in school was Harvey Markham, who'd had polio as a child and was left with both legs paralyzed. His father had outfitted a special Model "T" Ford for him, which Harvey could drive by using only his hands. The handicapped boy would pick up his able-bodied friend every morning. Speeding down a mountain one morning on their way to school, Harvey tried to engage the brake. It didn't hold. Then he took hold of two levers, one for the emergency brake and the other for the reverse gear. They broke off in his hand. The front wheels of the car jackknifed when they hit the bottom of the hill. Harvey was thrown clear through the canvas top. Frank was not so fortunate. He was thrown to the ground, and the car, standing for an instant on its hood, then rolled on him.

Harvey's injuries were minimal and so, apparently, were Frank's. A doctor advised him that he'd torn ligaments in his hip and that he should stay in bed for a few days. Then he should get on a horse to regain strength on his weakened side. (It wasn't until he was past forty, after he'd fallen off a horse while shooting a picture, that X-rays revealed Cooper actually had fractured his hip in the accident.)

Always one to follow the orders of his elders, Frank proceeded to ride despite the agonizing pain he was suffering.

He described to silent screen star Colleen Moore the long days he would spend riding, wearing only a pair of pants, with his chest exposed to the sun, anticipating the horse's every move so as not to jostle his injured hip. Should he guess wrongly, his reward would be a stabbing, lingering pain. He became so adept as a horseman that he and his steed eventually moved as one. As a result of the accident, his walk was stiff and somehow off balance. It was a readily identifiable gait, distinctive in that it could suggest emotion when photographed from the back.

With his schooling ended at Bozeman, Frank wanted to go on to art school in Chicago. His parents didn't approve. Despite his well-proven limitations as a student, they suggested a more conventional education. He selected Grinnell College in Iowa, where he would spend the next three years.

During this period, his father was elected to the Montana Supreme Court. Also at this time, Montana was in the grips of a recession. Despite his prestigious position, Judge Cooper knew that his time was limited there. The biennial session of the Legislature, with the attendant Supreme Court hearings, was the principal event in Helena. It was too little activity and too little money for Judge Cooper. The deaths of his cousins were an omen and an opportunity to revive his pioneer spirit. He and his wife would move to California.

Their younger son was dating a Grinnell coed he would later identify only as Doris. He thought he wanted to get married. He left school, returning to his hometown to work as an editorial cartoonist during the 1924 Presidential campaign. He expected the girl to follow him there. The job ended, partly due to the amateurish quality of his work. He was both disappointed and relieved when Doris informed him that she was going to marry an Iowa druggist instead. She didn't envision a future for herself with him in Montana. Neither, subsequently, did he, and Cooper moved to California to join his parents, and to find newspaper work. He was told he was not talented enough an artist, and was forced to take odd jobs. Frank worked briefly as a canvassing salesman for a local photographer, getting two dollars a day. He also sold advertising space for theatrical curtains. Any money he made wasn't enough to cover his already-developed spendthrift habits. These were for incidentals, for he lived with his parents, who gave him lodging and catered to his enormous appetite. Yet, his bankroll was dwindling. He couldn't always depend on his parents to tide him over, since they were commuting between San Diego and Los Angeles while the elder Cooper looked after his clients' interest. Once, when he tried to wire his father for money, the telegraph office wouldn't accept his collect telegram.

He'd been in Los Angeles three weeks when he ran into two friends from Montana, also the sons of lawyers, named Jimmy Galeen and Jimmy Calloway. The two told him they were doing riding and stunt work at the movie studios for ten dollars a day. That was very good money for the time, and they suggested he do likewise. They got him together with Slim Talbot, one of Montana's most notable rodeo stars, who'd drifted into movie work and was now recruiting other cowhands. Yes, Cooper could get such work too, but first he'd have to go through an apprenticeship paying five dollars a day. Once he'd completed it—an intensive regimen requiring him to leap onto horses, then fall off them, with attendant bruises and contusions—he could qualify for the higher salary . . . which Cooper eventually did.

"I quit trying to draw when I started falling off horses for a living," Cooper said about the field he drifted into. In his first 1½ years in the movies he was in fifty films.

William Wyler tested him for Universal's Mustang two-reelers. "It was all routine, but it taught you the business of movement," Wyler told his biographer, Axel Madsen. "It was all action. We didn't have real actors, but cowboys who could ride. I made a test of cowboys one day. The test consisted of riding down the Western street, making a flying dismount, running up to the camera, counting to ten and making a Pony Express mount, which was getting on a horse already running. That was the test. Years later, Gary Cooper told me he had been one of the hopefuls in my test. He wasn't fast enough, I guess, because he wasn't hired."

"Some days," Cooper said, "I was a cowboy before lunch and an Indian in the afternoon." It was while working as an extra in *The Lucky Horseshoe*, with Tom Mix, that he definitely decided to stick with acting, and what convinced him was Mix's weekly salary of $17,500 to his own $50.

Myrna Loy, a twenty-year-old neighbor from Helena, was also trying to get her start in show business. Cooper had only vague recollections of Myrna Williams, the name she was born with, since she'd lived in Helena only two years before he and his brother Arthur went to school in England. He was four years her senior, and among children, that much of an age gap is generations apart. Previously, the girl and her family had lived on a cattle ranch outside Helena, moving into a house on Fifth Avenue, six blocks away from the Coopers, so that the girl could attend public school. Although their parents knew each other, Myrna herself had an even-dimmer recollection of the fledgling actor.

She was a dancer at Grauman's Chinese Theatre that year when she was spotted by Rudolph Valentino, who remolded her into an Oriental siren. Frank Cooper had yet to change his name and, even then, his career wouldn't blossom as fast as Myrna's.

Nevertheless he persevered. He had a series of photographs taken in the styles of Valentino, Ramon Novarro, Wallace Reid, and Tom Mix. Casting offices were papered with the pictures, but no offers ensued.

Valentino had already been held up as his first acting model from a very improbable source. A friend of the family's from Montana, trial lawyer Wellington Rankin—his sister Jeanette was the first woman to be elected to Congress—gave him his first sage advice. "Look at this fellow Valentino," he said. "After all, what does he do? Look how this fellow puts over an idea. He thinks of what he is doing. He thinks it so strongly that it becomes obvious to the audience. When he looks at a girl, he's thinking of taking the clothes off her. You know that when he walks up and kisses her, he is sort of halfway beyond that kiss already."

As part of his efforts to become noticed by studio powers, Cooper took up with Grace Kingsley, the film society columnist for *The Los Angeles Times*. He accompanied her on many assignments, meeting movers

17

in the industry, but the main impression he made on them was negative. The ploy may have seemed too transparent. Esther Ralston, later to costar with Cooper in several pictures, remembered Miss Kingsley as "an older woman and a brilliant writer. It would be like him to escort her around completely on a friendship basis. That would just be good business."

He next made contact with Nan Collins, a studio casting director, who also took a motherly interest in him. There were already two Frank Coopers in films, and she suggested his name be changed to Gary, her hometown in Indiana.

He invested sixty-four dollars in a makeshift screen test. The money included horse rental. The footage was shot on a vacant lot at the corner of Third Street and La Brea, with the cameraman stationed behind a rail fence. It ran for about twenty seconds, Gary Cooper astride the horse, galloping toward the camera. Just before he reached the fence, he pulled the reins and jumped off his mount. He then leaped over the fence and swept off his hat as the camera caught in close-up, as he later described it, "a ghastly grin."

He was permanently yanked from the extra ranks early in 1926 when Hans Tiesler, an independent producer, starred him in a two-reeler, *Lightnin' Wins*, opposite Eileen Sedgewick. It was one of many "Poverty Row" productions being shot on the fringes of the movie colony at the time, without the backing and the liberal budget of a major studio. Gary Cooper proved adequate. His career as an actor could be said to have begun.

Chapter 2

Bob McIntyre, Samuel Goldwyn's casting director, was hiring riders for *The Winning of Barbara Worth,* staring Ronald Colman and Vilma Banky, and based on the popular romantic novel by Harold Bell Wright, published in 1911. Cooper was sent to the Goldwyn studio by Nan Collins to see if he might be hired as a rider.

The venerable Henry King, now in his nineties and looking back over a monumental fifty-year career as a director, recalled his first impression of Cooper, who was seated outside McIntyre's office one day, his knees up and his arms encircling them. When King asked the casting director about the young man, McIntyre replied, "He's just a rider. He wants to get into pictures. He says he has a test."

King instructed the casting director to set up a screening of the footage Cooper had been lugging from one casting office to another. In the meantime, he would talk to the fellow.

The director perceived that this was an unusually handsome young man, who, despite his rough edges, possessed the quiet dignity of a genuine American Westerner. When Cooper finally summoned the courage to speak, King also realized there was a great deal of ambition beneath that self-effacing exterior. "I want to play the part of Abe Lee," Cooper said.

19

The part called for an actor of considerable accomplishment, since the noble, tragic Abe Lee, whose love for Barbara Worth was unrequited, was an engineer who discovered the fault in the big dam that no one else believed was there, and died alerting Willard Holmes, the ultimate winner of Barbara Worth, of the impending flood.

"That part is already taken," King informed the presumptuous, gangling newcomer. The Goldwyn company was waiting for Harold Goodwin to finish *The Honeymoon Express* at Warner Brothers before shooting the Abe Lee scenes. King nonetheless looked at Cooper's homemade screen test and told McIntyre, "Well, anyway, he can ride a horse."

He called Cooper back into his office, and said, "I'm taking about ten riders up to the location. I have nine of them already, and I'd like to take you. You get fifty dollars a week and we keep you in the camp."

"I'll take it," Cooper said, "on the understanding that if you have a little part you'll give it to me." Slightly amused at the young man's pushiness, King agreed.

Given the paltry salary, it obviously wasn't a monumental decision on King's part to hire yet another aspiring actor. More important matters had to be looked after. Interiors were being shot at the studio and location shooting would then follow.

The *Barbara Worth* company went on location to the Nevada salt flats. Much of the then staggering $670,000 budget was expended in building three separate towns in the vast Black Rock Desert near the Idaho border.

"One day," Frances Marion, Goldwyn's $3,000-a-week screenwriter, wrote in her autobiography, "Mr. Goldwyn's secretary asked me if I would take a look at her 'boy friend' who was standing outside. Through the window I saw a tall, lean cowboy slouched against the wall. 'That's our man!' I said. 'Bring him in.'"

What she saw in Cooper, as did several mooning secretaries at Goldwyn, was his insistent sexuality. She was convinced Cooper's magnetism might be effectively deployed somewhere in the picture, given the more subtle approach of Ronald Colman. When she suggested this to the director, King said he would give the boy a closer look.

For eight weeks in the latter part of 1925, the hardy troupe endured sandstorms and heat reaching 130 degrees to film the exteriors for the superspectacle, without so much as a leave of absence to visit a real city. For this reason the temporary desert settlement, dubbed Barbara Worth, Nevada, and incorporated by the state, with King himself appointed Mayor, was outfitted with its own newspaper, movie theater, and recreational center. A railroad station was also built, and a total of 1,200 extras brought in to add to the 1,200 members of cast and crew already there.

Drinking water had to be hauled in from two hundred miles away, although a well was drilled to supply water for bathing. Meals were catered by a Chinese cook with whom Cooper bunked, a clear indication of his standing in the actors' pecking order.

Barbara Worth (the town), was finally destroyed when the flood scenes were filmed, though its Barbara Hotel had already been wiped out by one of the area's daily sandstorms, which arrived regularly at noon and departed at two.

As shooting continued and Harold Goodwin was further detained at Warner Brothers, director King decided to put Cooper in the Abe Lee costume.

"All you have to do," he instructed, "is keep your eyes on Vilma Banky." Goldwyn's exotic European import, a hothouse flower, was out of her element in the stark desert setting, but she was proving to be a trouper. So, surprisingly, was the tyro actor.

"Do you know," King told film historian Kevin Brownlow, "the man stood there from eight in the morning until twelve? No matter where Vilma Banky went, his eyes followed her . . . whether we were shooting or not. . . . Well, he did some other scenes for me and while he didn't have much to do, he did them well. So I thought to myself, if he can do the scene at the hotel—where he rides across the desert for twenty-four hours to bring the news to Mr. Worth—then I'm not going to wait on the man from Warner Brothers. I didn't say anything to anyone. I didn't want any arguments—how do you know how good he is, or how good he isn't?—or anything."

The most dramatic scene called on Cooper, completely exhausted and near death, to come with the news of the impending break in the dam. King talked to Cooper as he wet his face and covered it with clay. "Tired . . . tired . . . tired." He kept the actor walking while he rehearsed scenes with other actors. "Tired . . . tired." Cooper was required to trudge around the camp for an hour before he was called before the cameras.

"If I told you to come up to this door," King said, "and fall flat on your face—even if it smashed you to pieces—could you do it?"

"Yes, sir," Cooper replied.

"Don't break your fall with your hands. Fall like a corpse."

"Yes, sir."

"How tired would a man be if he'd ridden twenty-four hours on a horse?" the director asked.

"Mighty tired."

"Well, I want you to be that tired, and to knock on the door like a tired man. You've got to be tired in mind as well as body. You look across the room, but you can't move your feet. You collapse, but you fall full length . . . just as though you died."

Separately, he told Colman and Paul McAllister, another actor in the film, that they should catch Cooper under the arms as he fell, then carry him over to a bed. The two other actors rehearsed their movements before Cooper was called back to join them.

Prior to filming, King had blocked off the set with a black cloth, so that no outsiders could see what was going on. One, however, was an incorrigible snoop.

Goldwyn had come to understand that Gary Cooper—an untrained actor—was being cast in one of the biggest parts in his biggest picture of the year. He'd already seen the previous day's rushes and, although he found Cooper adequate, he didn't feel a mere cowboy could perform the most dramatic scene.

King explained that, since Goodwin was delayed, there was no harm in using up film until he arrived. Goldwyn was only slightly mollified, but this was enough for King. He returned to the set, resumed talking to Cooper, wetting his face again and pasting on more dirt. Dust caked Cooper from the top of his head to his scuffed boots, with only the two cracks of his eyes squinting through.

"And you know," King recalled, "he knocked on that door like he could hardly touch it. Ronnie Colman stood up, opened the door, and revealed the most pathetic case I've ever seen in my life. I don't think anything will remain in my memory as long as the sight of Gary Cooper standing full length in that door . . . and falling flat on his face. As he went down, Ronnie Colman and Paul McAllister grabbed him, and Cooper's face missed the floor by two inches. They carried him over to the bed and I said to George Barnes, the cameraman, and Gregg Toland, his assistant, 'Right, over here, quick! If I let this makeup deteriorate, we could never replace it.' "

At this untimely juncture, Goldwyn called for King to come out of the black canvas enclosure.

"Sam," King said impatiently, "what *is* it?"

"Why didn't you tell me that boy was a great actor?" Goldwyn asked.

"Because he isn't," King replied. "He's just a cowboy from Montana."

"He's one of the greatest actors I've ever seen in my life," Goldwyn insisted.

"How do you know?" King asked.

Goldwyn sheepishly admitted he'd been watching the filming through a hole in the curtain. "Henry, let's put him under contract," he urged.

"Sam, I have a tentative agreement with the boy."

"Listen," Goldwyn responded, "we're partners. Anything you two do, I'm part of it. And anything I do, you're part of it."

"Sam, we'll take care of it." With that, King hurried back before Cooper's makeup caked and fell off.

Later, Goldwyn insisted that King not speak directly to young Cooper about a studio contract. It would be better to go through channels. Cooper would be sent to see Goldwyn executive Abe Lehr. When Lehr started talking about a seven-year contract, Cooper was bewildered. All he'd thought of was getting the part, and here he was in the midst of a discussion using such esoteric words as options and escalations. He was forced to think where he wanted to be seven years from now. Cooper didn't think it greedy, given Tom Mix's phenomenal salary, that he should be getting one thousand dollars weekly at the end of that time, compared to the sixty-five dollars he was presently getting. (His fifty-dollar weekly salary was increased when he was cast as Abe Lee.) Lehr balked at the money, though Cooper's starting salary would still be sixty-five dollars.

He assured his associates that the contract would be worked out in some way. He felt there was no rush to sign the cowboy, since Goldwyn wasn't known for making Westerns and hadn't voiced any ambitions to produce others in the future. Cooper, as a result, continued working on the film without any permanent contract being signed. It's entirely possible, as the actor later maintained, that King thought Goldwyn had signed him, and Goldwyn felt McIntyre had gotten the commitment from him, while the casting director himself was waiting for Nan Collins to come around with a counteroffer. If this was the case, his being signed to a studio contract wasn't of sufficient enough import for any of the studio executives involved to personally want to follow through. They had no assurance, despite the rare flash of brilliance of which any amateur might be capable, that Gary Cooper could sustain a role, much less a career, in films.

Not even after Frances Marion saw the footage already shot was there any sense of urgency in signing him. Miss Marion was delighted to see that her faith in Cooper was justified, but concerned that the performance he was delivering would work to the picture's detriment. "This boy's going to steal the picture," she told King. "And if you leave that scene in, where he rides twenty-four hours across the desert, you better shoot it over with Colman, because he'll be the hero instead of Colman."

That scene might have been reshot with Colman doing a far, far better thing than he had ever done before, as he would later do in the film version of *A Tale of Two Cities*, had the British actor been more jealous and zealous. Consequently, the original footage in which the Abe Lee character sacrificed his life was retained. Goldwyn and company were glad that Colman didn't raise any objections to the ending, for the studio was being pressed to have the picture ready in time for the grand opening of the Forum Theatre on Pico Boulevard. All involved were working night and day to get the picture completed in time.

The effect on the opening night audience was galvanic. Goldwyn, King, and their associates were delighted with the impression Gary Cooper made.

Thanks to Goldwyn's saturation publicity, *Barbara Worth* was a hit. There were cheers on its opening night in New York. However, it never attained the classic status of King's *Stella Dallas* of the year before, also made for Goldwyn. Some reviewers felt it was hardly worthy of the talents of Goldwyn, King, Vilma Banky, and Ronald Colman. A practically illiterate review in *Variety Weekly* called it "finely interpretated." Though many reviewers singled out Cooper's work for praise, cued in by the advertising which singled out the fifth-billed Cooper as a "dynamic new personality," *The New York Times*, in an extremely critical analysis blaming the picture's pedestrian quality on the mediocrity of the novel, failed to mention Gary Cooper at all.

Nevertheless, he and the film rode a tidal wave of critical and public support. The image stuck. Some of it grew out of the period Cooper started in. During the 1920s, the morality play was still the order of the day, and it was generally conceded that the man who strayed in the first reel would find his way back to the fold in time for the last. Some of it originated in the Code of the West, until it wore a groove in the public memory. Gary Cooper, at the outset of his career, was identified with this powerful American archetype, and he never strayed far from it in the future.

Yet, over the next few days, no one from Goldwyn bothered to tell him how admirably he'd acquitted himself in this challenging role.

Nan Collins, in the meantime, sent Cooper over to Famous Players-Lasky, the forerunner of Paramount Pictures, where director John Waters was preparing a Western, *Arizona Bound*. Waters had recalled Cooper's makeshift screen test.

The actor was summoned by B. P. Schulberg, production head. Studio executives were about to start a meeting when Cooper's presence in the outer office was announced. Schulberg thought it would be a good idea to have them all look the actor over at the same time.

"I was a little nervous," Cooper recalled. "Schulberg's secretary told me to go right into his office. So I walked in—but I didn't get much past the door. In his office were twelve men seated at a large table. All were executives and all were looking directly at me. I never faced so many big men at one time in my life before. I knew that I blushed because I could feel my face and ears getting hot. I stammered and couldn't think of a blamed thing to say. I don't know exactly what happened but I finally got out of that office with a contract in my hand."

As Schulberg later described it, "It was his blush that won us all. I hope he never loses it. He sold himself to us immediately during that severe test. Because of his natural ability and winning personality, he has a great future."

He was signed to a contract calling for $200 a week. The studio announced that he would first costar with Clara Bow and Esther Ralston in *Children of Divorce*. Although it became popular folklore that Clara Bow was instrumental in his getting the part, the two had not yet met. She was not influential enough at the studio to demand him as her costar, since she was a lagging thirty-eighth in box office standing among studio stars that year. Next, Cooper was scheduled to star in two Westerns, *The Last Outlaw* and *Arizona Bound*.

Now that he was beginning to achieve a measure of security, Cooper bought himself a jazzy red Chrysler roadster.

"She had fright in her, this girl," Whitney Bolton of the *New York Morning Telegraph* wrote upon her death in 1965. "She had defiance that was a flower of fright. She had a kind of jaunty air of telling you that she didn't care what happened; she could handle it."

The problem was that Clara Bow couldn't. She was a cuddlesome, five-foot-four-inch, 115-pound package from Brooklyn when, in 1921, at the age of sixteen, Clara won the Fame and Fortune contest sponsored by *Motion Picture Classic* magazine to pick "The Most Beautiful Girl in the World." Her rewards for winning the hyperbolic title were a silver trophy, an evening gown, and the promised efforts by the magazine publishers to "try to help the winner gain a role in films."

This was one of the few bright spots in her thus far dreary life. Another was her early introduction to sex in the byways of Coney Island, where her father found erstwhile employment as a waiter at Nathan's.

Robert Bow was a poor provider, and his family lived in extreme poverty. His wife, Sarah, was mentally unstable, the deaths of her two previous children in their infancy having permanently upset her fragile emotional equilibrium. She was sinking quickly into madness when Clara won the contest. The girl was awakened one dark night by her mother bending over her cot, a butcher knife held to Clara's throat. "I'll kill you myself before I'll see you an actress!" the deranged woman threatened. The terror of that moment never left Clara Bow—and may help explain the chronic insomnia that plagued her the rest of her life. Threatened for sins yet to be committed, Clara Bow was spurred to take her pleasures with reckless, driving abandon.

"I think wildly gay people are usually hiding from something in themselves," she once told the press, although the statement had the imprint of the studio publicity machine. "The best life has taught them is to snatch at every moment of fun and excitement, because they feel sure fate is going to hit them over the head with a club at the first opportunity."

By the time her mother Sarah Bow was permanently placed in a mental institution, Clara had already begun her acting career in several bit parts in pictures shot around the New York area.

In 1923, the same year her mother died, she signed a three-month personal contract with B.P. Schulberg of Preferred Pictures, which would later be absorbed by Paramount. She moved to California to pursue her movie career and the contract was extended.

One of her early assignments was on loanout to First National in 1924, in support of Colleen Moore, the brunette American gamine, in *Painted People*. Miss Moore was among the top box office draws. She recalls Clara as having long dark brown curls and not the bright red hair that she later affected, which made a dazzling sight as she sped down Wilshire Boulevard in her Kissel Kar roadster, with her seven chow dogs, their manes dyed an identical red.

"Clara didn't like her part in my picture," Miss Moore said. "She was so unhappy that she quit and we put a blonde in her place. I liked Clara. A very warm, sweet, generous girl. What great potential. But she wasn't a finisher. Many older women, like Adela Rogers St. Johns, tried to take her in hand and educate her.

Her mind was like a sponge, but she didn't have the concentration or the ability to see it through. She was quite ingenuous. People would go into shock over her salty language. It just came out. She'd learned it in the alleys around Coney Island."

Paramount was not finding it easy to sell her to the American public. Their campaign to promote her as "The Brooklyn Bonfire" was a dismal failure, and Elinor Glyn's coinage of the word "It" a few years previously to describe animal magnetism hadn't yet caught on or been associated with Clara. Then, suddenly, late in 1926, her career began to take off in one of the most dizzying propulsions in movie history. She was ill equipped to handle it emotionally or, with her eighth-grade education, intellectually.

Gary Cooper, as a new contract player at Paramount, witnessed her creation as a star. Paramount was grinding out 104 pictures every year, and many new players would have to be highlighted. It was a propitious time for an actor to be there.

Cooper's signing had to do with the declining fortunes of William S. Hart. Three years previously, the popular Western star had met with Jesse Lasky, Vice-President in charge of Famous Players, Hart's releasing corporation. He was told that his days of independence were over. Hart couldn't believe his ears. He had run his own production company for years, using his first-hand experience in the West to produce and sometimes write and direct his own starring vehicles. All had succeeded, and Famous Players had profited from distributing them. But the new bureaucracy at Paramount wanted change.

"We would have to produce your pictures, select your stories, select a suitable director to direct that particular story, change your directors whenever necessary, select your cast, and be entirely in control of your productions," Lasky told him.

Hart was to be relegated to the plain and simple post of actor; his marquee value as a movie star was all that Famous Players was interested in. "I was being told that I did not know how to make Western pictures," Hart wrote in his autobiography.

"The sales organization must be considered," Lasky said. "The sales organization must have a voice in the selection of all stories and their treatment."

"But Jesse, this is all wrong," Hart protested. "It is the tail wagging the dog. . . . It will stifle all imagination." Hart refused these conditions. Lasky seemed to cave in, but then reneged in the contract. Hart refused to sign and moved to United Artists, which had a reputation for creative autonomy. Cooper was now able to move into the Western-star vacuum created by Hart's departure.

Paramount, under Adolph Zukor, was booming. It was Zukor's brilliant merging under one roof of production, distribution, and theater ownership that made him the biggest power in films. In 1916 Zukor had merged Famous Players Film Company with Lasky's Feature Play Company to form Famous Players-Lasky, then the largest production-distribution firm in the industry. Between 1916 and 1921 Zukor virtually created the big-studio system and established business procedures the entire industry would adopt—a company made its own films; kept its own writers, directors, and stars under contract; made its own short subjects to accompany its own features; had its own publicity and marketing arms; and owned the theaters. The independence of pioneers like D. W. Griffith and Thomas Ince was crushed. In 1926, Famous Players-Lasky assumed the name of its distribution and exhibition arm, Paramount Pictures Corporation.

Though it discovered some of the greatest talents in movies, Paramount's interest in total control over all elements of the business was sometimes counterproductive. By making secret deals with their agents and neglecting to pay them money that was due, Paramount risked losing the Marx Brothers over a matter of a few thousand dollars, at a time when the Marxes were their top box office stars. They signed up the eccentric comedian W. C. Fields, then refused to let him direct, shoving him into conventional romantic stories where he didn't belong, like *Her Majesty Love*. Not satisfied with distributing the extremely successful Popeye and Betty Boop cartoons from the independent Fleischer Studios on the East Coast, they courted Max Fleischer behind Dave Fleischer's back and finally ousted both of them from their own studio. After Paramount took over the Fleischer Studio, the quality of the cartoons plummeted. The key element in decision making at Paramount became quantity. With theaters that changed bills twice a week, the executives were constantly under pressure to meet the quota of 104 films a year.

Despite these abuses, the American film industry reached its peak of artistic and commercial achievement in the last years of the silent era, with Paramount and Metro-Goldwyn-Mayer setting the standard.

This was the maelstrom Clara Bow was being sucked into as she filmed *It,* her first starring role. Cooper was given a bit part as a newspaper reporter. They didn't get to know each other, however, until a New Year's Eve party in 1927. "I had never before known an actress," he told Dorothy Spensley of *Photoplay*, forgetting that he'd been dating Carole Lombard. He called Clara "a new type of girl, glamorous, full of fun, devoid of jealousy. I was grateful to her and admired her . . . we went around together."

It wasn't surprising to Colleen Moore that Clara Bow should attach herself to Cooper as "many women later did the same thing. It was probably hard for him to get away. She was a very sexy little girl . . . probably oversexed . . . and she was so pretty and so cute."

"Some of his peers, perhaps jealously, regarded him as an opportunist," Joe Morella and Edward Z. Epstein wrote in *The "It" Girl*. "Cooper's enemies had claimed that, in these early days, Gary had no second thoughts about sleeping with anyone who could further his career . . . bedding down Clara Bow, the leading ingenue on the lot, was hardly an unpleasant way to climb the ladder, if that's what Cooper had in mind.

And, in all fairness to Cooper, it must be noted that it was evident to all who knew them that Clara Bow and Gary Cooper were genuinely 'hot' for each other."

In her case, however, it wasn't an exclusive commitment, and she continued seeing other men, particularly Victor Fleming, a virile director of forty.

Cooper had bedded many script girls and secretaries in the past, but now the tables were turned and it was he who felt exploited by the inconstant twenty-two-year-old "It" Girl.

He started filming his first costarring role at the studio, in support of the girl who was upsetting his private life. He would be third billed below the title after Esther Ralston, a very ladylike actress, and Clara. *Children of Divorce* attempted to cash in on the ideas of marriage and sex that had been good box office since Cecil B. DeMille made *Don't Change Your Husband* in 1919 and *Why Change Your Wife?* in 1920. It was adapted from a five-part novel by Owen Johnson which had been serialized in *Redbook* magazine. The story was worked on by Adela Rogers St. Johns, a second time by Hope Loring and Louis D. Leighton, and once again by Dixie Willson, in a revision that would never be used. It had similarly gone through several changes of directors before Frank Lloyd took over. The first four parts detailing the activities of several generations in a family visited by divorce were fairly well dispensed with. The picture concentrated on the off-spring of shattered unions, trying to find their place in the world. Hedda Hopper was in the picture and later, when she switched to gossip, she became Gary Cooper's closest friend in the press.

"Both Clara and I were delighted to have this lovely young cowboy playing opposite us," Esther Ralston said. "About a week after we started, Gary was fired. They decided to put Douglas Gilmore in his place."

The move was justified, as Hedda Hopper would later attest. Even an accomplished actor would have been thrown by the complicated logistics of the role.

"Gary's job was an All-American high in Hollywood miscasting," Hedda said. "I'll never forget the first day of shooting. It still holds my private record for the most painful performance I ever witnessed. The set was my swank Park Avenue apartment. The characters were supersophisticated Manhattan youths merrily going to hell. The scene was a cocktail party and Gary's job, of all things, was to breeze into the room and make the rounds from one flapper to another, sipping champagne out of their glasses, cadging a nonchalant puff from their cigarettes, and tossing sophisticated wisecracks as he strolled along. Mister Personality Snake in person. He was a New York man about town, the script read, yet only a few months before he'd been riding the range in Montana."

Director Lloyd supervised twenty-two takes before giving up. He called the older actress over for a private discussion. "Hedda, you've got to do something. You've got a son. Go talk to this big boy and snap him out of it."

"It's only a film they're running through that thing," she told Cooper, "not bullets."

"I can't do it," he said. "I just can't do it."

Shooting resumed with his replacement, but Gilmore proved to be no more up to the job than Cooper had been. It might have been then that Clara Bow created a tearful scene in the front office. Whether she did or not, Schulberg asked Esther Ralston to meet with him at the end of the day.

"You know, Esther," he said, "I like that other boy's face. He's got something. I think we ought to give him another try. I'm going to put him back in again. But, Esther, can you do anything with him? He's afraid to touch you. He's afraid you'll break or something. Couldn't you just loosen him up a bit?"

The actress was wondering how much she would have to sacrifice for her art. "Just what did you have in mind?" she asked the studio production head.

"Take him to lunch," Schulberg urged. "Talk to him. Be friendly. Make him comfortable with you."

"Of course, I will. I'll do the best I can."

First, however, the studio had to find Gary Cooper. Deeply depressed, he'd taken off for points unknown to think out his future. At the first serious test of his ability, he'd been found lacking. Maybe he could find work as a cartoonist in Chicago. Aimlessly, he'd driven into the Mojave Desert to the east of Los Angeles, stopping at a ramshackle hotel when he reached the point of exhaustion. The following day he returned west, driving down the California coast through Malibu, then east to Hollywood. He hadn't eaten in all that time. Finally he stopped at Henry's Sandwich Shop, a hangout near the studio. It was there that Frank Lloyd found him and told him he was back in the picture.

Esther Ralston, as promised, invited Cooper to have lunch with her. As they chatted, she was bubbling and encouraging. Cooper, however, was as tongue-tied as ever. He was, typically, groping for words. Finally they came trickling out.

"Esther . . . can I tell you a secret?"

"Of course, Gary, what is it?"

"I'm in love."

Miss Ralston wasn't sure how she'd cope with the admission. Had she gone too far in loosening him up?

"Oh, no," she protested, "you're just imagining it."

"No, I'm not," he replied. "I'm in love with Clara."

Although she'd recently married George Webb, Miss Ralston laughingly admitted that, given her own supposition, Cooper's admission "didn't do my ego any good. But it was the start of an interesting thing. It was a time for Gary to really unfold. He seemed to develop shortly after that. Before he'd grunt and point, a man of few words. He was always very reserved, but very kind. Actually he was more sensitive than talkative. He was a gentleman, always well groomed, not just another cowboy."

After Cooper's return, Lloyd wisely decided to film the difficult scene last. Throughout the shooting,

Cooper's legs shook uncontrollably. Lloyd ingeniously devised scenes where only his head and shoulders showed. He put him behind big sofas or dressed him in long bathrobes and polo coats.

What Lloyd had greater difficulty disguising were the scratches Clara inflicted on her lover during their violent arguments off the set. "A black eye," Adela Rogers St. Johns recalled, "even when bestowed by one's ladylove, is no help to the cameraman. Nor were the reconciliations, which took place all over the lot, much quieter, though Gary always forgave the red-head."

Hedda Hopper was nonplussed when, one day, she idly asked Clara how she and Cooper were getting along. "All I can say," Clara answered, "is that he's hung like a horse and he can go all night."

Although Esther Ralston never heard Clara's graphic description of her lover's sexual equipment and technique, she said, "I wouldn't put it past Clara. She was a little untamed minx. She could have held back with me, thinking I was a prude or straitlaced or something. Maybe she thought that kind of frank talk wasn't part of my New England heritage. Yet, she tried in other ways to shock me."

One day, while the company was on location in Pasadena, both actresses were sitting on the sidelines while Cooper was filming a scene.

Clara turned to her costar. "Esther, do you like Gary?"

"Yes, I do," she answered, "very much. I think he's a wonderful man."

"I like him very much too," Clara replied. "You know, he's so kind to me. He always lets me take my dog in the tub when he gives me my bath in the morning."

"Yes," Esther said, "isn't that just like Gary?"

In spite of the sophisticated subject matter in *Children of Divorce*, a scene was inserted to allow Gary Cooper to still be on a horse. The script called for him to break up a lawn party by jumping over the bar. To add to the challenge, he had to use the unfamiliar English saddle for the difficult jump.

On another occasion, after completing an orgiastic party scene in which he was jostled by drinkers and dancers, Cooper was quoted as remarking, "I'm in the wrong line of work if that's what may be expected in a business career." So, apparently, were several of the men behind the camera. The film, which had been budgeted at $1 million, was found to lack spark by studio executives.

Josef von Sternberg was called in by Schulberg. His solution was to scrap half the film and reshoot it. That much footage would normally require five weeks of work, but the director, in a display of bravado, said he could accomplish the feat in three days. Despite the fact that the sets had been struck and all the stages were occupied, Schulberg okayed the plan when von Sternberg erected a tent for use as a stage. He would have two days to get ready and three to remake half the film.

Shooting had recommenced when the tent was pelted by a three-day rainstorm. "We waded through the new scenes," von Sternberg said, "now and then dodging a heavy burst of water that penetrated the canvas overhead. The crew that helped me and the poor actors that I mercilessly put through their new paces had to take a prolonged rest cure when I had finished with them."

Teutonic and abrasive, von Sternberg didn't believe in coddling actors, and the impression he usually left was one of cruel insensitivity. Cooper felt demeaned after several confrontations. He refused to look at the director as he received instructions.

Von Sternberg, in his autobiography, slyly interpreted this as evidence of Cooper's natural reserve. "He was shy, as most actors are, but in his first contact with me he carried this to an extreme, developing what is known as 'klieg eyes.'" This burning irritation of the membranes in the eyes "was due to his reluctance to look at the director when receiving instructions; he preferred instead staring at the arc lights."

Von Sternberg got along better with Clara Bow. She took all his criticism in stride, maintaining a frivolous attitude throughout. Esther Ralston recalled the day on the set when Clara sat popping her chewing gum as the makeup men prepared her for her big death scene. "All right," von Sternberg called out, "we're ready to take it." Esther knelt down beside the dying Clara, trying to work up some tears. Just as the cameras started to roll, Clara Bow jerked the gum out of her mouth and stuck it behind her ear. Esther broke up.

"She was defiant and childlike," Esther said. "She seemed to say, 'All right, you've put this particular crown on my head. Now I have to wear it.' "

When the picture was released in April of 1927, *The New York Times* said, "There are moments when the players are so perfect in their attire and hair arrangement that they impress one as catering to a public that admires clothes and good looks infinitely more than histrionic ability."

Gary Cooper's reviews weren't encouraging. Yet the public saw something in him that critics didn't. "Even in that terribly miscast part," Hedda Hopper recalled, "his scenes revealed something so terrific that they fairly shouted, 'Star! Star!' You couldn't put your finger on what it was then, and I suppose you can't now. It's his pure inner power."

It would take some time for Cooper to understand the extent of his appeal. The one person who might have assured him of it was in no position to do so. While *Children of Divorce* was being prepared for release, Clara was hurriedly thrown into another picture, *Rough House Rosie*. Paramount, having discovered the formula to her success, was now paying her $7,500 a week and was getting its money's worth. The strain of too much work as well as too much living caught up with her, and Clara suffered her first nervous breakdown. It was rumored that the reason for her collapse was her inability to choose between her two suitors, Cooper or director Victor Fleming.

Studio executives continued being condescending toward Gary Cooper even after he was an established star. "Gary Cooper did his level best," Adolph Zukor wrote in 1953. "His determination enabled him to climb to greater heights than most of the quicker talents ever attained." It wasn't determination, however, that was creating his reputation. It was the combination of sexual magnetism and the romantic aura he projected. Never before had a Western hero made the transition to matinee idol. Gary Cooper just might.

Paramount was paying Cooper $300 a week when he went into his first important Western starring role. *Arizona Bound*, with an $85,000 budget, was a routine program picture which took only two weeks to film at Bryce Canyon, Utah, but it began to establish Cooper with the public. He was doing his own stunt work, and was even seen jumping from a horse onto a swiftly moving stagecoach. "Cooper is a tall youth, with a boyish smile and enough swagger to give him character," *Variety* said. *Exhibitors Daily* agreed: "Gary Cooper has the physique, the ability to ride, as well as histrionic ability, for a Western hero and Paramount has done well to assign such parts to him. He is equally effective in the action business and he and Betty Jewel, who is charmingly vivacious as the heroine, make an appealing pair."

The same two were again teamed in *The Last Outlaw*. *Variety Weekly* found Cooper promising, but voiced some reservations about the tired vehicles he was being burdened with: "Paramount can stand a western star and has a personality bet on Cooper, but they're not doing right by him if *The Last Outlaw* is a sample of the best story material they can offer."

Cooper's work in *Barbara Worth* brought him his most important break to date—a supporting role in *Wings*, an ambitious air spectacle and the first motion picture of its kind. William Wellman, the director, knew that Cooper was ideally suited for the role of Cadet White.

When ex-World War I pilot John Monk Saunders outlined to Jesse Lasky the aviation story he hoped to sell as a movie, Lasky was excited by its cinematic potential but dubious about its feasibility. Saunders felt it had to be done on a grand scale or not at all; Lasky doubted that any studio could afford it. Saunders then had an inspiration that was to establish a Hollywood precedent. "Why not get the material from the War Department?" he suggested. "It's certainly in their interest to cooperate."

To Paramount's astonishment, the War Department agreed and lent millions of dollars worth of equipment and uniforms. This in turn increased the value of the film by millions. A good image for the Army Air Corps was the only condition the government required. Thus, *Wings* was the first of many cooperative ventures between Hollywood and the American Defense Establishment, accounting for all the highly emotional messages about the gallantry of fighting forces in U. S. films over the years.

William Wellman had been an ace war pilot himself. Though his career was to include such well-remembered films as *Public Enemy, Wild Boys of the Road, A Star Is Born* (the Janet Gaynor version), *Nothing Sacred, The Ox-Bow Incident, The Story of G.I. Joe,* and *The High and the Mighty,* Wellman's love of flying and his primitive flair for spectacle would never find better expression than they did in *Wings.* The aerial sequences are staggering, and combine the thrill of flying a small plane with the epic panorama of Wellman's re-creation of World War I battlefields. The film took a year to complete and cost $2 million.

Cadet White was a small part, but Wellman knew it had to be memorable. Thirty-five actors tried out for the scene, but none could match Cooper's magnetism. Wellman signed Cooper and sent him to the location at Kelly Field in San Antonio, Texas, for six months of aerial photography.

Cooper met Charles (Buddy) Rogers and Richard Arlen on the chartered train. Clara Bow, added to the cast to furnish some glamour, was arriving separately. Rogers and Arlen were buddies at Paramount, and indulged in their usual banter. Rogers recalled that the newcomer in their midst said only three words during the trip: "Hello, yup, and good-bye." Cooper preferred to keep to himself.

"My God!" Arlen exclaimed. "Doesn't he ever talk? He reminds me of Long Tack Sam."

Rogers didn't know who this character from Arlen's past was, but he and his friend began calling Cooper Silent Sam.

"We didn't realize at the time that *Wings* was going to be a strong or big picture," Rogers said. "We were three punk kids in a silent movie, and we became pals. We didn't have to learn many lines, you know. We didn't know the talkies would ever come along."

Arlen, although an American, had been a pilot with the Canadian Air Corps during World War I. Rogers learned to fly while in Texas. His instructor was a second lieutenant he knew only as Van, although in later years he would gain considerable renown as Air Force General Hoyt Vandenberg.

"My little second lieutenant would take me up. The minute we'd get up one thousand feet or so, I'd shake a stick at him and he'd have to hide so the cameras wouldn't spot him."

The actor in each plane, in addition to acting as his own pilot, also was his own cameraman and electrician. Cameras were mounted on the front of each plane to catch the action.

"We'd stay up an hour or two," Rogers recalled, "for as long as we had gas. When the shooting was over, Van would land the damn thing. Every day, we had to find the same kinds of clouds that we'd photographed the day before. There'd be a telephone call that clouds were eighty miles away, and we'd jump in our planes and go find them. Once, we had to wait eighteen days for the clouds to return."

Much of their waiting was spent at the St. Anthony Hotel, where another film company, that for *Rough Riders*, being directed by Victor Fleming, was also quartered. The hotel became, as Wellman described it, "the Armageddon of a magnificent sexual Donnybrook. . . . To begin with, all the young actors fell in love with Clara Bow, and if you had known her, you could understand why. . . . She took care of it— how I will never know. She kept Cooper . . . Arlen . . . and a few whose names I can't remember, plus a couple of pursuit pilots from Selfridge Field and a panting writer, all in line. They were handled like chessmen, never running into one another, never suspecting that there was any other man in the whole world that meant a thing to this gorgeous little sexpot—and all this expert maneuvering in a hotel where most of the flame was burning."

Cooper was not fooled. He ended the affair, though he was to stray back to her many times. Victor Fleming was so tolerant of Clara's wanderings that he would continue to be her occasional lover as well as her best friend. Later, when the world came to know the extent of Clara Bow's emotional disintegration, Cooper ungallantly claimed their relationship was a publicity stunt. In fact, it had been uncommonly generous of Clara Bow to allow herself to be photographed with an unknown such as Cooper and to permit him to share her limelight as The "It" Boy. Elinor Glynn went along with it too, saying she found men from Montana "lean clear through."

Wellman saved Cooper's single scene until last. He knew once it was done he'd have no excuse to hang onto Cooper anymore, and he liked having him around. The director lugged the tent in which the scene would be shot to every location. The night before shooting, Wellman rehearsed the scene in his hotel suite. The next day it was performed in one take, and Wellman knew he had it. "Print," he said, and the movie was finished.

As Wellman was taking a shower, Cooper surprised him by entering the room and asking if he could do that scene again. "Look, Coop, you're the only one who could get away with asking for this in the whole troupe. I'd tell everybody else to go to hell. Why do you want to do the scene again, anyway?"

"Well, uh, I picked my nose in the middle of the take," Cooper replied.

"Listen, you son of a bitch! You keep right on picking your nose and you'll pick your nose right into a fortune."

Thanks to its major 1970 rerelease, *Wings* is one of the most familiar of silent films, but it is far from being one of the best. The acting is sentimental, stock silent-film stuff. Silent masterpieces like *Underworld, Docks of New York, The Wind, Sunrise,* and *Greed* balanced complex characterizations, genuine conflicts, technical wizardry, and brilliant visual concepts. *Wings* had smashing spectacle and pictorial sweep, and that's it. When *New Yorker* film critic Penelope Gilliatt pointed out to Wellman in 1971 that the cars and clothing styles of the nonaerial scenes are all of the period of the film's release date (1927) rather than the film's historical period (1917), he admitted it was the first time he'd ever noticed it. *Wings* nonetheless won the best picture Oscar of 1927.

In *Wings,* Richard Arlen and Buddy Rogers are two fresh youths who project nothing more than freshness and youth. When Richard Arlen goes off to war, Julia Swayne Gordon and Henry B. Walthall, as his parents, assume poses of deep sorrow. Buddy Rogers returns home with the news that their son is dead and they fall into their mournful poses again. The performances are pretty much on this level throughout, with one major exception in Cooper. He holds the screen as powerfully as Emil Jannings or Erich von Stroheim. Playing a seasoned veteran in the aviators' camp, casually eating a candy bar while saying, "Luck or no luck, when your time comes you're going to get it," he makes a perfect contrast to the callow recruits Arlen and Rogers. The scene lasted one minute and forty-five seconds before the character went out to do "a flock of eights before chow." "In my opinion," Cooper said, "those 105 seconds were the most valuable in my life." The scene was so good it made the rest of the picture an anticlimax. Cadet White suffers a fatal collision performing his "eights." There is a beautiful aerial shot of the Red Cross truck rushing to the site of the crash. After those genuinely moving moments, *Wings* embarrassingly reverts to cornball emoting for the next hour and a half.

Within the next few years, four actors would emerge as the greatest male stars in films. Three of them—Clark Gable, Spencer Tracy, Humphrey Bogart—had solid apprenticeships in the theater. The fourth, Gary Cooper, had no such legacy to bring to films. Igonrant of technique, he relied on instinct. He also knew about the camera, courting it as if it were a lover, and seducing it.

The same couldn't be said about Clara Bow. She was still entertaining Cooper in the satin-canopied bed in her Spanish bungalow on Bedford Drive in Beverly Hills. She seemed oblivious to the very apparent defects that were beginning to show in the formula acting that had made her a star and now threatened to turn her into an outmoded caricature. Cooper was more fortunate—he would be credited with the creation of a uniquely photographic style of acting, one devoid of gimmicks and seemingly lacking in technique, relying wholly on sincerity—the "natural." He'd felt totally comfortable before cameras since childhood, for his mother was an amateur photographer whose constant subjects were her two sons.

Chapter 3

In 1927 Paramount discovered it had a lot of desert footage left over from its production of *Beau Geste* and decided to make a sequel. Colleen Moore, the number one box office star, requested that Cooper be loaned out to costar with her, but Paramount kept him to play opposite Evelyn Brent, a new star, in *Beau Sabreur*. Miss Moore would have to wait.

Evelyn Brent had just come into her own in Josef von Sternberg's instant classic, *Underworld*, playing gun moll to a Chicago crime boss. She had been discovered during a visit to World Film Studios in Fort Lee, New Jersey, when she was fourteen, and she suffered a nervous breakdown before she was twenty. She and Cooper embarked on a mild affair during filming. To commemorate the passing of Clara Bow from his life, fan magazines stopped calling Cooper The "It" Boy, referring to him now as The Big Fellow.

Beau Sabreur was to cost over $500,000. The unpronounceable title meant Handsome Swordsman, although in Cooper's case he would be an inept one, since he suffered a serious gash during a fencing scene.

Cooper was believable as a romantic figure, despite the awkwardness of making love to a leading lady who was a foot shorter than he. Directors hadn't thought of digging trenches for him to stand in, which they would do later.

The success of *Wings* spawned a host of imitators; among them was *The Legion of the Condemned*, Cooper's next assignment at Paramount. He was second-billed to Fay Wray, soon to marry John Monk Saunders, the screenwriter of *Wings* as well as *Legion*. *Wings* was to typecast its writer and its director, William Wellman, for the rest of their careers. World War I aviation figured importantly in nearly all the scripts Saunders, a Rhodes Scholar, worked on, stretching from Howard Hawks's *Dawn Patrol* in 1930 to Edmund Goulding's remake in 1938, perhaps culminating in the haunting 1931 film, *The Last Flight*, a powerful account of the gradual crack-up of a small band of flyers after the war. Director William Wellman's passion for flying highlighted an otherwise disappointing career, but even his aviation films, such as *Thunderbirds* in 1942, were effective only during the aerial sequences.

Legion's plot concerned "a band of flying daredevils to whom life is but a hollow mockery and death a tempting solace" . . . a sort of French Foreign Legion of the sky.

Paramount attempted to establish Cooper and Miss Wray—later to achieve immortality as King Kong's love object—as "Paramount's Glorious Young Lovers" to compete with the romantic teams of two rival studios: Metro's Greta Garbo and John Gilbert were erotic and heavy-breathing; Fox's Janet Gaynor and Charles Farrell were antiseptic. Cooper and Wray were wholesome and passionate, but the public didn't buy them, perhaps because action picture fans, predominantly male, felt ill at ease with love stories. Nevertheless, the studio continued to pair them in several subsequent pictures.

In the mid-1920s, Colleen Moore had saved First National Pictures from bankruptcy. First National had been formed in 1917 to combat Adolph Zukor's consolidation of Famous Players-Lasky the year before. First National was a consortium of theater owners banding together to consolidate the exhibitor's power in opposition to the production and distribution company Zukor was creating. Charlie Chaplin immediately signed up with First National to distribute his independent productions. In retaliation, Zukor began buying up theaters to fight the exhibitors' circuit, and Paramount was born. First National was later bought by Warner Brothers, combining distribution and production in a similar oligopoly.

Now Colleen Moore and her husband, John McCormick, First National's production chief, planned to make *Lilac Time*, an old Jane Cowl play being revamped to suit the vivacious film actress' talents. It was planned as a million-dollar production, a war story using hundreds of extras, a whole village being blown up and airplanes being destroyed in vivid dogfights, roughly similar to *Wings*.

The executives at First National were not aware of the parallels between the two pictures; *Wings* had not yet been released. But *Lilac Time*'s love story was dangerously similar to the popular *Seventh Heaven*, which was then playing in movie houses across the country. "We had to rewrite the story almost completely," Miss Moore said. "There were many writers on it before Adela Rogers St. Johns finally put it together to our satisfaction." It was designed as a silent picture, although a theme was to be recorded as background ("Jeanine, I Dream of Lilac Time" was to become a hit).

"We'd been looking for a leading man," she recalled, "but nobody seemed quite right. We decided we'd have to find an unknown." She spotted Cooper in an old Western short feature when she went to the movies one night with her husband on Catalina Island, where they were filming *Oh, Kay!* "I thought this most attractive young man was exactly right for our picture. I called the studio the next day and suggested he be hired.

"Gary was a long, lanky, kind of sleepy young guy," Miss Moore said. "He couldn't act at all. George

Fitzmaurice, the director, had an awful time with him.

"He was pure Montana. He didn't travel in international circles as yet. He didn't talk much. He didn't have to. The small bit of talking he did do was about himself and Evelyn Brent. I found him bright, but no intellectual and not a great reader. He didn't have to be. Gary Cooper was a natural.

"Everybody liked Gary. I said this boy was going to be a huge star. 'Why's that?' they asked. I answered, 'Because there's not a girl in the front office who hasn't been down here to take a look at him.' They hadn't come down on any of my other pictures."

In addition to interiors at the studio, the company went on location to the mountains between Santa Ana and Capistrano, where an entire French village had been constructed. Judge and Mrs. Cooper often visited the location. "They couldn't have been more charming," Miss Moore said, "nor more British."

Fitzmaurice didn't want to use stock footage of the flying sequences, and it was over these mountains that entirely new aerial scenes were shot.

He conferred with his top stunt pilot over the small crash that was needed to cap a comedy scene. In her story, Colleen Moore had climbed into an idling plane and soon found herself wildly taxiing all over the air field. After a great deal of Mack Sennett-style slapstick, the plane was to smash through a small patch of trees to end its runaway ride.

The stunt pilot asked Fitzmaurice, "Where do you want the plane to hit the ground?"

Fitzmaurice waved his hand in the general direction of the spot, saying, "Oh, right about there."

The pilot walked over to the spot, drew an "X" with the toe of his shoe in the dust, and said, "Okay." He then went back to the plane and made several adjustments on the wings with a saw.

With cameras turning, the pilot drove the plane straight through the trees, tore up both wings, continued taxiing for a second, and dove nose first into the ground—precisely on his "X"! Unfortunately, the camera operator wasn't expecting such precision, and went on panning past, until the plane was clear out of camera range, and he had to jerk back to locate it again.

Lilac Time was a smash because of Miss Moore's enduring appeal. In days when theaters changed their attractions every week, *Lilac Time* ran for six months at the Astor Theatre in New York. If Gary Cooper's notices were tepid, some critics finding his interpretation too restrained for the hearts-and-flowers story, his appearance opposite one of the top stars in films was a clear indication of his growing prestige.

The talkies had arrived and every contract player at Paramount was required to pass his orals. The test took on the character of an Inquisition. A soundstage was built at the studio and each actor was instructed to go into a booth to see if his voice would pass muster for talking pictures. He'd record in the morning, and get the verdict by afternoon.

Buddy Rogers recalled the discussions he had with Dick Arlen, Jack Oakie, and Gary Cooper. Because of their friendship—all were bachelors about town at the time—they had become known as the Four Musketeers. "They say you have to have a voice like Clive Brook or Ruth Chatterton," one of them said. "They're bringing a lot of those actors out from New York."

"My God!" Cooper said. "Do I have a voice?"

The four would hang around the recording studio to see how the other actors fared. One morning, Wallace Beery walked in. Three or four hours later, the door opened, and a young assistant director came out, yelling, "He has a voice! He has a voice! Wally Beery has a voice!" The four rested a little easier, thinking that if Beery's gravelly delivery was acceptable, they also might have a future in talkies.

Esther Ralston, for one, had few doubts about her ability to make the transition. "I'd been brought up in the theater, playing Shakespeare, and it didn't bother me any. I went right out in vaudeville, though, to get my bellows. But all the producers were so frightened. I was offered a long-term talking contract by Paramount, but my husband, who was my manager at the time, insisted on a raise of $100,000 to also use my voice. They wouldn't pay it, they were so frightened, which was probably very sensible at the time."

Asking for more money may have been exactly the wrong gambit. Although Miss Ralston made more talking pictures than silents, her tenure as a major star was over. Louise Brooks, one of the studio's great silent stars, found the transition "a splendid opportunity . . . for breaking contracts, cutting salaries, and taming the stars." Those who remained, as the Four Musketeers did, were in for an arduous adjustment, not only to a new medium, but to much greater personal discipline. "People will tell you the reason a lot of actors left Hollywood when sound came in was that their voices were wrong for talkies," Miss Brooks told Kenneth Tynan. "That's the official story. The truth is that the coming of sound meant the end of the all-night parties. With talkies, you couldn't stay out till sunrise anymore. You had to rush back from the studios and start learning your lines, ready for the next day's shooting at 8 A.M. That was when the studio machine really took over. It controlled you, mind and body, from the moment you were yanked out of bed at dawn until the publicity department put you back to bed at night."

Buddy Rogers said that after his friends' contracts were renewed for talking pictures, each actor was assigned his own dressing room. His social life didn't change much. "I read about all the wild carrying-on, but I didn't get in on one damned party. I didn't drink and didn't smoke."

The four actors saw each other every day. "Coop always did Westerns, and I would always get the musicals. He wanted to do a musical, and I wanted to do a Western. We were under contract, but that had nothing to do with anything. We'd be given a year's booking. I'd look at my assignments. 'Oh! I'm going to make a picture with Nancy Carroll. It's called *Abie's Irish Rose*. Nice!' Then the next picture. 'Oh! I'm going to work with Mary Brian this year.' We had four pictures lined up, but had no say as to what they would be."

The talkies were a new medium, and the films of that transitional period from 1927 to 1932 are quite awkward. They were basically silent films with occasional dialogue that actors had to shout at primitive microphones.

Gary Cooper was, like so many other actors, the victim of crude recording instruments and sound technicians who had only months before been radio operators on boats. He was miscast, awkwardly directed, required to interpret mawkish writing. That he shone at all is a tribute to his skill and natural ability; that he has moments of brilliance is miraculous. In his 1929 film *The Shopworn Angel*, the crackling soundtrack intruded on the mystical spell of the silent film, and the written subtitles distracted from the flow of the audible dialogue. The film was crippled by a wedding scene finale with blaringly spoken "I do's." Nonetheless, the public was pleased with Cooper's voice, as well as costar Nancy Carroll's, and his career in talkies was assured.

He could share the glowing notices on the set of his new film with the new girl in his life. She was a spicy cinnamon confection known as Lupe Velez, and they were the stars of *Wolf Song*, the story of a young Kentuckian who goes West to seek his fortune. He meets Lola, the daughter of a haughty Mexican overlord, and they elope.

The picture was released in two versions, one silent and the other part talkie. Lupe Velez sang two songs and Cooper one, "My Honey, Fare Thee Well." "The singing is quite good," said *The New York Times*.

Wolf Song proved to be a stepping-stone in Cooper's career. His director was Victor Fleming, who later made the famous MGM films *Red Dust, Captains Courageous, Gone With the Wind,* and *The Wizard of Oz*. Fleming had more of a flair for powerful images than he did for movement or for plausibility, often prolonging his striking visuals.

Fleming visualized *Wolf Song* as a study of the ebb and flow of sexual tensions. His direction of Cooper was as strong as any the actor received in silent films. Wellman and Waters had exploited his comfortable easygoing camera presence. Fleming used Cooper as an irresistible sex object. Slouching insolently against a post, peering lazily out from under the jaunty angle of his wide-brimmed hat and the lush curly locks of his long hair, he is simultaneously strong, silent, and shy, sullenly exuding sexual energy while playing hard to get, seeming both more innocent and more knowing than his open-faced trapper companions. Fleming set up Cooper in one of his powerful compositions and let his underplaying act as counterpoint. With a slight furrowing of the brow Cooper could express deep concern when Lupe Velez's father says he'll kill him if he comes near his daughter. Cooper then considers his threat, a slight grin appears on his face, and we *know* he's going to make love to her. When two toughs get into a fight over another girl, Cooper whisks her into a back room and when they come out Cooper makes it clear simply through a change in the way he carries himself that he's taken very good care of her. In contrast to this superb screen acting, Lupe Velez goes through the entire picture as if she were making a silent—right up to the chest-heavings that attracted so much attention in 1929 ("As a heaver, Lupe's a champ," commented *Variety*).

There is a rumor that Cooper and Velez filmed a nude swimming scene but it is probably not so. There is a nude scene, however. Cooper and his trapper friend Louis Wolheim bathe together in a hot spring, getting ready for a dance in the village that night. Wolheim surveys Cooper's body and says a woman is going to get hold of him some day and never let go. Cooper replies that a lot of women have tried and he's still going. Stills exist of the scene—one is in this book—but it does not survive in the University of California Archives' sole print of the film, possibly the only one extant. It's probable that the scene was shot but eliminated in some markets, giving rise to the idea that it was a Cooper-Velez bathing scene.

Few critics liked the picture, although with the help of a cross-country promotion tour by the stars, it was a commercial success. "There is something immensely droll and appealing about long, lanky, curly headed Gary Cooper," the *Chicago Tribune* said, "with his rare sweet smile. Good actor!"

When Cooper and Lupe Velez had started the picture, she was romantically involved with singer Russ Columbo, who was given a supporting role to be near her. Before filming was ended, Cooper moved out of his parents' home and into Lupe's hideaway at 1826 Laurel Canyon Road. It was to be the year's noisiest romance, with Lupe supplying most of the din.

"Hollywood history has never had another like her," Adela Rogers St. Johns wrote, "so kind, so merry, so warm-hearted. Hollywood to this minute has no more vivid memory than that of Lupe Velez at the Hollywood Legion fights. Visiting celebrities were always taken there not to see the bouts, but to see Lupe rooting, putting on a better show than the one in the ring. . . .

"Strange, how up to a given moment it seemed so funny, tiny, tempestuous Lupe Velez and six-foot-three of slow-moving Cooper; her firecracker Mexican accent and her sparkling laughter against the slow drawl and slower smile of the big cowboy; Lupe's public demonstrations and declarations of love and Gary's embarrassment and adoration."

Mrs. St. Johns once invited the lovers to her Malibu Colony home. She came back from an afternoon swim to find Cooper asleep on a couch and Lupe kneeling beside him. "Now I yield to no one in finding Cooper the most attractive man that's ever been in Hollywood, but Cooper asleep and snoring gently with his mouth open is a good deal like any other man asleep and snoring gently with his mouth open."

Lupe, noticing Mrs. St. Johns' arrival, said, "Is he

not beautiful? I have never seen anyone so beautiful as my Gary."

Cooper had woken and overheard the compliment, which struck him as amusing. Lupe turned violently on him. "You laugh at your Lupe's love?" Now it was a hair-pulling, scratching, one-way fight. Lupe adored scenes.

They created several in public. F. Scott Fitzgerald told Sheilah Graham he'd been pushed aside as a nobody when the two lovers arrived at a nightclub, to the delight of headwaiters and photographers. A Paramount executive, fearful that the affair would jeopardize Cooper's naive image, told him that his career would go farther if he gave Lupe up. There was still a considerable public which found his romance with a Mexican distasteful. There were limits, however, to Cooper's ambition, and he wouldn't drop the girl he thought he loved simply to advance his star status.

Nor would he drop her for his parents, who were scandalized. Cooper had always been a dutiful son. "Despite his success and fame," Hedda Hopper wrote, "Gary was never anything but their kid around them." Esther Ralston found Mrs. Alice Cooper to be "a wonderful mother, beautiful and gracious. She looked like Queen Mary. I think probably his upbringing and his respect for her attached itself to all womankind. Maybe Clara Bow and Lupe Velez were an escape from that. I doubt whether his mother approved of either of them." Mrs. Cooper's Church of England attitudes hardly meshed with the free spirits her son had taken up with. When he'd been involved with Clara Bow, he at least spent *some* nights at home. (Cooper was now twenty-eight.) Try as they might, his parents could never accept Lupe as the proper choice for him. Mrs. Cooper more than once tried to revive his interest in Evelyn Brent.

Lupe Velez didn't give a hang for public opinion. She was a pleasure-bent girl of twenty, a devout Catholic who knew there would be Sunday absolution for Saturday night sins. She wasn't the total peasant Hollywood thought her to be. Her father was a Mexican army colonel and her mother an opera singer. Born Maria Guadalupe Villalobos in 1909, in San Luis de Potosí, a Mexico City suburb, she was shipped off to a San Antonio, Texas, convent school at a time when Pancho Villa was attempting to wrest control of her homeland from the Constitutionalist party led by Alvaro Obregón. As she would later describe her days at our Lady of the Lake Convent: "Studied English. Liked to dance. Guess I wasn't much of a success as a student."

The volatile political climate in Mexico was stabilizing somewhat by the time Lupe was fifteen. In one of the last violent uprisings after Obregón took power, her father was killed. She had to return home and work as a salesgirl to help support her family. She took dancing lessons and tried to go on the stage. For her tiny, five-foot, 109-pound frame, she had abundant 37–26–35 curves. She was dancing in Mexican burlesque, which didn't sexily smirk like its American counterpart, when she was spotted by a Hollywood talent scout and signed to a three-year contract at Hal Roach Studios, where she made a series of modest comedies. Jean Harlow and Carole Lombard were working there at the same time.

The following year, Douglas Fairbanks was looking for an actress to play a wild mountain girl in *The Gaucho*. Dolores del Rio was already an established star, and this was a featured role. Lili Damita was briefly considered before Lupe won the part. She emerged from the picture a star, at age nineteen, and was signed to a five-year contract by United Artists.

When U. A. loaned her in 1929 to costar with Cooper in *Wolf Song*, Lupe was drawing a weekly salary of $2,500 to Cooper's $750. Again, Cooper was thought to have attached himself to a bigger star for career purposes. Cooper felt compelled to comment on the issue in *Photoplay* in April 1929: "It happens that I have made friendships with women who have aided me in my work and that they have been happy contacts. It was that way with Clara. In Evelyn Brent I found the companionship of a woman who was wise and brilliant. I was first attracted to her as a woman who had her feet on the ground and was not riding the clouds. In Lupe Velez I found a girl who takes the same joy out of primitive, elemental things that I do. In each friendship I have found that the most casual linking of our names caused dynamite. I am going to marry. I want, like every man, a home and a family."

If he was an opportunist, Esther Ralston, for one, found him the least obvious kind. "Gary was genteel . . . reserved. I don't think he would have used a woman merely for his own ends. I think it was more apt that women threw themselves at him. He was so personable and charming, and such a nice guy."

"Yes, he was a great ladies' man," Buddy Rogers said. "It was his height, his slimness. He was a very attractive guy and tremendously popular with everyone."

"There are two types of men who appeal most to women," Mrs. Jack Warner said. "One is the macho type. The other is the mother-love type of thing that a woman has for a boy. Some little boys you meet you just adore. Gary had this endearing boyish quality, and I don't think he ever lost that." Judging from his romantic rondelays, Ann Warner thought Cooper was probably a very sensuous man.

Stuart Heisler, who'd known Cooper since his *Barbara Worth* days and would later direct two of his pictures, was more plain-spoken. "Coop was probably the greatest cocksman that ever lived. They fell over themselves to get him to take them to bed. He couldn't stop screwing around. The women wouldn't let him. They'd go lay down for him in his portable dressing room by the soundstage. I guess he had the reputation for being a wonderful lay."

To Cooper, sex was to be enjoyed as often as the flesh was willing. Totally uninhibited, genitally well endowed, he took as much satisfaction in giving pleasure to his partners as he did in receiving it. Clara Bow's testimonial to his prowess received wide circulation. Women, so often involved with selfish lovers, were eager to dally with a man who was as handsome as he was sexually adept.

There was another aspect to Cooper's character. He loved women, but he also liked them. Consequently, there were few recriminations from the women he casually bedded. It was a pleasant interlude for all concerned, with few regrets, other than the probability that it wouldn't happen again.

In Lupe, Cooper found an equally sexy woman. "I guess I was in love with Miss Velez," Cooper wrote in *The Saturday Evening Post* in 1956, "or as much in love as one could get with a creature as elusive as quicksilver. . . . You couldn't help being attracted to Lupe Velez. She flashed, stormed, and sparkled, and on the set she was apt to throw things if she thought it would do any good. But she objected to being called wild, which was a word the reporters seemed to favor."

She was also extremely professional in her approach toward her craft, and totally reliable. She wasn't jealous of other women, except when they tried to encroach on her man. She was generous with her laughter, with her praise, and with herself.

Indicative of her singular lack of professional jealousy was her continuing close friendship with Estelle Taylor, the wife of Jack Dempsey, who'd virtually stolen *Where East Is East*, a Metro production filmed later in 1929, from the Latin star. They would remain so close that Miss Taylor would be the last person to see Lupe before she committed suicide in December of 1944.

She was equally generous with her family, and could laugh at their newly revived materialism. Their lot had considerably improved since she'd become a star.

Lupe entered Esther Ralston's dressing room one day. "Oh," she said, "I do not know what to do about my mother."

"What do you mean, Lupe? What's the matter?"

"I just don't know what to do."

"Why, you've given her diamonds and beautiful bracelets, and that fur coat, and the house."

"Yes," Lupe replied, "but now she wants rent."

"Rent?" Esther asked, incredulously.

"Yes. She say, 'For nine months I carry you. I want rent.'"

In February 1929 Lupe arrived at the Santa Fe Railroad station in Pasadena, wearing a wedding ring as well as an engagement ring. Cooper was there to see her off to the East Coast for a publicity tour. Lupe denied to the press that she and Cooper had recently slipped into Mexico to get married. "The scene at the station was one that will not easily be forgotten," a *Los Angeles Times* reporter wrote. "In that last frantic moment of good-bye, not being able to open the window to give Gary another farewell kiss, Lupe decided the thing to do was to break the car window. Only the restraining hand of those with her prevented this catastrophe."

There was a dichotomy in Gary Cooper's nature. Although he felt uncomfortable with such public displays, he also took pleasure in them. He couldn't have been an actor if he hadn't possessed a strong streak of exhibitionism. In his dressing room, he was a practicing nudist. When a childhood friend visited him, he was only slightly taken aback that Cooper should greet him buck naked. Soon after, Lupe called, and as Gary and Lupe discussed the delights they would be sharing that night, Cooper developed an erection which he did not bother to conceal from his guest. "It was one of the most uncomfortable experiences of my life," his friend, who asked to remain anonymous, said.

Cooper made a formal statement to the press that he was not engaged and not even thinking about marriage. He said it was unwise for a leading man in films to marry—"puts him in second class"—and he didn't elaborate.

What he refused to comment on was the announcement three months previously by Lupe's studio, United Artists, that the two would be marrying the very month he was denying any such plans.

Yet the affair continued.

Chapter 4

Elsa Maxwell said, "Gary Cooper used to wear the most awful clothes with a heavy watch chain strung across his middle." During his romance with Lupe, he had "unlaxed a lot," as Hedda Hopper put it. Now he was rakish, blooming color. Mrs. William Goetz remembered Cooper as the first man of unquestioned masculinity to wear a hot pink dress shirt with a grey flannel suit and a black tie.

Lupe had also encouraged him to be more serious about his craft, taking him to Josephine Dillon, Clark Gable's considerably older first wife, for drama and voice lessons. Mrs. Gable had been helping Lupe improve her English.

The household the lovers shared included various relatives of Lupe's whom she was supporting, as well as a pair of wild eagles that had free run of the big house. Cooper had trapped only one eagle at first, but Lupe sent him out to get a mate. Cooper had to scramble over the cactus-spiked hills of Catalina Island before he returned bruised and scratched with a second eagle for the aviary.

To Alice Cooper, her son was living in outback country with aborigines. She could not—would not—accept the way of life he'd chosen for himself. Neither would his studio, continuing to insist that the alliance with Lupe would ruin his career.

Cooper was torn. He said at the time, "I used to think when I was an extra working two days a week that it would be great to be somebody in the movies and have people point you out and say, 'There he goes.' Everybody likes attention, but in this business there's too much of it sometimes."

Despite makeup that looks ludicrous today and gestures too animated for the stoic he was to become, Cooper in his earliest films projected a persistent concern with what's right. He made the most trite contrivances seem interesting, because you could always see him thinking. Almost twenty-five years later, he would teach Roberta Haynes, his costar in *Return to Paradise* and a newcomer to films, a hard-earned lesson: "You don't necessarily have to think about the lines, but think of *something*."

Cooper's first talking picture would be Owen Wister's *The Virginian*, directed by Victor Fleming. This would be the third film version of the 1902 novel. Cecil B. DeMille's 1914 interpretation was one of the first features made in Hollywood. The second version was based on a 1923 Broadway adaptation and was presented by B. P. Schulberg. The first film made two lines famous: "This town ain't big enough for the both of us" and "Smile when you say that." The latter was already a cliché when Buster Keaton burlesqued it in *Go West* in 1925.

Victor Fleming made brilliant use of sound in *The Virginian*. He was one of the first directors to master the medium. Cooper peeks in on Mary Brian while she's trying to teach a schoolroom full of children, and the unison on their rendition of "Three Blind Mice" is thrown just off kilter enough to be funny. "I'm afraid that herd of yours is 'bout to stampede," says Cooper.

The "high-sign" between Cooper and his friend Steve—an imitation of the whistle of quail—is repeated ironically on the soundtrack (from an actual quail) at the poignant moment when Cooper is forced to hang Steve for cattle rustling. Fleming used sound the way D.

W. Griffith used meaningful props in silent films. Fleming even managed to avoid the overmodulation that marred many early talkies—and made them unbearable in theaters where anxious managers cranked their volume up till the soundtrack became a deafening roar—by reducing the recording level and reducing the chances of both distortion and excessive volume. The effect was noted by *The New York Times*: "The sounds, whether footfalls, horses' hoofs (sic), rumbling wheels, or voices, are remarkably well recorded and reproduced."

The Virginian often succeeds simply by imitating the best elements of silent film technique. Most directors, in their eagerness to make "all-talking" pictures, turned their backs on the long tradition of excellence in image-making that stretched back to what D. W. Griffith was doing in 1910. Contrary to the claustrophobic nature of many early talkies, Fleming made ingenious use of perspective, with foreground figures hundreds of yards from important background figures. The scenes outdoors very clearly encompass the whole outdoors.

Perhaps the best use of good silent movie storytelling comes at the moment when Cooper first realizes his best friend Steve is involved in cattle rustling. He sees a steer with its brand changed. He sees a fire at the smoldering stage. He sees Steve's horse, with a branding iron in the stirrup. In a strong closeup, he tests the iron with his bare fingers and the camera is close enough to see them recoil in pain. The revelation hurts us as well as him.

There were other highly effective visual devices. As Steve is about to be hanged, the shadow of the next man's gun falls darkly on Cooper's face. When he is then forced to shoot down the villain, Trampas, the man who lured Steve into cattle rustling in the first place, it is Steve's gun The Virginian does it with, and closeups of the large *Steve* on the handle remind him that the reasons he must gun down Trampas are multileveled, complex, and deep in his heart.

All of these touches raise the film above the general level of sound pictures of the time. In fact it would greatly influence later talkies. Its critical and popular success was such that Paramount was compelled ("by popular demand") to rerelease the picture in 1935, when there were many more technically accomplished talkies to meet the demand. It has its flaws as well. The picture has no incidental music whatsoever. The title is accompanied by the sound of lowing cattle; after a while it sounds silly. Throughout the movie, the action scenes tend to have no dialogue, and the dialogue scenes tend to have no action. There is, in fact, very little action at all, especially for a Western, a fact that was not lost on contemporary reviewers: "It may not be a yarn jammed with thrills, but it is one that always compels attention," said *The New York Times*.

The Virginian poses the kind of conflict that would be reworked in a more sophisticated fashion in *High Noon* in 1952, but it would be essentially the same as in the 1929 film: a showdown looms on the hero's wedding day. His conscience tells him he must face it; his wife tells him he must not. He can't live with the love of his life if he rises to the occasion; he can't live with himself if he doesn't.

Fleming exploits Cooper's amazing ability to look spontaneous. For roles more consistent in this seeming artlessness, Cooper would have to wait for microphones sensitive enough to pick up the kind of half whisper he could deliver through clenched teeth.

Toward the end of his career, Gary Cooper mentioned several other pictures as his favorites, then revised his statement and cited *The Virginian* as his favorite of all his nearly 100 films.

Cooper visited Lupe Velez on location at Truckee, 7,000 feet up in the California Rockies, where William Wyler was directing her in *The Storm*. Wives and lovers joined the cast and crew on weekends, and the railroad cars they were sleeping on bounced with great ardor on Saturday nights. On one Sunday, the company watched enthralled as Cooper took Lupe's lipstick and painted large areas of her exposed skin.

When in Los Angeles, Cooper wasn't spending all his nights at Lupe Velez's Laurel Canyon home. She had been away on location or making personal appearances for a great part of the year, and Cooper had taken a flat at 1919 Argyle Avenue in Hollywood. The press reported his new address with the news that Cooper had been arrested for driving forty-five miles an hour in a twenty-five-mile zone on Wilshire Boulevard.

Joe Sternberg was a Paramount director who admired Erich von Stroheim so much that he changed his name to Josef von Sternberg. He came across Marlene Dietrich when he took a leave of absence from the studio to go to Germany to direct *The Blue Angel* starring Emil Jannings. Once abroad, von Sternberg started bombarding Jesse L. Lasky, Paramount's vice-president in charge of production, with memos raving about Dietrich. He urged that she be brought to America. Sidney Kent, a studio executive, was going to Europe on business, and Lasky asked him to determine whether von Sternberg's interest was personal or professional. It would prove to be both. Kent was as impressed by Marlene Dietrich's potential as von Sternberg. "SHE'S SENSATIONAL," he wired back. "SIGN HER UP."

Von Sternberg was to direct all of Dietrich's first American pictures. *Morocco* would introduce her to audiences at the same time it was affording Gary Cooper a chance to play his first unsympathetic hero. He was an American private in the French Foreign Legion, ruthless with women, yet attracted to a cabaret singer newly arrived to the desert city. The feeling is more than mutual. At picture's end, she has thrown away her high heels to follow her hero to an uncertain future in the desert.

Film cultists would come to consider *Morocco* Cooper's first great motion picture. Yet, it wasn't his film at all, and no one knew this better than he. The film belonged to von Sternberg and Dietrich.

Von Sternberg may well have been the most brilliant lyricist of light and shadow the American cinema ever produced. He was able to make black and white look more radiant than color. Charlie Chaplin was largely responsible for getting von Sternberg's avant-garde film, *The Salvation Hunters*, released by United Artists. Chaplin was to be the first in a long series of von Sternberg associates to admire his talent but find him an intractable and inflexible collaborator.

Von Sternberg emulated his idol's immaculate dress, including von Stroheim's white gloves and cane. He once told actor Clive Brook, "The only way to succeed is to make people hate you. That way they remember you."

To British film historian Kevin Brownlow, he said, "I am ice cold. You cannot direct unless you have contempt for your camera, contempt for your lights, contempt for your actors." When asked if this wasn't too strong a statement, von Sternberg amended it to "indifference."

His soft inner core of sensitivity plastered over with a cold and hard surface became the model for leading characters in his films.

Very little happens in the hour and a half of *Morocco*. There is a shot early in the film in which a crowd of Moroccans, milling through one of the city's byways, pass back and forth under an overhanging trellis which throws its shadows on their passing headgear. As the shot goes on (for some length), it becomes clear that the subject is not the crowd of people, who become irrelevant, but the shadows gliding mysteriously over and around them. In the same way, the dramatic scenes are not shots of people doing and saying things to each other; von Sternberg is photographing the emotions that passed through his characters and lie unspoken under the elliptical dialogue revealed in such minimal manifestations as an enigmatic look, a pair of initials carved on a tabletop, a fan languorously waved, a broken string of pearls, or a pair of high heels removed at the start of a barefoot trek across the sands.

The general style of *Morocco* consists of long, sultry takes before a camera that never moves. Cooper, during the five-week shooting schedule, much of it in the scorching desert, had no concept of what von Sternberg was trying to achieve. "First, he directed almost entirely in German," he recalled, "and I didn't understand a word. Second, he was introducing ingenious camera effects never seen in Hollywood before. It was bad enough not knowing what he was talking about, but I didn't even know what was going on."

Adolphe Menjou was in the cast, and the nominal star of the picture went to him for advice. Cooper came away from the meeting encouraged, unaware that von Sternberg was totally contemptuous of Menjou. Von Sternberg, in fact, was unenthused with the casting of both men. He'd compromised. Since Dietrich had shown her legs throughout *The Blue Angel*, he wanted to put her in pants, finding the vaguely lesbian connotation delicious. The studio had at first opposed it, but von Sternberg was eventually allowed to have his way. He thought that Cooper was harmless enough, but found Menjou a distinct liability. He agreed to their casting after realizing that the film would either succeed or fail on the merits of a generally unknown personality: Dietrich.

Cooper recalled that von Sternberg "had a habit of compelling the whole cast to stand around him in hushed silence while he coached Miss Dietrich in German. In one of those meetings I saw my chance. I opened my mouth wide and yawned. An actress gasped. Adolphe grinned. Von Sternberg stopped, pawed the air a minute, and then continued. I yawned again. About the fourth yawn, with von Sternberg's collar shrinking to the choking point, he let me have it in perfect English."

Cooper replied that if von Sternberg would only speak more English he might be able to stay awake. Von Sternberg stormed off the set, but he did manage to throw his actors an English phrase or two when shooting resumed the following day.

Cooper wanted to play the Sydney Carton role in *A Tale of Two Cities*, a film project Paramount was considering. He'd even made up as the character and taken photographs which he showed to the studio brass. They didn't see him as a Charles Dickens character, however, and the project was abandoned.

Cooper was affronted. There followed a drawn-out dispute over his salary, which he lost. To teach him a little humility, he was assigned in support of Clara Bow, who hadn't yet matched the success of her silent pictures in the talkies. The film was to be *City Streets*, based on a story by Dashiell Hammett.

Clara Bow now became involved in a scandal that virtually drove her out of films. Her private secretary, Daisy De Voe, sold a lurid account of Clara's love affairs to a tabloid and then was brought to trial for embezzling money from her former employer. The press played the story big, stopping just short of calling Clara a nymphomaniac. Because of the turmoil, Clara could not do *City Streets*. B. P. Schulberg thought his new girl friend, Sylvia Sidney, might fill the role. The emphasis of the film was changed, and Gary Cooper was now the top-billed star.

Civilized, refined Rouben Mamoulian was an unlikely choice of director for one of those hard-hitting gangster films the studios turned out in the late twenties and early thirties. The opening montage of beer trucks rolling, some of them directly over the camera's head, emphasizes the deadly serious nature of a business that represents boisterous good fun to its customers. The dissolve from a keg of foaming beer to the river with a victim's hat floating in it connects in one vivid stroke frothy spirits with literal death. A brief montage of stark, lonely shots depicts Sylvia Sidney's lengthy prison internment in the most desolate visual shorthand; a dialogue scene between two wary inhabitants of the asphalt jungle is represented on the soundtrack by the natural voices and on camera by closer cuts to two separate china figurines, both cats, underscoring the fact that beneath casual chitchat the two are arching their backs.

Cooper's character has more place in this environment than it would first appear. A cocky cowboy adrift in the big city, he projects a totally unassuming nature while performing every impossible stunt in the book, combining a strong sense of bravado with perfect nonchalance. He could throw anything, flip anything, and shoot anything, flinging a monogrammed handkerchief in the air and firing a hole directly through the "M."

Cooper was now doing five pictures a year, filming one picture during the day and another at night. Sometimes two of his films would be released virtually at the same time. His normal weight of 180 pounds, slim enough for a man almost six-foot-three, dropped to a dangerously low 148 pounds. Cooper was tired from overwork and depressed by violent conflicts with his parents and the studio that his continued association with Lupe Velez engendered. He was suffering from jaundice. He was also nearly broke, since he'd never neglected to indulge himself and Lupe while still partially supporting his parents. Finally, he dropped from depression and exhaustion. Adela Rogers St. Johns claimed he'd had a nervous breakdown, due to his realization that the affair with Lupe had to end.

Paramount executives were now aware how dangerously ill their increasingly valuable property was. He'd worked for five years without a day off, often when making two films at once, as much as twenty hours a day. His bosses agreed to allow Cooper to take a five-week rest cure in Europe . . . if he went alone.

Stuart Heisler, who would have one of the longest professional associations with Cooper, which started when he was an editor on *The Winning of Barbara Worth* and ended with his direction of *Dallas* in 1951, described an incident during Cooper's departure which was never reported by the press. "If Coop was going to take the Twentieth Century to Chicago Lupe Velez wanted to know why he was going and she wasn't going with him. His departure was all set up. Coop didn't have anything to do with it, except to get down to the station and get on the train. He was there talking to a couple of people. She sneaked around and saw him. He was standing right outside the train. She shouted, 'Gary, you son of a bitch!' Then she took a shot at him, but she missed. By that time Coop had slammed the door and was inside. The train pulled out, but a hell of a lot of people were wise. Some woman had taken a shot at Gary Cooper.''

Chapter 5

"It's a sort of open house for celebrities . . . dignitaries . . . royalty on the loose . . . other congenial characters."

That's how Paramount executive Walter Wanger described Villa Madama, with its notable frescoes by Raphael, when he gave Gary Cooper a letter of introduction to Dorothy di Frasso. American-born, she'd entered the ranks of European nobility in 1923 with her marriage to Italian Count Carlo di Frasso. Her previous husband had been Commander Claude Graham White, famous on both sides of the Atlantic as a heroic aviator and philanderer. The marriage had been brief, ending in divorce in 1916.

Dorothy was well into her thirties when she married the elderly Italian count; some called it an acquisition on her part. In her second marriage, she'd anticipated the vogue of Hollywood movie queens buying royal husbands. Already, in 1931, one of them was about to be passed along like a scepter from the previous top female box office attraction to her successor. Henri, the Marquis de la Falaise de la Coudraye, was divorcing Gloria Swanson to marry Constance Bennett.

Born Dorothy Taylor in Watertown, New York, the countess inherited $12 million from her father, a leather manufacturer, and was the sister of Bert Taylor, the President of the New York Stock Exchange. Her brother was intrigued by people in show business, having at one time been linked to Gertrude Lawrence. His wife, Olive, was a former actress. His sister was also fascinated by celebrities, who seemed to return the interest, and she embarked on a career of fun and frivolity unsurpassed on two continents. Having been disappointed once in love, she would take her pleasures with the same directness as any man. What with her handsome legacy, she could well afford to indulge them.

She'd already spent $1 million restoring Villa Madama—which would be confiscated by Mussolini as his guest house during World War II—and was already renowned as an international figure. Her first large dinner immediately established her as the top hostess of Italy—she entertained His Royal Highness, Crown Prince Umberto of Italy, at a nine-course dinner for two hundred.

Walter Wanger told the Countess di Frasso that Gary Cooper, an American actor, would be calling on her. Elsa Maxwell, more interested in the holiday jaunt she was planning with the Countess, said Gary Cooper was a short, unattractive man. Dorothy di Frasso decided that her staff could take care of his needs until she and Elsa Maxwell returned.

Cooper was told by his doctors he should take at least a year off. He settled for the five weeks the studio granted; he wasn't especially eager to be absent from the volatile industry during this period when quick adjustments to sudden change were required if an actor were to survive. He disembarked in Algiers, walking around the dock to get his bearings, when a group of African boys gathered around him, chattering in French. The only word he caught was "cinema." Some of them went running off, coming back shortly with fifty more children. Lacking a common language, they tried to communicate by making faces at each other. They grinned at Cooper, some of them making pistols of their fingers, yelling, "Boom! Boom!" He felt better already.

From there he went to Venice and Lido Beach, before going to Rome.

The very lean cowboy, with his infirmities, including, as one columnist put it, "a slightly broken heart," was quickly ensconced in a guest suite of the Villa to await the return of the Countess and Elsa Maxwell. Once she returned and took a look at him, his hostess immediately took charge of his recuperation. "A wonderful woman," Cooper would later say. "I could never be grateful enough to her."

The Count and Countess had come to an agreement about their marriage, and they went separate ways. "Dorothy seemed to have the money," Buddy Rogers said, "and her husband seemed to have the title. She was in the United States a great deal of the time, but I only saw him in Italy."

Inevitably, the thirty-year-old Cooper was showing his gratitude to the forty-three-year-old Countess in not quite the usual way. For she couldn't do enough for him.

As Cooper later said in *The Saturday Evening Post*, "The Countess . . . took me in hand like the lost lad I was. Her villa was a meeting place for the international set, and rubbing elbows with assorted noblemen, heiresses, and celebrated characters made me forget my fears.

"It was hard to tell whether the Countess threw one party that lasted all summer or a series of weekend parties that lasted all week. Guests just came and went as if the Villa Madama were a Grand Hotel. With the Italian contingent headed by Prince Umberto, the British contingent by the Duke of York, and the American contingent by Barbara Hutton, I was as out of place as a cowboy can get all at one time. . . ."

Mrs. Jack Warner thinks the popular conception that the Countess kept Cooper was inaccurate and unfair. "I think it's a better word to say that she sponsored him. He went to Rome looking like a cowboy. She introduced him to European society, and he came back looking like a prince."

71

He'd been introduced to the best tailors in Rome, who taught him how to dress. His manners became equally as continental. "Gary wasn't a real hick," Ann Warner said, "but he didn't know much about that life of social elegance that Dorothy did."

"Countess Dorothy did everything in the grand manner," Cooper said. "When I pronounced myself well enough to ride, she simply summoned the Italian Cavalry to keep me company."

Cooper was invited to join the horsemen on a "little steeple-chase course" they'd devised to exercise their horses on. He was one of only four riders to complete the course, marked by impossibly high hurdles and dangerous water jumps. Only then did he discover he'd conquered the notorious Tor de Quinto course, one of the most challenging in the world.

It was a tremendous coup for a horseman to complete the course on his first try, and significant that an American movie cowboy was one of the few to do so. Instead of being congratulated for upholding the honor of his studio, Paramount cut short his vacation. If Cooper was well enough to be frolicking all over Europe, as press reports had it, he could return to work. Paramount called him back to start work on *His Woman* with Claudette Colbert. The French-born actress was one of several Broadway performers signed to studio contracts between 1928 and 1930, including Ruth Chatterton, Kay Francis, Phillips Holmes, Walter Huston, Fredric March, Helen Morgan, Jack Oakie, and Sylvia Sidney. She'd been kept as frantically busy as her costar in the new picture, having appeared in her eleventh film in two years.

In late July of 1931, Cooper returned from his European jaunt aboard the *Majestic*. When the liner docked in New York, he was accosted by the press. In answer to a question, he said Lupe Velez had flatly refused his marriage proposal.

His mother visited while he was filming *His Woman*. Lupe Velez herself had recently returned to California from a trip East, and she confirmed Cooper's statement. "I don't love Gary Cooper," she said. "I turned Cooper down because his parents didn't want me to marry him, and because the studio thought it would injure his career. Now it's over, I'm glad. I feel so free. I went around New York, did whatever I wanted, had a fine time . . . I must be free. I know men too well; they are all the same, no? They fall in love with Lupe, very much, the way Lupe is. Then quick they want I should be somebody else . . . the doormat . . . they wish to conquer the fiery one, to tame Lupe. I die first."

She followed that up with another statement a week later, announcing, "I am ever so much in love again. Who is he? I'll never tell. Nobody is going to know this time because that spoils everything when the public knows."

Yet, she couldn't stop talking about Cooper. In a later interview, she placed the blame for their broken affair directly on Mrs. Alice Cooper. "I'm not good enough for him," she said. "I know that. But I tried to make him happy. I *did* make him happy. I would have done anything in the world for him. His mother! I hope she never cries the tears that I have cried. I hope she never knows the suffering I have known. I didn't hate her . . . that much. She said I wasn't good enough for Gary. She told him that when I was in New York, I was seeing other men. She told him that I wasn't faithful to him. He believed what she told him."

Mrs. Cooper, as Buddy Rogers remembers her, "wasn't a stage mother at all. She was just a normal mother concerned about her son. She was around a great deal of the time." Mrs. Cooper felt she couldn't let Lupe's statement go unchallenged—she was not a heartless meddler at all. Overcoming her British reserve, she allowed a fan magazine to publish "Gary's Mother Speaks at Last." She and Lupe Velez were to exchange more words in print than they ever had in person.

"I have no ill-feeling toward Lupe Velez," she stated. "I wish her continued success. I think she is a fine little actress. I wish her happiness. My only regret is that she finds it necessary to talk so openly and so violently for publication. Her love for Gary, I should think, would make her want to keep it a secret thing, rather than to allow it to become public property. . . .

"It shocks me, of course, to read in headlines that I have invaded Lupe's home . . . to get various personal knicknacks that belong to Gary. I have not been inside her home since before the break. And to hear stories, no matter how grossly exaggerated they may be, that she demands of Gary that I be kept from bothering her. I haven't seen Lupe for months.

"And preposterous stories that I threatened to kill myself if Gary married Lupe, and that if he did, I said it would break my heart. And that I made a long trip to New York upon Gary's return from his vacation abroad this summer, not to see my son, but to tell him that his sweetheart was unfaithful to him. Do mothers do that? Certainly I don't. And the stories, too, that I had told friends that Lupe wasn't good enough to marry my boy. . . .

"I have never set down any dictates about the kind of girl my son should marry. I rely too much on his innate good taste, his judgment, his intelligence. He knows whom he wants to marry, and he will marry her when the time comes. It will not be the duty of his father nor myself to select his wife for him. . . .

"Perhaps I have not entirely approved of any of the women with whom Gary has been romantically associated. But does any mother entirely approve of her son's choice, or her daughter's? Very seldom. And very few of them raise objections. Our children have their own lives to live. We have ours. We cannot live theirs for them.

"There are qualities, of course, that I should like to see in Gary's wife. The most important are respectability and fair-mindedness. I leave the matter of beauty and talent and charm up to him. I don't care whether she is blonde or brunette, or whether or not she is an actress. After all, why should I?"

Mrs. Cooper, in answering Lupe's accusations, denied some charges Lupe had never made. It took no great perception for the general public to realize how violent her opposition was to her son's marrying Lupe.

Cooper was trying to avoid the imbroglio. Not only did he have to film *His Woman* with Claudette Colbert in New York; he had to make long-range career decisions. Obviously, he wouldn't be able to continue working at such a breakneck pace. Suddenly, with no overtures on his part, a solution presented itself. Stuart Heisler was on a film-editing assignment in New York when he was approached by Jack Moss, an associate producer on the Cooper-Colbert picture. "I'd gotten to know Jack very well," Heisler said, "and had a damn good opinion of him. One day he asked me how well I knew Cooper. He wanted to get a chance to really talk to him."

Moss informed Heisler that Cooper was being handled badly, and that he needed someone to oversee his career. When Cooper and Jack Moss got together, they discovered they had a perfect rapport, and Moss became Cooper's personal manager. The teaming was to be the turning point of Cooper's professional life. Not only did Moss engineer an immediate $1,000-per-week increase in Cooper's salary to $1,750, but he was the advisor who steered Cooper into making some of the most distinguished pictures and vastly popular entertainments in the history of films. Within a short time, Moss would also be handling the careers of Henry Hathaway and Heisler, whom he would guide in their transitions to film directors.

To assure that his stay in New York wasn't totally humdrum, his friend Walter Wanger—they often courted and bedded the same women—interceded for Cooper. Wanger had invited Tallulah Bankhead to the opening of *The Third Little Show*, starring Bea Lillie. Then he called, saying that a business engagement was forcing him to cancel their date.

"Don't be alarmed, Tallulah," he said. "I'm sending a most attractive young man in my place."

Bankhead, the toast of England before returning to America to embark on a career in talking pictures, blistered Walter Wanger's ears. She wasn't accustomed to being shunted off to a blind date. Wanger insisted she would like the fellow.

"I must confess I was as fascinated as the next gal by the screen Cooper," Bankhead said. "In my book Gary and John Barrymore were the two most beautiful men I had ever looked upon. I use the word beautiful in its classic sense."

Yet, throughout the evening, he continued talking in the same monosyllabic "Yup" and "Nope" he'd used in *The Virginian*. "His reticence set me off into a torrent of words," she wrote. "Thus do I manifest my nervousness when faced by a gentleman dedicated to the proposition that silence is golden. But I got a great kick out of being with him." Especially when he deposited her on her doorstep, and beyond, at the end of the evening.

Two days later, a New York columnist wrote that the two were engaged. Reuters, the British news service, wired her on the following day: "CONFIRM ENGAGEMENT TO GARY COOPER."

Tallulah wired back: "IT'S JACKIE COOPER I'M ENGAGED TO."

One of the Reuters newspapers ran the story of her impending "marriage" under a headline: TALLULAH ENGAGED TO JOHN COOPER. Under the banner were two pictures, one of the actress and the second of John Cooper, a retired professional golfer.

The threatened Dorothy di Frasso immediately sailed for New York. When she and Cooper were seen in public, she was identified by the press as a mysterious countess. Once assured that Tallulah wasn't poaching on her territory, the Countess returned to Italy while Cooper resumed his work.

Cooper never claimed to be an easy study, and preparation for his work was often exhausting, particularly during a period when he was in precarious health. While filming *His Woman*, he found the only way he could keep going was to get himself into character, fix the scene in his mind, then stretch out on whatever was handy to take a nap. At the moment, he needed as many catnaps as possible to conserve his energy, but he would follow that procedure during healthier times throughout the rest of his career.

He wasn't in completely good health when shooting had started on the picture. Cooper and Colbert were bogged down by a tepid, melodramatic script and, though they would perform competently, were miscast to boot. Shooting exteriors along the Eastern seaboard and interiors at Paramount's Astoria studio was both exhausting and demoralizing. Cooper lost twenty pounds, which he'd just managed to gain back during his European trip, and was anemic and again dangerously underweight. He needed a break, his doctor again insisted, of at least six months, and perhaps a year.

Shooting lasted until late September. After that, the studio wanted Cooper to make three additional pictures in Hollywood.

He was mentally and physically unable to resume the accelerated treadmill the studio had kept him on over the past five years.

After leaving his doctor's office, he ran into Jimmy and Willie Donahue, whom he'd met through the Countess. They were going on an African safari and invited the actor to join them. Then, he had dinner with Jerome Preston, who owned a farm on the shore of Lake Nyasa in Tanganyika. Preston and his wife urged him to accompany them on their trip. "So I took the rest of my savings and went to Africa," he stated. "I stayed there for five months. Resting at the Prestons' home, going on safari in the high country of Tanganyika, did me a world of good."

Cooper wrote a polite fiction to his parents, saying he would be sailing up the Nile alone. The press would soon inform them otherwise.

His recurring jaundice totally disappeared and Cooper began gaining back badly needed pounds as he recuperated on the Preston ranch. His hosts, in the meantime, had gone to Nairobi to escort Dorothy di Frasso and her entourage back to Tanganyika. The big-game hunting safari took them to the slopes of Mount Kenya. Sunday supplements recorded the progress of the group, which consisted of members of New York society, the international set, and one Hollywood star. Readers avidly followed the progress of the intrepid group.

Yet, as Cooper said, "When a report reached New York that we were dressing for dinner, the conclusion was that Africa had gone soft, and that we were a symptom of its decline."

He'd decided that if he lost the fight with the studio, which Jack Moss was currently waging for him, he'd have enough money to buy a ranch in Kenya. At the moment, that looked like a real possibility. Paramount announced the signing of a young British actor as the successor to Gary Cooper. Cooper's initials were transposed when Archibald Leach was given the name of Cary Grant. Soon, three roles originally planned for Cooper—*Hot Saturday* with Nancy Carroll; *Madame Butterfly* with Sylvia Sidney; and *The Eagle and the Hawk* with Fredric March and Carole Lombard—were assigned to the newly named Grant. Jack Moss wired him not to be unduly alarmed. He knew for a fact that Paramount had assured its exhibitors that Gary Cooper would soon be starring in four consecutive pictures. The studio had already announced that the first would be *The Broken Wing*.

While he sailed to Europe, then on to Africa, much of Hollywood assumed it was his Italian-based benefactress who'd called him back and, what's more, that she was paying all expenses.

"Coop had no career at the time," Buddy Rogers said. "He was down and depressed and sick. Dorothy came into his life at the right moment."

During the early 1930s, such Italian luxury liners as the *Conte Grande* and the *Conte Rosso* transported the *haut monde* from America to Europe and back. In the following year, the Italians would launch the *Conte de Savoia*, one of the first passenger liners to be equipped with gyro stabilizers.

William Goetz, a studio executive who'd recently married Louis B. Mayer's daughter Edith, heard of Cooper's sailing for Europe as the guest of the American heiress, and topically, wittily observed—in a remark later attributed to both Robert Benchley and Alexander Woollcott—"I've always wanted to go to Europe on the Countess di Frasso."

Edie Goetz remembers that the Countess was of a forgiving nature and wasn't affronted for long. That the Goetzes later became very close friends of Gary Cooper also indicates the actor didn't take umbrage. Yet, an undercurrent of not-so-veiled contempt was developing toward Gary Cooper, and Goetz's remark typified the attitudes of many.

Even after he was respectably married and becoming part of the Establishment, his relationship with the Countess was still cause for ridicule. When Clare Boothe Luce's *The Women* opened in New York in December of 1936, one of the characters was the Countess de Lage, "a silly, amiable middle-aged woman, with carefully waved, bleached hair." None of the men in the women's lives was ever seen in either the stage or film versions of the Luce work, but an offstage character was Buck Winston, a dumb cowboy taken over by the Countess, who decides to make an actor out of him, only to lose him to another woman. The real-life inspirations for the two characters were quite apparent.

Dorothy di Frasso occasionally made Cooper the butt of her stories, so the actor seemed to be getting it from all sides. The Countess, as Buddy Rogers recalled, liked to tell an anecdote about their African safari.

"The sun was setting," she said. "Coop was sitting away from the rest of us, silhouetted against the sky. He had an elbow on his knee . . . looking down at the ground . . . concentrating. It was the most beautiful picture I'd ever seen. 'Oh, darling Coop,' I said, 'what are you thinking?' He looked at me for a minute. Then he said, 'I've been wondering whether I should change my brand of shoe polish.' "

Rogers insists Cooper was the first to laugh at the story. If it painted him as less than an intellectual, Rogers felt, "He was as deep a thinker as any of us."

And, to the amazement of Paramount, he was of even greater public interest, thousands of miles away, than most of the stars cavorting in Hollywood. The safari was chronicled almost daily in the press. People were intrigued by the idea of a movie star on a hunt for dangerous animals.

While the African idyll continued, one of the other women in Cooper's life was still talking for publication. One of Lupe Velez's final words about their affair came in October of 1931. "When Gary and I were in love it was terrible," she stated. "He took me away from my mother too much. I hate young men; they are so conceited."

Her new attraction, it would soon become known, was an aging John Gilbert, with whom she took a European vacation in November.

Lupe was a fiercely loyal friend, as she proved the following August when her friend Estelle Taylor divorced Jack Dempsey. Throughout their marriage, Lupe insisted that the boxer wasn't good enough for her friend. When Miss Taylor came to the same conclusion, Lupe was constantly there to hold her hand during court proceedings.

For the moment, however, she was playing mother hen to the faltering Gilbert. "He hides in that big gloomy house like a bear with a sore ear," she told Adela Rogers St. Johns. "His wife [Ina Claire] told him she is a better actor than he is, which is true, but no wife should tell a man such a thing. I will make him laugh. That will cure him."

Mrs. St. Johns once overheard Lupe talking to Gilbert. "Big baby," she said, "you let Hollywood get you down. I say to Hollywood, look out, here comes Lupe. If my heart hurts me, I go to the fights and holler whoopee. Hollywood says, 'That Lupe, she is the wild one, nothing ever gets her down.' "

The actor was sitting out an enormous contract with Metro while the studio decided what to do with him. Louis B. Mayer had intensely disliked Gilbert since he'd overheard the actor telling a story about his mother, Jolly Della Pringle, a repertory show actress. The train of her dress had rolled up in a curtain after a performance. "That's the last time I saw my mother's ass," Gilbert cracked.

"That man is a monster!" Mayer later fumed. "A degenerate!" To the studio chief nothing was more sacred than a mother's love.

Nevertheless, Mayer was too shrewd a businessman to intentionally sabotage the career of a potentially valuable commodity. The actor was being forced to reestablish himself with the public, as were many great silent stars at the time. Gilbert's voice could have been trained. Yet, the actor did nothing to save his career, and the prudish Mayer had neither the time nor the inclination to save it for him.

Lupe's efforts on Gilbert's behalf were doomed to fail, for she couldn't shore up the erosion of his self-confidence. Once she realized she couldn't help him, their alliance ended. John Gilbert would become the most famous casualty in the transition to talking pictures.

Late in 1931, though no agreement had been reached in his contract dispute with Paramount, Cooper wired the studio that he would be taking an additional leave of absence. He would be gone a total of six months.

Had he known the precariousness of the studio's very existence, Cooper probably would have come back immediately to try to salvage his career elsewhere. In the following year, Paramount would lose $21 million. The expanding company had bought many theaters with company stock, which it agreed to repurchase at a fixed high sum. The value of the stock was dropping rapidly. Creditors forced the company into receivership.

Investors tried to force out company founder Adolph Zukor. But it was determined that he, if anyone, could salvage the situation. There were certain decisions that only an innate showman could make. Among them was what to do about Gary Cooper.

After arbitrators were assigned to reorganize the corporation, Famous Players-Lasky was liquidated as a producing entity, and Jesse Lasky and B. P. Schulberg were ousted. No matter how lightly Cooper had been regarded by studio executives in the past, they had the box office receipts proving he was one of the studio's top draws. Among male actors, only Fredric March was more popular. They had to get Cooper back to work at any cost. In its current delicate condition, Paramount couldn't risk its future on an as yet untested talent like Cary Grant.

The studio agreed to Moss's demands. In the new seven-year contract being drawn up, Cooper would be getting $2,500 a week in addition to approval of scripts.

The change in his fortunes hadn't come a moment too soon. The safari ended, and Countess di Frasso suggested a spring caravan to the watering places of the Riviera. Despite the Countess' largesse, he'd gone broke at Monte Carlo, not from gambling, but from the accumulated expenses of the last few months—and no income.

When he returned to California, he was met at the train by reporters. He confirmed that his love affair with Lupe was over and that he was "out of love temporarily."

He described his time away as a "six months' finishing tour," returning with many pieces of luggage holding new suits and ties and shoes, even dressing gowns and ascots. In answer to a question, Cooper declared that Italian tailors were superior to the British. "Even the Prince of Wales is buying his suits in Rome." Gary Cooper had indeed come a long way.

In addition to his once-scruffy wardrobe, the "old cowboy" brand of tobacco had been replaced by a milder American brand. Despite his new polish, Cooper denied that he brought back an English valet, as had been rumored.

When asked if he was romantically interested in the Countess di Frasso, now the houseguest of Mary Pickford, he replied, "She and her husband were very pleasant and hospitable when I was in Rome. I stayed at their villa as their guest for some time."

Cooper leased a house in Beverly Hills—the only one he would ever live in decorated specifically to his personal taste—and he accessorized it with a selection of the sixty mounted specimens he'd shot during his safari. Having the run of the house was a chimpanzee he'd captured during a game hunt. Also soon installed as a houseguest was Elsa Maxwell, recruited by the Countess to do some subtle spying, as well as by her host to put on entertainments for such friends as Clark and Rhea Gable, William Powell and Carole Lombard, and Irving Thalberg and Norma Shearer.

It came to be said around Beverly Hills that Dorothy di Frasso was the houseguest at Pickfair who stayed and stayed and stayed. This was surprising, since she and Mary Pickford hadn't known each other very well. They'd met in New York for the first time, prior to the Countess following Cooper to California.

"Oh, Mary darling," she said, "in a week or so I'm going to Honolulu. It's my first trip. I'm going to stop by Beverly Hills for a day or two. Could I stay with you?"

"Why, of course," said Miss Pickford.

The Countess, as Buddy Rogers recalled, stayed the better part of a year, "and we loved every minute of it. It was champagne and caviar . . . she lived it up good. A character! She used to call me Pearly Teeth. Mary didn't like it. It's the only time she ever got mad at Dorothy. She said, 'And what about you and that awful oversized cowboy of yours?' "

Dorothy di Frasso had come to California in pursuit of Gary Cooper, and this made Cooper extremely uncomfortable. He was grateful to her, but not in love. Yet, she clung to him.

When Colleen Moore held a party and invited "everybody in Hollywood," the actress recalled that Dorothy di Frasso couldn't match the sleek good looks of most of the women there. "At the time Dorothy was a little fat," Miss Moore said, "a nice round European type, although she was an American." She slimmed down in very short order.

His Women was released to mild commercial success and general critical disapproval in December of 1931, the same month that Clara Bow—who had somehow survived several personal scandals—married cowboy actor Rex Bell. In her prime, she'd made $100,000 a picture, but those days were in the past. She retired from public life in 1935, finding little solace in past glories, wondering what the future held for her and her troubled mind.

When author Richard Lamparski asked her why she decided to accept a Hollywood offer, Tallulah Bankhead replied, "Darling, they offered me all that money, and I thought I'd go to Hollywood to fuck that divine Gary Cooper."

She'd starred in three previous pictures for Paramount, all filmed in New York. "The screen had just started to talk," press agent Dick Maney wrote, "when Miss Bankhead interrupted it in 1931." She'd actually made one other film in Hollywood, *Thunder Below*, before being cast opposite Cooper, Charles Laughton, and Cary Grant in *Devil and the Deep*, the story of a jealous husband, a faithless wife, and two of the men in her life. Much of the action took place aboard the submarine the husband commanded, which in his insane jealousy he deliberately steered into the path of an oncoming steamship. Cooper would be playing the submarine lieutenant who saves the lives of those aboard.

Tallulah Bankhead was an original—a celebrity famous for being famous, a legend before her time. Even before she'd become established as an actress, her cavortings at the Algonquin Hotel as handmaiden of sorts to the literati at the Round Table had made her a well-known personality. Cooper's doctors were still advising rest and quiet, and the volatile actress seemed hardly the prescription he should be taking.

Tallulah had an androgynous quality—and she capitalized on it. She'd been born into one of Alabama's most distinguished families. Once she became an actress, she was outside the ken. She might as well admit to all the vices and perversions that would make her socially unacceptable in the loftiest quarters.

The first was lesbianism. When she first arrived in New York, she was exposed to a group of actresses living in the same hotel, who were known as The Four Horsewomen of the Algonquin. After she'd scored an immense success on the London stage, English girls flocked to the stage door, as admiring of her reckless beauty as they were of her prodigal talent. She'd had an affair with Lord Napier Alington. They hoped to marry. Then she was invited to tea to meet his formidable mother. The two seemed to get along well. Tallulah's manners were impeccable, but she couldn't control her irrepressible ways. "You think I'm in love with Napier," she said to Lady Alington. "But it's *you* I'm mad about!"

Next was her use of cocaine. "It's not addicting, darling," she'd assured one and all. "I've been taking it for seventeen years." People weren't sure that she was joking. Finally, she admitted to the greatest vice of all—she was a Democrat.

Tallulah had spent nine years in England, and when she returned to the United States to embark on a film career, she was close to thirty. After she moved to California, she leased the house of silent screen star William Haines. She held open house every night. In her desire to prove her domesticity, she took up petit point. While guests milled about, she'd sit with a basket filled with colored threads, holding the material she was working on. She'd slowly raise the needle, hold it poised above the target for effect, then drive it home to emphasize a point. Night after night, she'd sew, the rings under her eyes getting darker. People would leave and she'd continue her petit point until dawn. Once, having run out of thread of a particular color, she combed the town for it, and, unable to find it locally, had it flown in from New York. A friend observed, "Tallulah is the only person I know who succeeded in making a vice out of needlepoint."

Despite the suggestions of lesbianism, she was deeply attracted to Gary Cooper. During the filming of *Devil and the Deep*, Tallulah made no secret of her feelings—and Dorothy di Frasso did not appreciate her candor. As far as she was concerned, Cooper had far too many admirers already.

Also relayed to her was one of Bankhead's throwaway lines. The hostess at a big Santa Barbara house party was irritated because Cooper, who'd accepted her invitation, hadn't shown up. "Forgive him, darling," Tallulah said. "He's probably worn to a Frasso."

Jean Howard, a blonde beauty who'd performed in the *Ziegfeld Follies* in 1931, was in Hollywood trying to break into films. She was a friend of Dorothy di Frasso's brother and his wife—Bert and Olive Taylor—and as a favor to them, Cooper agreed to play opposite Jean Howard in her screen test.

Jean had some people in for poker one night, and Tallulah was included. Dorothy di Frasso looked on her foul-mouthed wise-cracking as if Tallulah was blaspheming in church. Olive Taylor attempted to quiet Tallulah, who by this time was several drinks past that point.

"You're a charming girl," she told Mrs. Taylor, "but don't be impressed by your sister-in-law. She's nothing but an old whore." Some people laughed at the outpouring of malice and wit that followed, but others were outraged. Tallulah was quite surprised when wine was thrown in her face. Only then did she realize that she was way out of line, that she'd reached a point in her personal life anticipated by Mrs. Patrick Campbell in her career as an actress. "Watching Tallulah onstage is like watching someone skate over thin ice," she'd said. "The English want to be there when she falls through."

Other actors by this time were beginning to notice and admire Cooper's work. Costar Charles Laughton came to *Devil and the Deep* with a very flattering conception of Cooper. "He's the greatest actor in Hollywood," said Laughton, who'd conquered both London and Broadway in *Payment Deferred*. "He acts from the inside."

Laughton's performance, however, would be considered the tour de force, while Cooper was an also-ran, his characterization being described by *The New York Times* as "sympathetic and vigorous." The material he was handed wasn't of much help. He'd had to say things to Tallulah such as "You look to me very lovely."

Cooper was not as attentive to Tallulah as she desired. There'd already been too many tempestuous actresses in his life. "When he wasn't before the cameras," Tallulah later said, "he sat cross-legged whittling on such lumber as was available."

Being exposed to a great actor such as Laughton, Cooper came away from the film with a new dedication to his craft, and also a greater recognition of the need for preparation.

"Ever since *Devil and the Deep*," he said, "I've made a habit of reading all the background material I can get on the character I am to play next. Pretty soon this dusty research begins to get personal. This stuff, as I read it, is happening to me."

Tallulah noticed during filming that Cooper was spending a lot of time in discussions with a naval officer who'd been hired to advise on authenticity. Since the actor was playing a submarine officer, he was learning from the technical advisor how a sub was actually run.

"What's that got to do with acting?" Tallulah wanted to know.

"The point is," Cooper replied, "if I know what I'm doing I don't have to act. I just push this and pull that the way I'm supposed to."

Tallulah had made an all-out effort to establish her screen career, and it hadn't worked. When she'd made her first picture, the bloom of youth was already gone. She didn't suggest the same vitality and excitement on film that her electrifying performances conveyed onstage. Instead of unleashing the force of her own personality, she seemed to be imitating Garbo. Her face didn't move; her eyes didn't come alive. She didn't suggest the uncensored thought. Tallulah wasn't born for the movies.

She made another film after *Devil and the Deep*, a loanout to Metro, before Paramount dropped her as a contract player. Even after Hollywood found her professionally unacceptable, her humor blasted forth. One of her targets was Elsa Maxwell, whom Tallulah considered a gauche opportunist.

The two women were together in a group one night, while Tallulah was regaling them with a past adventure. "Yes, yes," the portly Elsa would say insistently, "I was there. Go on."

Throughout Tallulah's recital, Elsa was the Greek chorus: "Yes, yes, I was there. Go on."

Angrily, Tallulah concluded, "and Napier and I fucked in the bathtub. *And you weren't there, Elsa!*"

Soon, Tallulah wouldn't be there in Hollywood either. The only interest expressed in her as a film actress came from Mayer at Metro, who, thinking she might still have picture potential, set up a meeting.

"I'd like to offer you a contract," he said, "but there's a problem."

"What's that?" she asked.

"Well . . . uh . . . I hear you like girls."

"Of course I like girls! Some of my best friends are girls, and—"

"No," Mayer interrupted. "I hear you *really* like girls."

"Oh!" She suddenly realized. "You mean like . . . ?"

Tallulah had pointed to a pile of studio stills on Mayer's desk, on top of which was the photo of a reigning Metro queen. The point was economically made, yet it canceled her last chance to remain.

She decided to give a bang-up farewell party for herself. When a friend dropped in with Elsa Maxwell one night, Tallulah told the other woman, "Why don't you come, Elsa? Johnny Weismuller and a lot of people will be coming." The screen's new Tarzan had supplanted Cooper in her life. "If you do come, I'll get a piano and we'll have some fun."

Elsa, a musician, often entertained at parties. So did Tallulah, in an hilarious, caterwauling imitation of Elsa Maxwell.

"Yes, I'd love to," Elsa assured her.

Afterward, Tallulah confided to a friend. "She won't come."

"How do you know?"

"When word gets around that I'm not on the crest of the wave, she won't come." Tallulah proved to be right. She returned to New York with instincts intact. She realized who wished her well and who didn't.

In the early thirties, Gary Cooper was still being used by Paramount in all-star vehicles the studio made to show off its rich vein of contract talent. He and Tallulah Bankhead had already appeared in their costumes from *Devil and the Deep*, playing themselves in *Make Me a Star*, the film version of the George S. Kaufman-Moss Hart play, *Merton of the Movies*.

Next, he was put into a vignette grab-bag picture. Released in the third year of the nationwide Depression, *If I Had a Million* took wish-fulfillment to the brink of overdose. The motion picture played before people who were lucky to have a dime in their pocket. It is of little interest today but it did serve as an exercise and prelude to one of the most anticipated films of Cooper's career, *A Farewell To Arms*.

Eleanor Boardman had originally been announced as Cooper's costar in the film based on Ernest Hemingway's novel, and it was a bitter disappointment to her, a huge star of silent pictures, when Paramount decided instead to cast Helen Hayes. The stage star had won an Academy Award for Best Actress in her first movie, *The Sin of Madelon Claudet*, the previous year.

Helen Hayes was another star of the theater who shared Charles Laughton's great respect for Cooper's natural style. Despite her experience and prestige, the young Hayes had great trepidation about costarring with Gary Cooper. "When I act, I'm pretending," she said. "He'll show me up. He *feels* what he's doing!"

Cooper was experiencing the same anxieties about Hayes. "I can't act. How can they expect me to play in a picture with someone like that?"

The first meeting of the two stars was awkward. Director Frank Borzage, trying to break the tension, instructed them to go immediately to the publicity department to shoot stills, which he would supervise. He had them strike several intimate poses, ending up with Cooper and Hayes lying on a couch.

"Miss Hayes," Borzage said, "that shot is so beautiful, I think I'll shoot the whole picture horizontally."

Both actors started to laugh. The ice was broken. They could embark on the project, in which, owing to her Broadway fame and her recent Oscar, Miss Hayes was top-billed.

Cooper should have made a great filmic Hemingway hero. His ability to handle terse, unaffected speech paralleled Hemingway's gift for endowing meaning to the plainest utterances. Cooper's roles of triumphant moral strength, and the audience expectation he built up for this type of character, were particularly apt for Hemingway's often-unstated but always-felt personal code. The actor's sportsmanlike life paralleled the writer's. His kinship with the whole style and personality that Hemingway reflected in his writing is illustrated by the personal friendship that was to develop between them.

If Cooper failed to make an even minimally recognizable Hemingway hero, it is probably due to Hollywood's reluctance to make anything resembling a real Hemingway film.

Hemingway's 1930 novel was purchased by Paramount almost immediately upon publication, despite the conclusion of a studio reader that "this is a magnificently written story and a great one, but it is not a story for a picture."

The eventual decision to buy the rights to the novel for a hefty $80,000 must have been prompted more by the name value of a bestseller than by its inherent potential. Paramount executives nonetheless decreed that audiences wanted nothing more in the early 1930s than a hot screen romance between Gary Cooper and Helen Hayes.

It was one of the prestige productions of the season. The film's producer-director Frank Borzage had also won an Oscar the season before for directing *Bad Girl*. One of his specialties was depicting the travails of lovers caught in adverse conditions; it was Borzage who'd directed the silent classic, *Seventh Heaven*.

Hemingway's novel popularized the disaffection and loss of values experienced by America's "Lost Generation" in Europe during and after World War I. Depression-era cynicism, post-World War II world-weariness, and sixties radicalism can all be seen as lineal descendants of this first sign of twentieth-century angst. The book's place in the social and literary history of our time is pivotal. The film trivializes the conception from first to last, to the point of replacing the bleakness and rain of Hemingway's last pages with an "upbeat" ending.

Nor did it ignite what should have been a fiery romance between Cooper's Lieutenant Henry and Hayes's nurse Catherine. Their attraction to each other is indicated chiefly by clever contrivances. In one scene, his detachment of ambulances, on its way to the front, passes the hospital where she works. Cooper is aware of the hospital as his conveyance roars past; Hayes hears the rumble of the ambulances heading toward the battle zone and knows that one of them carries her lover. Little chance for fire there.

When Cooper informs a priest, "Don't mind us, Father, we're in love," it's a fact we have to take on faith. There were too many contrasts between them—his relaxed, informal acting and her theatrical mannerisms; and the somewhat preposterous fifteen-inch difference in their heights.

A Farewell to Arms is not a bad film. It is, in fact, finely wrought, carefully prepared and grandly staged, more fluid and accomplished than many another major film of 1932. It is not that it errs on the side of Hollywood vulgarity and simple mindedness. Indeed, there are magnificent touches and magical moments. But it is altogether too stately and deliberate.

But the film's antiwar sentiment—the theme of the novel, the title, the characters, and everything else Paramount paid its money for—is reduced to elliptical suggestions.

A Farewell to Arms may be the only film of Cooper's career in which "I don't know" is given as his reason for fighting. When Lieutenant Henry performs the rash act of desertion, it's less out of disbelief in what the war stands for than out of sheer passion for his beloved Catherine. Hemingway's questioning faith also bites the dust, allowing Cooper in the final reel to pray rather shamelessly to God to let Catherine live.

About the altered ending, there has been considerable misunderstanding. Two endings were actually filmed, one less depressing than the other, and it was up to each individual exhibitor to choose the one that appealed to him. Though neither ending is faithful to the potent and important ending of the novel, neither is an uncompromisingly rosy finish. In the "sad" ending, Catherine dies on her hospital bed just as the armistice is declared and Cooper carries her lifeless body to the window while bells ring out. It replaces Hemingway's total despair with as much optimism as is possible. The "happy ending" makes it equally clear that Catherine will die as a result of her miscarriage, but the "pollyanna fadeout" arrives while she's still alive and embracing Henry, allowing for enough ambiguity to suit deluded romantics.

With compromise going on all around him, Cooper nonetheless managed to reach an intensity beyond anything in his previous screen portrayals. Carrying on a scene of suffering in a diner across the street from the hospital, he succeeds in shocking us with his grief—and simultaneously in silencing the patrons of the eatery—by crying out, "She can't die!" In the final death scene, he's big and lumbering. He can hardly talk through his tears, as he tells the dying Catherine he'll never stop loving her. Had this kind of deep feeling pervaded the rest of the film, it might be easier today to forgive Borzage for maintaining Hemingway's bestseller title and obliterating virtually everything else.

Symptomatic of Cooper's continued growth as an actor were the unanimous critical raves he received for his portrayal, overshadowing even those of the distinguished Miss Hayes.

"Gary Cooper, particularly in the closing scenes, is revealed as an actor with a greater emotional depth than he has ever displayed before," Martin Dickstein wrote in the *Brooklyn Daily Eagle*.

He was, according to the *New York Daily News*, "as natural and convincing an actor as might have had years of stage training—which isn't the case. Gary is a true product of the celluloid. His performance as carefree Lieutenant Henry is thoroughly ingratiating."

Of tangential human interest are the reactions of two of his leading ladies, one in Cooper's future and the other in his past.

Teresa Wright saw the film many years later, even after she'd starred with him in the forties. "I'd always wanted to see the picture," she said, "and someone ran it for me at the studio. I was amazed at this young, forceful, very sensual man. He was a very romantic character, with all the sophistication he exhibited in another part of his life. He was quite different, not at all the cowboy . . . very young and very good acting. He was truly playing the Hemingway character, attractive, but not all that nice."

When the picture was premiered in December of 1932, Lupe Velez and Johnny Weismuller, whom she would later marry, were seated directly behind Cooper and Dorothy di Frasso. During the screening, Lupe's voice could be heard throughout the darkened theater, singing the praises of Cooper the actor. Perhaps she wanted to show that she retained a fondness for him, or maybe to prove that she held no bitter feelings for him. Cooper didn't attempt to determine what her motives were. He may have already known. The previous July, the ever-accessible Lupe told an interviewer that Cooper had been the love of her life.

Although the war sequences had been used almost cosmetically in *A Farewell to Arms*, resulting injuries to Gary Cooper's eyes, ears, and left knee were decidedly real. Over the years, he'd been scraped, bruised, and cut in the action sequences of his pictures, injuries he would continue to suffer in the future. For the present, he was scheduled to be treated at a New York medical clinic. Mary Pickford suggested she and Dorothy di Frasso accompany Cooper on the trip, the three of them flying from the Burbank Airport together. As long as they were partway there, Dorothy thought they might sail on to Italy.

On September 24, 1932, the three arrived at the airport to take the flight East. They boarded the plane, yet like a *deus ex machina*, a message came for Miss Pickford. She would have to stay for more film work. Her luggage was taken off the plane and she returned to Pickfair, which, for the first time in several months, wouldn't have the Countess di Frasso in residence. Miss Pickford vehemently denied that her aborted trip was a ruse to get rid of the Countess.

When she and Cooper returned to California, the Countess took up residence on Bedford Drive in Beverly Hills, where she entertained at lavish parties which quickly made her the equal of Hollywood's top hostesses, Miss Pickford and Marion Davies. To lend further legitimacy to her continuing presence in southern California—although the old Count was never heard to complain of her absence—it was announced that she and Cooper were negotiating to release a seven-reel movie of their African safari, using 35,000 feet of film they'd shot. As a logical tie-in, Cooper would star for Paramount in *Safari*, a big-game hunting tale. Neither would be made.

Having starred in the first version of a Hemingway work, Cooper now, in late 1932, prepared to go into the first picture based on a story by William Faulkner, "Turnabout." It would also be his first loanout since going to work for Paramount Pictures. Metro would do the Faulkner story and Faulkner himself was brought in to write the dialogue, supplementing the work of adaptors Edith Fitzgerald and Dwight Taylor.

Director Howard Hawks, having read the story in *The Saturday Evening Post*, thought the tale about World War I fliers would make a good movie. Irving Thalberg at Metro approved the idea. When studio executive Eddie Mannix asked Hawks who he wanted in the cast, the director's first choice was Gary Cooper as the American aviator. He also thought Robert Young and Franchot Tone would be fine as the two young Britons.

There was no female romantic interest in the story, but Mannix said a vehicle was needed for Joan Crawford, and suggested that a female character be introduced into the proceedings. A sister was added to the naval officer being played by Franchot Tone.

Shooting was unexpectedly delayed when Cooper failed to appear for the first day of work. It was the first time he'd shown a star's temperament, or had demanded a star's perquisites. Fearing another physical breakdown, he asked for more time off. Paramount refused the request for a vacation. When he asked to be loaned out to play opposite Mary Pickford in *Secrets*, which would be her final picture, he was told he couldn't be spared. Now he was being cast opposite Miss Pickford's one-time stepdaughter-in-law, Joan Crawford, who'd been married to Douglas Fairbanks, Jr. Cooper would have gained much more social prestige appearing in the Pickford picture.

He was also unhappy that delay in completing the Metro film forced the cancellation of *Fly On*, in which he would costar with George Raft, the screenplay based on a story by John Monk Saunders, the creator of *Wings*.

Once all differences were ironed out to his satisfaction, Gary Cooper reported for work.

Today We Live, as the Faulkner picture would ultimately be called, was not a success. Joan Crawford wasn't believable as an aristocratic English girl, and the aerial sequences were beginning to look like photographed clichés. Cooper's notices were respectable. The only bright point, ephemeral though it would be, was that the picture afforded Joan Crawford the opportunity to meet and work with Franchot Tone, who would be her second husband.

Chapter 6

The couture dressés she wore were French and she'd made her mark on the international set in Italy, but Dorothy di Frasso was now settled in the America of her birth. She was catapulted to the ranks of the top hostesses in the film colony, the first woman with no ties to the movie industry to reach that exalted state. As a countess, she had solid credentials in international society, a group that Hollywood arrivistes dreamed of breaking into. It was not so much a matter of Hollywood accepting Dorothy di Frasso as it was of Dorothy deigning to include some of its glossier types in her circle. Some Europeans looked on the shifting of di Frasso's base of operations to Hollywood as a comedown in her social career.

Yet Hollywood of 1933 had progressed considerably from the brawling backward town of ten years previously. It was still a town, but its rough edges were being rounded and polished by the stream of distinguished people coming through. Recently, Mary Pickford had received at Pickfair Lady Mountbatten, the Duke of Alba, Charles Lindbergh, Prince William of Sweden, and the Crown Prince of Siam. Not to be outdone, Marion Davies—with William Randolph Hearst as unpublicized host—received Winston Churchill and the Baron de Rothschild.

Intellectuals were also drawn to Hollywood, such

as Albert Einstein and George Bernard Shaw. Some of them stayed to work in films: George S. Kaufman, Philip Barry, S. N. Behrman, Robert Sherwood, Charles MacArthur, Marc Connelly, S. J. Perelman, Dorothy Parker, and John O'Hara.

Escapist Hollywood films began having an extraordinary influence on fashion and interior design. When Adrian gave Joan Crawford a new look—which would evolve into one of fine tailoring and padded shoulders—millions of American women began imitating her clothes, walk, and charm-school speech. Jean Harlow's all-white bedroom in *Dinner at Eight* was one of the earliest examples of Hollywood Moderne, which was to be one of the greatest interior design influences of the thirties. A dewy-eyed, thirty-nine-year-old actress arrived from the New York stage to start her film career, and started another fashion trend adopted by Parisians and called La Vogue Mae West.

These were feminine influences, however. What about the men? For too many years, Hollywood's leading men—with their even features and cardboard lover postures—looked like shirt-collar ads. Western stars had a low-budget following; none of them had crossed over into major stardom, including the ostentatious Tom Mix. There were Rudolph Valentino and Ramon Novarro, but their appeal was an exotic one. Craggy types like Spencer Tracy and Humphrey Bogart were coming along. But the most influential male image, the strong silent type, was a creation of Gary Cooper. As Thomas B. Morgan wrote in *Esquire*, "Gary Cooper's *Gary Cooper* is second only to Charlie Chaplin's tramp among all the enduring symbols created by U. S. movies." The glorification of John Wayne was yet to come.

With Cooper, it was being proven that Americans didn't *want* their ideal to be a handsome knight astride a white horse, although that was what Gary Cooper often played. He hid it with a diffident shyness, being a half-heroic figure who wasn't afraid to do what was right but was scared to death of talking too much about it, who wasn't afraid to kiss a girl he scarcely knew, but was struck dumb when the moment came to tell her how much he cared for her. The Woodrow Wilson starry-eyed idealist, the most immediate role model, had gone out of fashion. An earlier, rough and ready Theodore Roosevelt man of action was again coming into vogue. He performed exciting deeds and left the talking to his admirers. Cooper could make the moral choice seem a matter of real, immediate moment. It was neither an abstraction nor a scenarist's conceit, though it probably started life as both. In the imagistic mass media of the twentieth century, the pragmatic American finds no need for abstraction.

Yet, in his personal life—which could never be truly private—Gary Cooper stood for something else, and it was everything the filmic Cooper would seem to abhor and hold in contempt. He was a social animal, with attendant ambitions, and he seemed to be carving out an everyday life—every night too—of rampant hedonism under the aegis of a much older woman. In Montana and points Midwest, they had a name for men like that.

If Cooper was suffering a crisis of identity, he didn't show it. His only cavil, years later, was at the "legend" that the Countess was responsible for transforming him into a continental gentleman. However, he never said the enduring story was untrue. He must have realized there were cracks in his public persona, and that his racy, rakish real life showed through.

Why, then, did his association with Dorothy di Frasso continue? Surely his mother, who'd made her feelings well known about the other women in his life, couldn't have approved of her son's involvement with a woman only thirteen years younger than herself. First, despite his stardom, Cooper had never circulated with the power elite. He was now hobnobbing with the most notable people in the industry, and it would have otherwise taken him years of achievement and dogged social-climbing.

Also, he felt enormous gratitude, for Dorothy di Frasso had nursed him back to health. Would the demanding hysterical girls of his past have done the same? If the Countess was a silly, superficial woman, she was also a caring one. She made life extremely comfortable for him, and he tried not to notice that he was strapped into a cashmere-lined straitjacket. He preferred not to think of what might happen should they part. The Countess was very popular, and it wouldn't be easy extricating himself from her tenacious clutches without alienating her influential friends.

Cooper was also caught up in a second social life in Hollywood, this one among actors his own age, centered in his dressing room complex. It was located at the end of the main street of the Paramount lot, next to Carole Lombard's. Others working out of this star boulevard were Marlene Dietrich, George Raft, Bing Crosby, Claudette Colbert, and Mae West.

In his dressing room, Cooper could be the closest approximation of himself. It was obviously an actor's room, with its systematic array of makeup on a dressing table, but it was also a rugged Western man's lair. The sofa was covered with an Indian blanket, there were four leather club chairs, and the walls were bedecked with a feathered Indian headdress, various Mexican and Indian artifacts, Mexican serapes, a rifle, several lariats, and stuffed animals.

Manager Jack Moss had moved his office from United Artists into Cooper's complex. "That became the hangout for actors or whoever was on the ins with Coop or Jack," Stuart Heisler said. "It became the meeting place in the morning for coffee. This was during the time Lombard was part of the group. She could tell a dirty story in the most beautiful way. Coop would come in, grab his coffee and a doughnut, then go into his dressing room to put on his makeup.

"Everybody had to bring in a new dirty story every morning: Lombard; a secretary, who was a big fat dame; a character man. Coop would once in a while stick around to hear the dirty stories. One morning Coop disappeared. After a while his dressing room door opened very quietly. When he stepped out it was the damndest sight! You never could have told one iota that that wasn't Abraham Lincoln. He had the top hat, the long dark coat. He just stood there. It was the most wonderful makeup I'd ever seen. Nobody should have played Lincoln but Gary Cooper." (Raymond Massey and Henry Fonda were to do so, but not Cooper.)

According to columnist Sidney Skolsky, "Most of these stars would drop into Coop's or Carole's bungalow after filming stopped at six o'clock. There was a warm feeling among stars then. Everyone didn't run away from the movie factory as soon as the whistle blew.

"Coop would be taking off his makeup, his shirt, or his pants—it didn't matter—they'd drop in on him anyway to shoot the breeze, to have a drink. Most people don't know it, but Bing Crosby named his first child, Gary, after Coop." The singer's eldest son was born that year. Bing Crosby was Cooper's closest friend at the studio, and their fathers had also become cronies.

While on loanout to Metro for *Today We Live* with Joan Crawford, Cooper had met the film's set designer, Cedric Gibbons. Normally, an elegant type like Gibbons, the most famous art director Hollywood produced, wouldn't have been a Cooper friend. The two men, however, shared an interest in art, and the actor often attached himself to people from whom he could learn. A coterie of beautiful, creative people revolved around Gibbons and his exquisite Mexican wife, Dolores del Rio. Among them was his screenwriter brother, Elliott, who was married to Irene, the famous costume designer at Metro.

When the Gibbonses invited Cooper to a party on Easter Sunday of 1933 in honor of their niece from the East, the Countess di Frasso wasn't included. She wasn't a daytime person, leaving Cooper free to accept the invitations for brunches and lunches on his own.

The actor was struck by the extreme self-possession in a girl so young, for Veronica Balfe was only twenty years old. He would have been surprised to discover she'd been mooning over his pictures since she'd been a girl in Eastern finishing schools. Known to everyone as Rocky, she was the product of Park Avenue, Palm Beach, and Southampton. Yet there was also a touch of rugged Western individualism in her ancestry, for her paternal grandfather, Harry Balfe, had created a fruit-growing and cattle-raising empire in Clovis, located in California's San Joaquin Valley. Somehow he must have passed on his love of the outdoors to his athletic, adventurous granddaughter.

After her parents were divorced, her mother married Paul Shields, a Wall Street financier who was a former member of the board of governors of the New York Stock Exchange. Veronica's orientation became almost exclusively Eastern from that point.

"She was so much the merchandise of her factory," a woman who came to know her well said. "She had the hardness that comes from that little world. To put it unkindly, she had an ersatz Southampton snobbery."

Her older, monied background wouldn't mesh well with the first-generation fortunes still being made in Hollywood. It couldn't be ignored at a time when, in Hollywood, as Tallulah Bankhead put it, "they call any girl a debutante who's a high school graduate." Veronica Balfe was the genuine article, having been formally presented to New York society two seasons before.

She had often come to Hollywood with her mother in the past to visit her two uncles. They'd stayed at the Hollywood Hotel, where the young girl would often play with Hedda Hopper's son Bill.

"She's always been poised and pretty," Hedda recalled, "a little on the elegant side . . . just a little aloof and unattainable."

Rocky and Mrs. Shields, instead of spending the previous summer at the family compound in Southampton, chose to visit Hollywood again. While at a party at Constance Bennett's, David O. Selznick spotted the aristocratic brunette with the grey-green eyes and offered her a screen test. She'd had very limited acting experience in school theatricals. The signing of Veronica Balfe to an RKO contract was in no small measure due to her stepfather's financial interests in Hollywood, and she took another name.

Sandra Shaw balked at revealing her personal statistics, which would have been of interest to the publicity department, other than to say she was five-feet-five-inches tall and weighed 119 pounds.

Her contributions to the cinema were minimal. She was a girl thrown to her death in *King Kong*, a scene considered too gory and subsequently cut, and she played a bit part in *Blood Money*, in support of George Bancroft, Frances Dee, and Judith Anderson.

Unaware of her acting career, lacking in dedication though it would prove to be, Cooper assumed he was meeting a frivolous society girl. But this one had a mind, and her outdoor interests coincided with his. She swam and played tennis, and what's more, she was an expert horsewoman.

Cooper was attracted to her. So was another actor. "Gilbert Roland was one of her first little romances," a woman close to all parties said. "Rocky came out here with an old nanny who practically raised her. She was young, but very soignée. She had this overbearing elegance. Gary was stunned by this Eastern deb." Contrary to what became printed gospel over the years, his wasn't a courtship which started with their meeting and moved inexorably toward marriage. First there was the awkward matter of Dorothy di Frasso to deal with. Cooper saw Rocky regularly for two months of well-chaperoned dates before he inexplicably stopped seeing her.

"Then like all men who didn't want to get married," Rocky said, "he disappeared for three months. No, I don't know how I snared him. He was ready, I guess. I didn't use a lariat."

The insistent Dorothy di Frasso may have had a lot to do with it. In July of 1933, *The Los Angeles Times* reported that the Countess was going to Reno to establish her six-week residency in order to divorce the

Count—just as the American Countess in *The Women* would be doing when the play opened on Broadway three-and-a-half years later. This, the press reported, would leave Dorothy di Frasso free to marry Gary Cooper.

Lupe Velez impishly said to Adela Rogers St. Johns, "This time that Coop has got himself in a fix!" That he was inaccessible to reporters and, when finally confronted, denied all such plans, tended to support Lupe's observation. There was no graceful or considerate way to tell a strong-willed woman like Dorothy di Frasso that he had no desire to marry her. Yet, he was now thirty-two and wanted to start raising a family. Sandra Shaw, née Veronica Balfe, was uniquely suited to be his wife. She was the real-life equivalent of the schoolmarm the Western hero marries after his carnal flings with golden-hearted dance hall doxies.

That same month, still underage, Sandra Shaw appeared in Los Angeles Superior Court with Dolores del Rio as her guardian to get approval of a seven-year contract with Samuel Goldwyn, calling for a salary, should options be picked up, that would escalate from $75 to $750 a week. She thus served notice of her plans to stay around for a while.

Her stepfather and mother weren't pleased that she was seeing an actor of such famous wolfish propensities. Cedric Gibbons talked them out of their objections. Their resulting courtship—still chaperoned—was a throwback to the Victorian age.

As if to commemorate the beginning of a new era in his life, Cooper accepted his first role as a slow-thinking and slow-moving homespun type in *One Sunday Afternoon*. It was the story of a small-town dentist who thought he married the wrong girl, but after seeing years later the girl he lost, discovers how right his choice was in the first place. The James Hagan play was still on Broadway with Lloyd Nolan as its star when the picture was released in September. Comparisons with the stage actor's performance weren't odious.

Cooper could play an awkward character as effectively as James Stewart, who came to films in 1935.

His next role was the extreme opposite—Noël Coward's *Design for Living*. He was cast, improbably some critics said, as a witty sophisticate involved in a ménage à trois. Fredric March and Miriam Hopkins had already been cast when Cooper was tapped by Ernst Lubitsch to play the hypotenuse of the triangle.

This was very fast company for a Montana cowboy. Rushed in at the last minute to play a part not tailor-made for him, in a story not his standard fare, Cooper proved that brittle, sophisticated comedy was not his métier. The net effect brought him down to the level of a competent comic actor, rather than giving him free rein as a magnificent star personality. Yet, the part broadened his range.

The film that wasn't a prime Cooper showcase also sold short its other great talents. It didn't do justice to Noël Coward's original play, though its bisexual chic premise was years ahead of its time. The Ben Hecht screenplay retained only one line of Coward's: "For the good of our immortal souls." It was inappropriate subject matter for the gifts of Ben Hecht; nor was it to be one of Ernst Lubitsch's finer moments. *Design for Living* was intermittently charming, with several glorious moments. One wonderfully apt line, spoken by Hopkins to Cooper, summed up his enduring appeal: "You're sort of like a rugged straw hat with a very soft lining—a little bit out of shape—very dashing to look at and very comfortable to wear."

Ernst Lubitsch was so good at making a certain kind of movie, with a special brand of elegance that derived from explicit understatement, that his influence came to be known as "the Lubitsch touch." A Lubitsch closeup or fadeout could imply things that would be illegal to state explicitly. A German who had begun directing short comedies in 1914 at the age of twenty-two, he adopted his most distinctive style after being imported to the U. S. by Mary Pickford.

Noël Coward had concocted a witty theatrical conceit, delicately balanced, to be played by Alfred Lunt, Lynn Fontanne, and himself, with sly implications of offstage parallels and autobiographical references. Lubitsch correctly perceived that the possibility of this kind of thing coming off for the movies' mass audience was zero.

The wisdom of his next move—to junk every line of the play but one and to assign the task of concocting a more cinematic version to Hecht—is still open to question. Mordaunt Hall in *The New York Times* called it "slaughter."

Yet, the sly Lubitsch humor is called into play, bringing to the enterprise his own distinctive sophistication, and the stars give workmanlike performances.

The director, in regard to Cooper, had a well-formed opinion. Lubitsch later told Garson Kanin that Gary Cooper and Greta Garbo never made a film together because they were the same person. "They're essentially photographic creatures," he said, "bland, almost dull, except when a camera is aimed at them."

During the filming, however, Cooper pressed too hard, rushing his lines. He risked making no impression on the camera at all.

"Look, Gary," Lubitsch said. "Stop trying to save film. I have lots of film. You don't have to charge through a scene in one second, like a bull. Take two seconds. Do like Freddie. His pauses are valuable to me . . . they make a subtle point. That's what film is for—to make a point. Now, you are just as big a star as Freddie. Your pauses are just as valuable to me."

"But, they aren't!" Cooper exclaimed. He was being literal—March was making three times Cooper's salary. He nevertheless followed the director's advice and, as soon as he could, went to the front office to demand wages equal to those of his male costar.

The Depression was beginning to ease up that summer. However, the industry in 1933 was worse off than ever, since movie attendance had been cut in half in the last two years. Paramount was in receivership and reorganization. Nevertheless, Cooper came out of the meeting with a $6,000-a-week salary. He immediately bought a Duesenberg, christening it The Yellow Peril. It was so long, he quipped, that he had to start making turns in the middle of the block.

With a fancy new salary, he was assured of his worth. Taking time in August of 1933 to legally change his name to Gary Cooper, he also confirmed his identity. His next assignment as the White Knight in *Alice in Wonderland* should have underscored it.

Paramount was prompted to celebrate the seventieth anniversary of the publication of *Alice's Adventures in Wonderland* by Lewis Carroll with the first feature-length film version. Episodes were borrowed from the later *Alice Through the Looking-Glass*. The picture was assigned to director Norman McLeod, whom the publicity department described as "a veritable son of Barrie with a love of the whimsical." He directed the Marx Brothers' first two Hollywood movies, *Monkey Business* and *Horse Feathers*. The great designer and director William Cameron Menzies shared screenplay credit with Joseph Mankiewicz, but the Menzies style is principally evident in the bold and elaborate visual effects. It's unlikely he did any writing.

The production schedule suggests anything but meticulousness. Girls were being tested for the part of Alice in August; the script was completed in September; the picture was a Christmas release.

Although the book *reads* like a great movie, logical illogic defied screen adaptation. Many of the star actors simply appear uncomfortable under their cumbersome Halloween costumery. The startling compositions are arresting on first appearance, but are held on screen too long, becoming blatantly artificial. The picture is stiff and stuffy.

Everyone in the cast, Cooper included, walks through his part with a curiously spiritless delivery inappropriate to Carroll's adventuresome mood. Cooper as the White Knight is given some of the best dialogue and some of the worst direction of his career.

The conception is marvelous; the playing, apologetic. His shenanigans on and off his horse grow more wearisome with each repetition. Cooper has his funniest moments simply tilting back and forth in the saddle, threatening to topple off with every roll.

In a perceptive review, *Variety* pointed out that *Alice in Wonderland* managed to make its origin from a classic a hindrance. "Use of heavy names for most of the parts represents a dead loss other than for billing. . . . Each identity is concealed behind an elaborate mask . . . any one of Joe Cook's stooges would have served as well for the White Knight as played by Gary Cooper."

Like every actor's career, Gary Cooper's had hit a rough spell. His last significant commercial success had been *A Farewell to Arms*. But that was four pictures in the past and a year ago, and though its success made him worth his inflated salary, he knew he would have to start choosing his vehicles more carefully, with as much care as he was going about choosing a wife.

Dorothy di Frasso at last saw the handwriting on the wall. She and Cooper were finished. She invited both Rocky and Lupe Velez to lunch at the Vendome, a chic restaurant frequented by celebrities. She didn't have to say much. The contrast between her two guests was very apparent. Cooper had made the transition from Lupe, the peasant-urchin, to Rocky, a girl of breeding and class. One person could be credited for the change in Cooper's taste.

"I really got them," the Countess triumphantly told her friend Ann Warner later. Yet, she had been the big loser and subsequently turned bitter. "I taught him everything he knows. When I met him, he was still wet behind the ears."

Now, he had headed elsewhere. The press was beginning to pick up the trail of the new lovers. For some time, many reporters didn't know that Sandra Shaw and

Veronica Balfe were the same person. It only served to double Dorothy di Frasso's humiliation for Cooper to be linked to two other women.

Early in November, Louella Parsons reported a rumor that Cooper and Sandra Shaw had eloped to Phoenix, accompanied by John Gilbert and his new wife, actress Virginia Bruce. The columnist crowed that she exclusively broke the story of their engagement the week before. Jack Moss, Cooper's manager, confirmed the fact. Parsons was wrong about one point. The trip was actually a short holiday, chaperoned by Rocky's uncle, Elliott Gibbons.

Cooper went to New York for the November 22 opening of *Design for Living*. "Miss Shaw is a wonderful girl," he told reporters waiting for him at the train station, "a beautiful girl, a girl any man would be proud to win as a wife. . . . But Miss Shaw and I are not married. And as long as she will be here herself, with her mother, in a few days, I believe the social amenities would be best observed by allowing herself to discuss the matter."

Rocky had taken a later train, and when it stopped over in Chicago, she was asked if she and Cooper planned to marry. "Oh, I don't know," she replied. "Right now all I'm thinking of is getting some rest before continuing to Broadway." In conjunction with the opening of his new picture, Cooper would be making his stage debut at the Paramount Theatre in a skit directed by Lubitsch, with fellow players Sari Maritza and Raquel Torres. The theater was jammed; the skit was awful.

The engagement was announced less than a week later at a supper dance held at the Park Avenue home of Mr. and Mrs. Paul Shields. At that time, no date for the wedding had been set.

A little over two weeks later, Cooper announced that the ceremony would be held the following day, December 15, in his suite at the Waldorf-Astoria Hotel, with only close friends in attendance. In an attempt to keep an inquisitive press away, it was actually held in the Shields' mirrored white Chippendale drawing room. Only four other people were present: Mr. and Mrs. Shields; Barbara Shields, the bride's stepsister; and Jack Moss. The groom's parents remained in California.

The press located the newlyweds shortly after the ceremony. Still wearing their finery, Cooper and his new wife agreed to meet with them. Rocky was in a grey crepe and satin afternoon dress with matching turban, and Cooper wore a brown checkered business suit, tan shirt, and brown tie. His wedding gift to the bride, he told reporters, was a two-inch-wide bracelet of diamonds and cabochon rubies. Rocky's wedding ring, a simple platinum band, was worn with her square-cut fifteen-carat diamond engagement ring. In answer to a newsman's question, it was confirmed that the word "obey" was omitted from the ceremony.

That evening, they took a train West, traveling to Phoenix, where they spent a few days riding in the mountains. Then, the newlyweds settled on ranchland leased near Van Nuys where Cooper, when not making pictures, could farm. He planted lemon and orange trees. Rocky, away from the faster-paced life of Beverly Hills, tried to be content decorating the interior of the ranchhouse.

The newlyweds were lunching one day at the Vendome when Dorothy di Frasso entered, holding the pedigreed puppy Cooper had only recently given her. All eyes had been on the handsome couple, but they now followed the Countess as she walked up to their table. Cooper rose as she approached. He chatted with her, while his wife sat silently. Neither asked the Countess to sit down, though that was what she was expecting. She, perversely, turned their meeting into an endurance contest. The Countess and Cooper stood for forty minutes—Hedda Hopper, one of the most interested observers, timed the encounter—before she silently admitted defeat and moved on. Once she'd departed, Cooper sank into his chair with relief.

Dorothy di Frasso may have wanted to effect a truce with Rocky—she repeatedly said she would always be Cooper's friend—but this hadn't been possible. Separate factions sprang up as a result. The larger consisted of those who remained loyal to the Countess so that they would continue to be invited to her lavish entertainments. This group wanted to find a very young Rocky arrogant and difficult, and she didn't disappoint them. She didn't make any effort to win them over, perhaps sensing it was a lost cause. Gradually, however, a counterreaction set in. Cynics laughed that it had nothing to do with the Countess' moving back to Rome to reunite with her husband and embark on a project to introduce dog racing to Italy. Before departing, she threw a lavish costume ball for her Hollywood friends. Marlene Dietrich came as Leda *and* the Swan.

Years later, when William Goetz was trying to establish his International Pictures, Cooper agreed to star in one of the independent studio's productions. Goetz was grateful, but also curious. Why would the top box office attraction in films agree to make a picture for the most minor of producers?

"When I married Rocky," Cooper said, "everybody in this town was afraid to be friendly with her. But not Edie [Goetz's wife]. She had Rocky over playing tennis, and made my wife part of her life. I took a vow then that one day I would be in a position to thank Bill Goetz."

Cooper started the new year on loanout to MGM for a Civil War picture starring Marion Davies. It would be one of her rare forays into straight drama, and would meet with the same fair-to-middling reaction from the American public as her past comedies had done.

Operator 13 would be her last picture at Metro before her dressing room bungalow was cut in half and transported to Warner Brothers, where William Randolph Hearst had negotiated another deal. He was furious that Norma Shearer had been chosen as the star of *The Barretts of Wimpole Street*, since Marion desperately wanted the role. The budget of the film with

Cooper grew to $1 million, largely because of delays caused by Hearst's tampering.

This was definitely the female star's picture and Cooper caused no problems. It couldn't appreciably harm his career, and it might lead to a closer relationship with Hearst, one of the most powerful men of his time.

Marion Davies came to greatly admire her costar. "When you were working with him, he was very considerate," she wrote. "He would always back you up. Gary would give the star the benefit of the scene. Only a real man does that, and Bing [Crosby] did that, too. Other actors don't."

During the filming, director Richard Boleslavsky would call out, "I can't hear your voice. Kindly talk louder." Marion's voice would get lower, while Cooper's would get higher. Still, the problem wasn't resolved.

One day, Miss Davies angrily accosted the director. "Look. It's your job to get a voice level on us. I can't talk down to my toes, and if Mr. Cooper talks higher, they'll say he's a pansy."

Cooper wasn't sure he heard correctly. "*What* did you say?"

"Don't disturb us while we're working," she replied to her costar. She'd made her point, and neither performer had trouble with the director from then on.

Her personal cook catered lunch for the cast and crew of 100 people. The fare was hearty: beans and potato salad and tamales and beer. "I'd be watching Gary," she said, "and he would eat more than anybody in the whole cast. He'd have the beans, and God knows he loved hot peppers, and then after luncheon he'd just throw himself down on the grass and rest until we were called. Then he'd get right up and go, and he looked skinnier than anybody else."

The Coopers were now regular guests at San Simeon. The actor could keep up with Marion Davies drink for drink—whenever they could sneak them by the disapproving Hearst—although alcohol occasionally put him to sleep. Over trenchermen lunches, he would discuss horses (of which his hostess was afraid) and hunting and country life (in which she had virtually no interest). Yet, she found him "a good, wholesome person," and Hearst emulated his mistress' fondness for her costar. The two men would often ride over the California hills surrounding the castle, Cooper listening to the pronouncements of Citizen Hearst and possibly understanding some of them.

Cooper's rudimentary politics were innately conservative and Republican. This was due to several influences. He'd been raised close to the land, with long and hard labor often bringing forth meager yields, so he opposed government giveaways to those he felt didn't want to work. To be a Democrat was to be a free spender of his tax money. Paul Shields, his father-in-law, was a partner in the J. P. Morgan Company, and was also a Republican, if for somewhat different reasons. The higher echelons in Hollywood, which included both Louis B. Mayer and Hearst, traditionally supported the Republican cause. In fact, in the upcoming 1936 Presidential election, when Alfred Landon would be routed by Franklin Delano Roosevelt, winning only two states, a new axiom was born. As Maine went, so did Vermont—and Beverly Hills. Landon narrowly won those two states, yet Beverly Hills was the only community of any size to come up with an Alf Landon landslide.

After the loanout to Metro, the Coopers took the first of their summer trips to Southampton, to visit Rocky's family. They landed at Newark Airport to discover Lupe Velez holding court with reporters. When they were asked to pose for pictures with her, the Coopers declined. Lupe, recently married to Johnny Weismuller, was offended. "I'm happily married, and so is he," she stated. "I wouldn't pose with him. . . . What does Gary Cooper think he is anyway? He's no oil painting! He may be an idol to his mother, but he's nothing to me."

The actor returned to Paramount by mid-year for

filming of *Now and Forever* with Carole Lombard and Shirley Temple. It was, as Richard Watts, Jr., described it in *The New York Herald Tribune*, "a moderately pleasant sentimental melodrama about noble crooks and the reforming influence of a baby's smile." Not to mention the enormous box office receipts generated by the greatest child star at the peak of her popularity.

Playing the second-story man to little Miss Temple's daughter role, the child having a better defined concept of the differences between right and wrong, the top-billed Cooper again yielded to the true star of the picture.

Carole Lombard, as his girl friend, was amiable and cooperative. Despite the camaraderie they shared in the dressing room, the blonde screwball never felt she knew Cooper well. He was as quiet offscreen as in films, but she didn't respect him as an actor.

"Carole regarded him as a dilettante," Larry Swindell wrote in his biography of the actress, "markedly effeminate in his mannerisms, and not at all the stalwart he impersonated so effectively on film." If this was true, she was the rare one who saw Cooper in such a light. Certainly, none of the rowdy stunt men he'd bummed around with considered him so. Cooper was shy and reserved, the grown-up little boy who brought out the mother in many women. Apparently, this wasn't Lombard's type.

For the rest of 1934, Cooper wisely turned down several studio offers. They included *Fifty-Two Weeks for Fleurette* with Claudette Colbert; Ernst Lubitsch's *Carmen; The Grandduchess and the Waiter* opposite Miriam Hopkins; and *The Last Outpost* with Gertrude Michael and Claude Rains. Except for the last film, which eventually starred Cary Grant, none of the films was made. They needed the power of Gary Cooper's name—despite his recent uninspired showings—to get off the ground.

His next choice was a fortuitous one. Henry Hathaway had been an assistant director on several Cooper films, but the Shirley Temple picture was his first full-fledged directing association with the actor. Their second, *The Lives of a Bengal Lancer,* was an action-packed adventure—a romp. With sets left over from Cecil B. DeMille's *The Crusades* and atmospheric footage shot in India by Ernest Schoedsack in 1931, it was a lively entertainment bearing so little resemblance to the book of the same title that one of the credits read, "Suggested by Francis Yeats-Brown's book."

Cooper's role of a slow-witted Scotsman caught up in the struggle to preserve British Imperialism in India was both comic and tragic. He's abnormally harassed, particularly by a flippant younger officer played by Franchot Tone, continually bested by both underlings and superiors. He does everything wrong, but his heart is in the right place. The audience expects him to redeem himself in everyone's eyes, but is poignantly disappointed when the character is killed in a desperate attempt to do something heroic.

Seen by today's standards, it's unfair to quibble that we are given no explanation of what the fighting is about. India's side is presented more coherently than the goals of the British Empire, but the action and the moral choices are supposed to hinge on the latter. *The Lives of a Bengal Lancer* was a huge success, being reissued several times, a smooth and conventionally pleasing effort by Hathaway. Though he would play other romantic roles in the future, Cooper was evolving into a mythic symbol, his performance both engaging and touching. "Gangling Gary Cooper, every long inch an officer," *The New York American* said, "stalks strikingly through both comic and tragic sequences." Said *The New York World-Telegram,* "The acting is of a superior quality. Gary Cooper has seldom had a more sympathetic or effective part than McGregor, and he performs the task imposed upon him expertly and effectively. The direction is of a high quality and the photography is splendid." Cooper and Hathaway would often work together in the future. They seemed to bring out the best in each other.

Much of the picture was shot on location. Although Rocky paid a brief visit to her husband during its making, she usually stayed home. Neither did she accompany him on his fishing and hunting trips.

The couple were in their second year of marriage before they came to an understanding about his celebrity. She had a healthy ego, and didn't like being relegated to a secondary position whenever they appeared in public. Fans and reporters rudely pushed his consort aside in their zeal to get close to their hero. Rocky was itching for an argument about the matter. Her husband refused to fight about something beyond his control. She would just have to accept the adulation, which was part of his job. She was a big, strong girl, and knew how to take care of herself. Her mother advised her to do the same thing. "Don't ride on your husband's coat-tails," Mrs. Shields said. "Develop your own personality."

If she was to accomplish this, it would hardly be on a ranch twenty-five miles outside Los Angeles. Rocky was not a frontier wife; she admitted to being useless in the kitchen. Although she also had reservations about functioning in the movie colony, since her ties were to New York, she'd have a better chance of becoming her own person closer to town.

Because he was often away filming, Cooper realized that it was unfair to isolate his wife in the country, and he was persuaded to move back to the West Side. First, they rented a house in Beverly Hills. Then they built a Bermuda-style house in Brentwood, set in three acres which Cooper could develop. It was intended as a happy compromise. He could still lead a modified outdoor life, playing the gentleman farmer in his spare time; she would be closer to the few cultural activities available in Los Angeles, and would socialize with their neighbors. Over the next few years they came to know Tyrone Power and Annabella, the Van Johnsons, and Cesar Romero.

Hedda Hopper noticed that "the house, tasteful, unique, and gemlike as it is, fits Rocky, not Gary. There's just one touch of Coop in the front room, a zebra rug made from the skin of a trophy he bagged on his safari. In a little sitting room off his bedroom, Coop racks the guns and outdoor tackle he's so crazy about and I sometimes wonder if he doesn't gaze a little wistfully at that zebra rug and those guns. The rest of the house is a woman's, filled with gorgeous antiques and rich furnishings." Its interiors were created by one of the status designers of the day: Elsie de Wolfe, Lady Mendl.

Back at the studio, Cooper had gradually fallen away from the Buddy Rogers-Dick Arlen-Jack Oakie axis. It had little to do with the fact that Rogers was about to marry Mary Pickford, who remained Dorothy di Frasso's close friend. They were separated by diverse interests. "Coop was warm, but not outgoing," Rogers said, "while Oakie would be all over the place. Dick and I played golf together, and Coop didn't play. He was nutty about automobiles, and he'd often bring his cars by our dressing rooms. We lost touch because Coop was always driving off someplace, or going hunting and fishing."

Chapter 7

Rocky kept Gary Cooper on a very long leash. She gave him solitude and freedom. He even had license, if handled with discretion, to assert the prerogative of a star to dally with leading ladies.

"There must have been a tremendous sex drive in Gary," one of Hollywood's most important citizens said. "When he got married, he'd just gone through several violent love affairs. That proves something that never quite came out. After a few years of married life, Gary was probably chafing at the bit. It was so easy for him, and not only because he was a star. Any woman would have been in love with Gary Cooper. With that shy little smile, he was so naive looking, so much the lovable boy."

His long-term commitment, however, was to his wife. They were building a life together, too solid to be torn asunder by the scores of brief flirtations. After a faltering start in the movie colony, Rocky established herself as a noted Hollywood hostess. She wasn't the adjunct of a star, but a young woman who'd always belonged to a privileged world and had a well-developed sense of her own worth.

Many of her critics found it an overdeveloped sense, and with them—some of the most distinguished people in the community—she would be accepted only because she was Gary Cooper's wife. It could have been shyness that came off as arrogance. But if you seem to be looking down your nose at the movie mogul who was an immigrant tailor only twenty years ago, you'd better correct that misconception. Rocky often didn't.

Also, as an adjunct to a star, she would have been disliked no matter how agreeable she appeared. Wives through the Hollywood ages have borne the brunt, extricating their husbands from generally uncomfortable situations. Their husbands are the wonderful people, filled with charm and consideration, while they are the nemeses. In performing this thankless task Rocky occasionally gave the impression that her husband wasn't bright enough to do this for himself. She created resentment because Gary Cooper was an extremely popular man who, his fondest admirers felt, deserved better.

Rocky was not close to her in-laws. Mrs. Alice Cooper should have been pleased that her boy had married a girl of obvious respectability. But Rocky was a devout Catholic, a decided minus as far as Cooper's mother was concerned, and her simple dignity didn't mesh with Rocky's aloofness. Rocky had always been insulated by old money: Alice Cooper was from proud working-class origins. When Rocky's parents visited, they were feted like royalty. Meanwhile, Judge and Mrs. Cooper lived simply in the modest house their son bought for them at 529 North Cahuenga Boulevard, where he dutifully, regularly called on them. As far as Gary Cooper was concerned, a workable compromise had been effected.

His career escalated dramatically in the next few years: he was transformed from movie star to folk hero. From 1935 to mid-1941, he starred in fifteen movies. Some of them were the best ever made. Gary Cooper proved for all time that he was a real actor and not just a Hollywood personality as some of his detractors had claimed.

Directors working with him for the first time consistently bemoaned his awkward delivery. Later they would be amazed by the magic the sound mixers could accomplish in highlighting the great modulation within the limitations of his voice. Cooper's vocal cadences were off kilter, filled with seemingly unnecessary pauses, and his inflection was unconventional. He stressed the unexpected word: it sounded artificial on the set, but when it came bounding back from the movie screen it sounded utterly real. Even memorable. Cooper ennobled lines that were uninspired and undeliverable.

The first picture in this new phase of Cooper's career was a critical success and a box office bomb. It also forced intellectual critics to reassess Cooper as an artist.

Goldwyn had been looking for a property in which Cooper would return as a genuine star on loanout to the studio where he'd made his first strong impression in *The Winning of Barbara Worth.* Goldwyn thought a Ben Hecht screenplay, *Barbary Coast,* might work with Cooper and Anna Sten in the leads. Cooper didn't like the script. Nor did he care for *Dr. Socrates,* a W. R. Burnett book which Paramount had bought for him. He was consequently still open to suggestions from Goldwyn.

Knocking around Hollywood was a twenty-page treatment with a protagonist based on F. Scott Fitzgerald and also drawing on the autobiographical experiences of Edwin Knopf, the author of the screen treatment. It seemed ideally suited to both Cooper and Sten. Cooper would play an engaging and sophisticated writer who falls in love with a Polish farmer's daughter, to be played by Sten. It was the dilemma of a celebrated married man in love with a fresh and sensitive girl. The affair is doomed, and there is no alternative but to return to his wife—cool, lively, and aware. If the romance with the girl was to have any resolution, she would have to die tragically. The picture, in a few years, would be eerily paralleled in Cooper's own life.

The Wedding Night came to be known as "Goldwyn's Last Sten." This was the last of Goldwyn's dogged attempts to turn Sten into another Garbo. Anna Sten was a beautiful Russian-Swedish actress who already had impressive European credits. Goldwyn put her into two projects, *Nana* and *We Live Again*, both flops. He chose to try again, this time with Gary Cooper.

Both stars had already been assigned when King Vidor was named to direct. "This was one of a series of Sten films," the director said. "This was bought and planned for her. She spoke English well enough, but she never got rid of the accent."

Since Goldwyn insisted the actors' delivery be fast-talking, like Claudette Colbert and Clark Gable in their recent smash picture, *It Happened One Night*, this became a problem for Vidor. Sten was speaking in a foreign language, her words often out of synchronization with her actions, and Cooper's speech was naturally hesitant. "I felt like a dentist trying to pull syllables out of their mouths," Vidor recalled.

Though he'd recognized Cooper's star potential as far back as *Barbara Worth*, Vidor found that Cooper was having great difficulty saying his lines. "His type of quality was photogenic, and he had difficulty speaking more than one or two sentences at a time. We broke it up into individual closeups. I thought we were going to have trouble. The next day when we saw the film, he was so effective and had such an amazing quality. It came over so strongly and was so interesting that I said forget about the trouble. Gary was a sort of mumbler. It was part of his character, sort of hand over mouth. Like many others, he didn't think in articulation of words."

The day a love scene was being shot, Goldwyn arrived on the set while Vidor was rehearsing the actors. All work stopped as Goldwyn took Vidor aside. "Do you mind if I speak to them?" he asked. Vidor had no objection.

Goldwyn delivered a pep talk, describing his vision of the movie and the devastating impact his stars would make. "If this isn't the greatest love scene that's ever been on the screen," he concluded, "then the whole picture is going to go right up out of the sewer." Considering this an effective line, he made his exit.

The principals looked at each other. Cooper asked, "Did he say 'right up out of the sewer?' "

"He certainly did," Vidor assured him. The short scene, because of recurring laughter, required many takes.

The screenwriter had inserted a Robert Browning phrase, "earth's returns," and unfortunately put it in Anna Sten's mouth. The words would be difficult for anyone to say, but virtually impossible for a foreigner.

Vidor took the best take and incorporated it into the picture. As they left the preview, Goldwyn said, "King, get in the car."

Vidor did.

"You'll have to reshoot that scene," Goldwyn said. "That goddamn girl can't say 'earse returzs.' "

Vidor the realist and Goldwyn the romantic nevertheless succeeded in putting together a distinguished motion picture. "With the assistance of King Vidor," André Sennwald wrote in *The New York Times*, "Hollywood steps out of its emotional swaddling clothes in *The Wedding Night* . . . it displays an unusual regard for the truth and it is courageous enough to allow an affair which is obviously doomed to end logically in tragedy." Thornton Delahanty of *The New York Evening News* found the picture "neither spectacular nor hair-raising. Its situations are not trumped up for dramatic effect. The incidents are welded by the logic of a quietly tragic love story which Mr. Cooper and Miss Sten make eminently believable and in which the directorial hand of King Vidor is unerringly present."

What Vidor elicited from Cooper was extraordinary alchemy—awkwardness, finesse, intelligence, tenderness, sophistication, wry humor, smoldering masculinity—that few other actors could conjure up.

Despite its many laudatory reviews and its enduring poignancy, the $2 million picture failed with the public. Even though it was proven that the subject of Goldwyn's insistent publicity was a true actress, few mortals could live up to such an inflated buildup. In the future Anna Sten was consigned to lesser roles at other studios.

One person who had more than passing interest in Cooper's portrayal was F. Scott Fitzgerald himself. The writer was in Hollywood under contract to Metro and also on assignment from *Esquire* to write a series of essays, *The Crack-Up*. "Gary Cooper's appeal," he said, "is just that he can't act. But they think from his unwilling expression—I bet when he takes those silly clothes off he'd be twice as exciting as those silly actors."

When *The Wedding Night* failed, Goldwyn began concentrating on two other female stars, Merle Oberon and Miriam Hopkins. He again asked Paramount to lend Gary Cooper to star with the two actresses and his good friend, Joel McCrea, in *Maximilian of Mexico*. Because of prior commitments, Cooper couldn't do the film; the project as a result was canceled. Such was the power of his name.

Cooper was due at Paramount for another picture with director Henry Hathaway. The stage version of *Peter Ibbetson* eighteen years previously had starred a very romantic John Barrymore. Constance Collier, who'd appeared opposite Barrymore as Mimsey, now adapted the screenplay. Both play and film revolved about the mystic premise that two lovers separated in physical reality can find a lifetime together on an astral plane. Cooper's naturalness in such far-fetched romantic eyewash showed how much he had grown. He could get away with this nonsense because he convinced the audience that he ardently believed.

For a man to possess the temperament to deliver a performance of consistent passion, he has to have a temper. Cooper wasn't nearly as laconic and unruffled as his public image suggested. He now had the power to make his voice heard, and he often exercised it. He never asserted himself without provocation, however.

Associates said Cooper had a bad habit of shouting at them when he felt they weren't performing their jobs properly. He'd unleash a stream of profanity. Once the anger of the moment was over, he'd cool off and forget.

Stuart Heisler was on loanout from the Goldwyn Studio while working on Cooper's *Ibbetson*. He forgot what he did to displease Gary Cooper, but he remembered very well the torrent of abuse that erupted from the star in front of the entire company. "You big bastard!" Heisler yelled back. "You can't talk to me that way!"

Cooper was stopped short. He hadn't realized the ferocity of his words. "Oh, I'm very sorry," he said, also in the presence of the company. He never hollered at Heisler again.

After *Morocco*, Paramount had wanted to reteam Cooper and Dietrich in *Dishonored*. Cooper flatly refused, swearing never to make another picture with von Sternberg, Dietrich's mentor. Von Sternberg's Svengali influence ended after six American pictures with Dietrich. In one stroke, von Sternberg was out of Dietrich's life and the studio fired him for being too esoteric and expensive.

In attempting a dignified last word, von Sternberg's bitterness showed through. "When we first met," he claimed about Dietrich, "her pay was lower than that of a bricklayer, and had she remained where she was, she might have had to endure the fate of a Germany under Hitler."

Dietrich's affections shifted to John Gilbert, whose contract with Metro had expired. She went to Ernst Lubitsch, who'd been named general production head at Paramount in 1935, and begged that the faltering actor be given a role in *Desire*, a bad-girl, good-boy comedy about a swank jewel thief and the American automotive engineer she uses as a dupe. Gilbert, she urged, could play her criminal cohort. Lubitsch agreed, but had to drop him after Gilbert had a heart attack.

Dietrich, demonstrating hausfrau propensities, nursed John Gilbert back to health at his house in Beverly Hills. A battered roadster pulled up to the house one day—and out stepped Greta Garbo. Gilbert went outside to join her. Dietrich watched the encounter from the house, and from there it appeared that Gilbert was begging Garbo to resume the affair she'd broken off several years before. Deeply hurt, Dietrich fled Gilbert's house, eventually into Gary Cooper's arms.

Gilbert had lost both women. His daughter Leatrice told Charles Higham the moment her father found out about Dietrich's affair with Cooper, he went on a drinking binge. On January 10, 1936, the day after Cooper was announced as the star of *Desire* opposite Dietrich, Gilbert had another heart attack and died.

Desire started shooting in February 1936. The Gilbert role was reassigned to John Halliday. This was to be the first Dietrich-Cooper movie since *Morocco* five years ago.

Desire would have "the Lubitsch touch," though Frank Borzage would be the actual director. Lubitsch personally supervised as head of production.

The film was another in a series in which Cooper played the noble blunderer somehow saved by his own ineptitude. It was little more than an exercise in adroit congeniality, though Cooper was singled out by *The New York World-Telegram* for contributing "a buoyant performance in light comedy that could scarcely be improved upon." Dietrich proved as well that she didn't need von Sternberg's stylized glitter and masklike makeup anymore, and became far more human. The picture helped to promote her career. Now that she wasn't tied to solely one man, other directors would interpret in their individual ways her unfathomable mystery.

By 1936, Cooper had been in films ten years. Half of his life's output—forty-eight pictures—had been made in that time, and the remaining half would take an additional twenty-six years. The pattern wasn't beneficial to his health, but it was an effective foundation for establishing a star's reputation: make one big picture every so often, and a lot of little ones in between to keep your name before the public. Cooper was about to change all that.

He was back at his home studio, mulling over several Paramount offers. The most interesting was opposite Carole Lombard in *The Case Against Mrs. Ames*. Both stars turned the project down, which ultimately would go to George Brent and Madeleine Carroll. Lombard accepted an offer from Universal to make *My Man Godfrey*, which established her as a major star, and Cooper went to Columbia for *Mr. Deeds Goes to Town*.

Frank Capra's *Mr. Deeds* was Cooper's first time back at a minor studio since his days as an extra and bit player. Columbia had scored an important box office hit with Capra's *It Happened One Night* in 1934 and was now building on that success. Capra had great power at Columbia—the profits from his pictures were running the studio. When it came time to choose the star of his new picture, he knew whom he wanted.

"Who in Hollywood could play honest, humble, 'corn tassel poet' Mr. Deeds?" he asked rhetorically. "Only one actor: Gary Cooper. Every line in his face spelled honesty. So innate was his integrity he could be cast in phony parts, but never look phony himself.

"Tall, gaunt as Lincoln, cast in the frontier mold of Daniel Boone, Sam Houston, Kit Carson, this silent Montana cow-puncher embodied the true-blue virtues that won the West: durability, honesty, and native intelligence."

Cooper was shrewd to take on the part. It brought about a fresh burst of acclaim as critics and public alike discovered Gary Cooper all over again. The dashing figure was supplanted by the archetypal common man. By playing the stereotype as he had never been played before, Cooper, at age thirty-five, was about to emerge as myth. There was nothing accidental about it, as the star himself once confessed. "I looked at it this way," Cooper said. "To get folks to like you, as a screen player, I mean, I figured you had to sort of be their ideal. I don't mean a handsome knight riding a white horse, but a fellow who answered the description of a *right guy*." Bumbling as he was, it seemed as if Mr. Deeds himself were speaking, unaware that White Knights come in many forms and that he might be one himself.

Shooting started before a leading lady was cast. Capra was being bombarded from all sides by actresses, several of whom had turned him down for *It Happened One Night*. His inspired choice was Jean Arthur, a stalwart lady with a pungent voice.

Robert Riskin's screenplay was based on Clarence Budington Kelland's "Opera Hat," a six-part serialization in *American Magazine*. The shrewdly constructed story had a quality of spontaneity that was delightful.

Capra is a sentimental moralizer. To break down our natural resistance to simplistic sermons he hits us where we are the most defenseless: in the funnybone. The first half hour of *Deeds* contains so many quick, adroit jokes that we find ourselves in need of a breather just when Capra decides he has something to say.

He wants us to distrust his villains instinctively, and he doesn't give much larcenous information about them. With Douglass Dumbrille as the slick lawyer and Muriel Evans as a counterfeit heiress, we dislike them on sight.

The romance means so much to Capra's hero Longfellow Deeds that the story revolves around it. Before he's ever put Gary Cooper and Jean Arthur in the same frame, he's established that Deeds has a fantasy about rescuing a damsel in distress and made clear in one throwaway line that Deeds doesn't think much of a man who "talks about women as if they were cattle." The instant Jean Arthur fakes a fainting spell and lands in Cooper's arms we know the power of that moment in his consciousness—and his unconsciousness. Their first kiss is saved for the last frame in the movie. In a previous scene—where she hugs him so hard he runs, embarrassed, into trash cans—the kiss seems needed as its focal point. Capra makes the earlier scene work without the kiss so he can save it for its optimum impact.

Capra's story has heart, comedy, and a message. He not only had to make those three elements work, they had to support each other. When Deeds feeds donuts to a cab driver's horse to see how many he'll eat before asking for a cup of coffee, it's not merely a joke. It's a device used by Jean Arthur the reporter to turn Deeds into a public laughingstock. When Deeds grows furious at the unknown writer who prints such scandalous stories about him, and simultaneously tells Jean Arthur she's the only honest person he's met in New York, there is touching irony. But we wonder what he'll do when he catches on. Capra is setting us up for his homilies on the simple virtues. Eventually Jean Arthur has to admit she loves Cooper in a way that leaves no room for doubt; Capra carefully sees to it that this admission comes at the point where it won't stick out as a lump of sentiment and simply make us squirm. It comes when Cooper *needs* to hear it, before he'll rally to his own defense, save his own life and defeat Dumbrille's final scheme to bilk him of his inheritance. The temple Capra builds to the Common Man is made up of embarrassing elements standing alone, but together they form an invincible structure.

Capra has an idiot hero to champion, a cross between Harry Langdon and Clark Gable. He's a lover, but a stumble-bum. "When I had Gary Cooper read Jean Arthur one of his love poems," Capra said, "I knew I was playing with fire. It was a good bet the audience would laugh *at* it. To release the laugh purposely, I had Gary run away and fall over a garbage can."

He's a man whose only reaction when he inherits $20 million out of the clear blue Vermont sky is to wonder where the Mandrake Falls band is going to get a tuba player to replace him. This gets him credibly tagged a moron by Wall Street sharpies. At the same time, he must be a man possessed of natural instincts

GARY COOPER

HOLLYWOOD'S GREATEST LOVER

Getting Even With Their Former Masters

Doc: That's what they are going to get for kicking us off the pay roll.
Joe: But it will not put us back again very soon!

Top: A family in Montana in 1909.
Frank James Cooper, age eight, is second from
left in the front row. (AUTHOR'S COLLECTION)
Bottom: A cartoon in the *Helena Independent*, drawn
during the election of 1924 by Frank Cooper, who would
later change his name to Gary. (AUTHOR'S COLLECTION)

Top: Cooper, standing at left in white shirt, as an extra in *Tricks*, 1925. (AUTHOR'S COLLECTION)
Bottom: Gary Cooper (prone) as Abe Lee in *The Winning of Barbara Worth*, 1926. Other actor is unidentified. (COURTESY OF SAMUEL GOLDWYN, JR.)

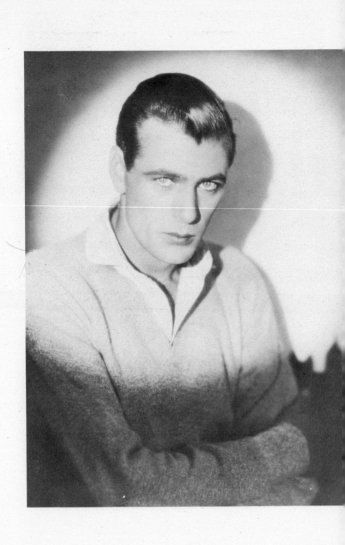

Opposite: A portrait, circa 1926. (AUTHOR'S COLLECTION)
Top: With Clara Bow in *Children of Divorce.*
(COPYRIGHT 1927 BY PARAMOUNT-FAMOUS-LASKY CORPORATION)
Bottom: Cooper, far right, with Charles (Buddy)
Rogers and Richard Arlen in his one scene
from *Wings,* 1927. (COPYRIGHT 1927 BY PARAMOUNT-
FAMOUS-LASKY CORPORATION)

P11-8

Opposite: Colleen Moore, the biggest star in
silent pictures, chose Gary Cooper as her leading
man in *Lilac Time*, 1928. (COLLEEN MOORE COLLECTION)
Top: With Lupe Velez in *Wolf Song*. (COPYRIGHT
1929 BY PARAMOUNT-FAMOUS-LASKY CORPORATION)
Bottom: The nude bathing scene in *Wolf Song*,
later cut from picture. (COPYRIGHT 1929 BY
PARAMOUNT-FAMOUS-LASKY CORPORATION)

Above: Cooper with his parents on
the porch of their Los Angeles home
in 1929. (WALT DAUGHERTY COLLECTION)
Opposite: Cooper in costume for *The
Texan,* 1930. (COURTESY OF UNIVERSAL PICTURES)

With Marlene Dietrich in a scene from *Morocco*, her first American picture, 1930. (COURTESY OF UNIVERSAL PICTURES)

Returning from his African safari, Gary Cooper, in 1932, showed off some of the sartorial influences of Italian Countess Dorothy di Frasso. (GENE ANDREWSKI COLLECTION)

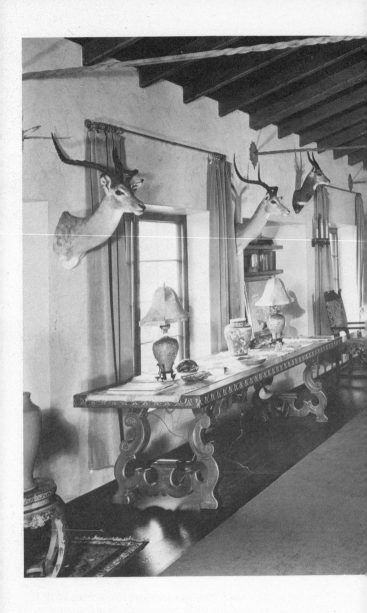

The living room of Gary Cooper's bachelor home, the only one he ever lived in specifically decorated to his personal taste, circa 1933. (GENE ANDREWSKI COLLECTION)

Opposite: Gary Cooper and Countess
Dorothy di Frasso, in the garden of the Del
Monte Lodge in California. (WIDE WORLD PHOTOS)
Top: With Tallulah Bankhead in *Devil and
the Deep,* 1932. (COURTESY OF UNIVERSAL PICTURES)
Bottom: With Helen Hayes in *A Farewell to
Arms,* 1932. (AUTHOR'S COLLECTION)

With Miriam Hopkins and Fredric March in *Design for Living*, 1933. (COURTESY OF UNIVERSAL PICTURES)

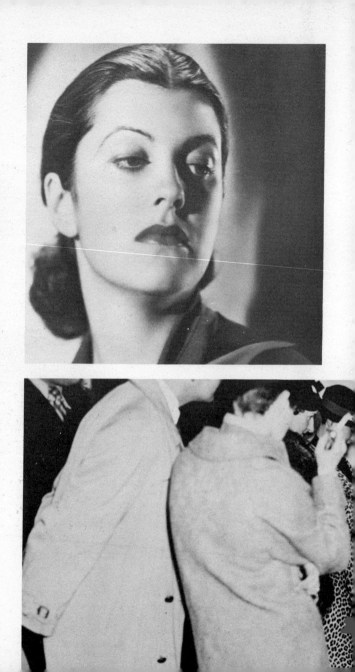

Opposite: Sandra Shaw, nee Veronica Balfe, during her brief acting career. She married Gary Cooper in 1933. (AUTHOR'S COLLECTION)
Below: Mr. and Mrs. Gary Cooper meet the press on their wedding day. (AUTHOR'S COLLECTION)

Top: Cooper and Marion Davies guest star
on Louella Parsons' "Hollywood Hotel" radio
program in 1934. (AUTHOR'S COLLECTION)
Bottom: Longfellow Deeds, the tuba player,
and Babe Bennet, as enacted by Gary Cooper and
Jean Arthur in *Mr. Deeds Goes to Town,* 1936.
(COURTESY OF COLUMBIA PICTURES)

Top: Ernest Hemingway (left) and Cooper hunting
with a guide in Sun Valley, in the fall of 1940.
(AUTHOR'S COLLECTION)
Bottom: On the set of *The Plainsman* with director
Cecil B. DeMille. (COURTESY OF UNIVERSAL PICTURES)

Opposite: Gary Cooper as Sergeant York.
(COURTESY OF UNITED ARTISTS)
Top: Cooper, about to be named Best Actor for
Sergeant York, at the Academy Award ceremonies
with his wife Rocky and Robert Taylor.
(ACADEMY OF MOTION PICTURE ARTS AND SCIENCES)
Bottom: The climactic scene from *The Pride of the
Yankees,* 1942. (COURTESY OF SAMUEL GOLDWYN, JR.)

Top: On the town with Ingrid Bergman.
(WALT DAUGHERTY COLLECTION)
Bottom: On the set of *Casanova Brown* in 1944
with his close friend William Goetz
(center) and an unidentified associate.
(EDITH MAYER GOETZ COLLECTION)
Opposite: Patricia Neal and Gary Cooper in one
of their few public appearances together.
(BEVERLY LINET COLLECTION)

A publicity shot from *High Noon* with Grace Kelly.
(COURTESY OF NATIONAL TELEFILM ASSOCIATES, INC.,
LOS ANGELES, OWNER/DISTRIBUTOR)

The showdown in *High Noon*.

Opposite: Candid wardrobe shot from
Return to Paradise. (ROBERTA HAYNES COLLECTION)
Above: A scene from *Love in the Afternoon*
with Audrey Hepburn, 1957. (ALLIED ARTISTS)

Opposite: Cooper, after cosmetic surgery, his hair dyed a soft brown, in 1958. (AUTHOR'S COLLECTION)
Above: On the set of *The Naked Edge,* Gary Cooper's final picture. From left to right: Deborah Kerr, Henry Ford II, Cooper, and his wife Rocky. Woman in the leopard jacket in the foreground is the first Mrs. Ford, a childhood friend of Rocky Cooper's.

Gary Cooper, shortly before his death, with his wife
Rocky and daughter Maria. (EDITH MAYER GOETZ COLLECTION)

superior to the worldly wisdom of the city slickers. That's where Cooper comes in.

As Gerald Mast points out in his book *The Comic Mind,* "Cooper can sustain an almost 150-minute film on this premise because the jolly good fellow who embodies that sap, Gary Cooper, is completely convincing, sympathetic, and affecting and because the comic contexts in which Deeds demonstrates his virtues are clever, sharply paced, and warmly textured. Gary Cooper, an actor of heart, is as important to the comedy of Capra as Cary Grant, an actor of the head, is to Howard Hawks's. . . . Jean Arthur, the woman of brain with a heart beneath, is also a Capra necessity. If *Mr. Deeds* seems Capra's best film, perhaps it is also because it is the only one with both Gary Cooper and Jean Arthur. As in the comedy of Hawks, the human truth beneath the Capra surfaces ultimately sustains the comic work."

Capra brings out the best comic as well as the best dramatic acting from Cooper. In the resulting miraculous character creation, it's hard to tell who, actor or director, needs who more. Without Capra, Cooper might never have had the chance to demonstrate how many sides of the human coin he could be at once. Without Cooper, Capra couldn't have made his greatest film. Cooper is genuinely hilarious when conducting a chorus of butlers to test the echoes in his newfound mansion, and he's genuinely disturbing when he goes into a blue funk and refuses to come out of it even to defend himself. Even when the story and the writing get too corny Cooper sees us through. And nobody else could do so much with a line that goes, "Nice day . . . er, nice night, uh, wasn't it, isn't it?" He could make any line of written dialogue sound like it was a thought coming out into the open air for the first time.

Perhaps because of *Deeds*, Cooper appeared in 1936 for the first time on the *Motion Picture Herald*'s exhibitors poll of Top Ten film personalities, where he was to remain, consistently, until 1958. It was a vote of long-standing public confidence surpassed only by John

Wayne and Bing Crosby. *Mr. Deeds Goes to Town* won the New York Film Critics Award for Best Picture. At Oscar-time, Frank Capra won another Academy Award for his direction. And at last, Gary Cooper was recognized by his peers. For the first time they nominated him for Best Actor. He lost the Oscar to Paul Muni for *The Story of Louis Pasteur*.

In May 1936, the month after the triumphant release of *Mr. Deeds*, Cooper and Jack Oakie left for New Mexico for location shooting on *The Texas Rangers*. Cooper dropped out before shooting started, to be replaced by Fred MacMurray. It is possible that his withdrawal from the picture was connected with a memorandum written by David O. Selznick to his New York representative, Katharine Brown.

The memo concerned Margaret Mitchell's *Gone With the Wind*. "Suggest you call this to Mr. [Merian C.] Cooper's and Mr. [John Hay] Whitney's attention for pioneer as possible color picture, especially if they can sell the very colorful man's role to Gary Cooper. Were I with MGM, I believe I would buy it now for some such combination as Gable and Joan Crawford."

In a single memo, Selznick named the man who was first offered the part—Cooper—and the man who eventually played him, Clark Gable. Cooper was tempted by the role of Rhett Butler in *Gone With the Wind*. "It was one of the best roles ever offered in Hollywood," he said, "and my screen character saw himself emerging from the film as a dashing-type fellow. But I said no. I didn't see myself as quite that dashing, and later, when I saw Clark Gable play the role to perfection, I knew I was right."

But was he? Or was he here merely rationalizing a major miscalculation? His next assignment was certainly no *GWTW*. He appeared as an unbilled guest star in *Hollywood Boulevard*, the story of a has-been actor making a comeback. The "B" picture starred John Halliday, who'd appeared with Cooper and Dietrich in *Desire*. *Hollywood Boulevard* featured many silent film stars, including Esther Ralston, who had been in England the last few years. Paramount gave her a supporting role. "I no longer had the star dressing room," she said, "just one that was assigned to feature players. I was very conscious of the fact I was walking on my old stomping grounds, but no longer considered *the* Esther Ralston."

She went quietly about her work. Walking to lunch one day, she passed by a grassy plaza on the lot. As she looked over to the sidewalk on the opposite side, she noticed Cooper walking by.

"Oh, dear!" she thought. "If he should snub me now, it would break my heart." Although they'd been good friends, circumstances had completely altered their professional standings. She wasn't going to embarrass Cooper by forcing him to acknowledge her. Looking down, she walked on. All of a sudden, she heard a cowboy whoop, saw those long legs jumping over the shrubbery and across the fountain in the middle. Cooper grabbed her and swung her around.

With humor and affection, he looked accusingly at her. "You were going to pass me by!"

She put her head on his chest. "No, Gary, I was so afraid it would be the other way around."

Cooper did not forget old friends. He was making an unbilled appearance as a guest at a bar in the same picture, solely as a favor to Halliday.

Cooper's manager, Jack Moss, casting about for a strong property, came upon the news that Clifford Odets, a leading playwright, was collaborating with Lewis Milestone, distinguished director of *All Quiet on the Western Front*, on *The General Died at Dawn*. Moss thought Cooper would want to bask in the prestige of a *succès d'estime*. He was right; Cooper took the role. Odets fashioned a story of oppression in China, and the antihero played by Cooper was required to overarticulate such lines as, "You ask why I'm fighting for oppressed people? Because I have a background of oppression myself!"

Both Odets and Milestone thought they would merge social consciousness and cinematic escapism.

Theirs would be as great a failure as Cooper's picture with Capra had been a triumph. *Mr. Deeds*'s message was tangential to the basic comedy. Film was effectively used as a mass medium to turn public opinion toward social objectives. In acknowledging life as it was during the Depression, the Capra film influenced the thinking of millions. It's impossible to see the film and not be affected by the values it espouses.

The turgid, pretentious approach of Milestone and Odets was doomed. In their artiness, they treated the action and intrigue condescendingly. If they didn't believe in it, why should the audience? Still, Cooper delivered embarrassing lines as if they were heartfelt, leaving his coworkers awed by his ability.

"With Gary," Milestone said, "all you had to do was put him someplace . . . on a chair, in a bed . . . light him, and tell him what he was supposed to think about. What you got was a picture of Hamlet. He was so photogenic, it was fantastic. We tried to stay on the subtle side, yet Gary Cooper's personality would always come through."

One of his fellow players learned the same lesson. Akim Tamiroff, trained at the Moscow Art Theater, was determined that Cooper wouldn't steal any scenes from him. Cast as an Oriental, he'd withstood great discomfort to have a rubber impression of Oriental eyes glued over his own. "For three days I act rings around him," Tamiroff said. "I have him stopped. Against my acting he can do nothing. I have won every scene. So I look at the rushes. On the screen I am there. Everybody else is there. But what do I see? Nothing! Nothing that is, but Gary Cooper."

As a logical progression, Cooper would soon be working for the first time with Cecil B. DeMille, the Grand Old Man of Hollywood, in *The Plainsman*. It was considered a further step upward to be collaborating with the great showman. DeMille was reputed to prize historical accuracy above all, employing researchers to dispel old myths so that he could create new ones. As a jingle had it:

> *Cecil B. DeMille,*
> *Much against his will,*
> *Was persuaded to keep Moses*
> *Out of the War of the Roses.*

There was a personality clash at the outset between the two men, for Cooper found DeMille to be as tyrannical as von Sternberg. "No one is to leave the set without my permission," DeMille ordered on the first day of shooting. If he intended to cow the cast and crew, he succeeded. With everyone, that is, but Gary Cooper.

Cooper would not work under such autocratic conditions. Before the entire company, the great star meekly raised his hand. "Please, sir, may I leave the room?"

The point was made: no one orders an emerging living legend around, not even an established living legend. The two men became friends. They had to be for DeMille to get away with some of his more outrageous conceits.

The characters in *The Plainsman* wander around uttering a historical fact here and a theatrical cliché there, grown-ups playing Cowboys and Indians. Much of the exterior footage was shot indoors, in front of rear projection screens on which appear further absurdities. When Cooper and his cohorts fire their pistols precisely on cue to fell Indians who obviously dropped dead on a previous shooting day, they look like a bunch of hicks at a shooting gallery.

Cooper's characterization as Wild Bill Hickok to Jean Arthur's Calamity Jane is unique in his career. He in no way resembles anything historical or even human. Instead, he is a typical DeMille caricature—an idealized historical personage reciting passages inscribed in marble.

Despite DeMille's hackneyed direction, Cooper managed some fresh and interesting touches. He eschewed Hollywood's International Standard speech in favor of a nineteenth-century Midwestern twang. In his relaxed moments he dispensed with his usual halting spontaneity, which was appealingly folksy, and in intense moments, he was powerful.

"How in the hell can you read those goddamn lines?" Howard Hawks asked Cooper.

"Well," he replied, "when DeMille finishes talking to you, they don't seem so bad. But when you see the picture, you kind of hang your head."

No one loved *The Plainsman* but the masses, and no one had a higher estimation of Cooper as an actor than DeMille.

"Gary is an embodiment of the old saying that art consists in concealing its own artfulness," DeMille wrote. "After seeing him on the screen, any young man might say, 'Shucks, I could do that.' The young man would be wrong. Gary Cooper, off screen as well as on, is an affable, modest American gentleman; but he is also an accomplished artist in his profession."

DeMille's praises were at odds with what Cooper professed to believe shortly before the picture was released. "I think movie acting is a pretty silly business for a man," he told *The New York Daily News*, "because it takes less training, less ability, and less brains to be successful at it than any other business I can think of."

Considering how long and hard he'd worked at his craft, one wonders where he suddenly developed such contempt. Could it have been during his recent first meeting with Ernest Hemingway? In the fall of 1936 Cooper realized an ambition of several years' standing when Marlene Dietrich, who'd met Hemingway two years previously on the *Ile de France*, arranged for the two men to get together. Cooper had come away from the encounter questioning his values.

Cooper went for the first time to Sun Valley, Idaho. A. E. Hotchner described the immediate friendship that developed between Hemingway and Cooper in *Papa Hemingway*. "They respected each other's hunting skills and knowledge of the outdoors, and they were

always completely honest with one another. Cooper was
an unaffected, compassionate man; and neither of them
played the role of author or actor, which also had a lot
to do with it. They shared rough jokes, swapped philan-
dering secrets, and enjoyed their mutual disdain for the
encroaching years."

They were the titans in their respective fields.
Hemingway was a serious artist with movie star pa-
nache. His exploits invariably landed him on the front
page. He was a committed activist, and this quality especially appealed to Cooper. In fact, Hemingway's
showy masculinity and cocksure proclamations of eternal verities may have thoroughly intimidated Gary
Cooper. Was there something condescending in the way
the literary lion referred to the actor? Friends called
him Gary; intimates who knew his preference called
him Coop. Only those in the Hemingway circle used the
comic "Coops."

After three years of marriage, the Gary Coopers
discovered that they were going to have a child. For
some time, Cooper had been trying to limit himself to
two pictures a year. The impending birth gave him another reason to slow down. He would stick to the
resolve for the rest of his film career. Cooper was working with Henry Hathaway in *Souls at Sea*, based on a
true incident in which an officer was forced to cut away
some of the passengers clinging to a lifeboat after a
shipwreck. George Raft costarred.

Paramount executives, after seeing the first rushes,
were so impressed that they decided to make the film
into a road show attraction to rival Metro's *Mutiny on
the Bounty* of three years ago.

The production would have a gestation period almost equal to Rocky's pregnancy, for the shooting
schedule was expanded from three to seven months.
Filming was organized so that Cooper could spend
much time off with his expectant wife. Raft, the less
important actor, was stuck at the picture's headquarters
on Catalina Island for the entire seven months.

As the film neared completion, Paramount decided to cut back some of the scenes and release it as a regular feature. Whatever the studio decided seemed to be all right with Raft, who would be nominated for a Best Supporting Actor Oscar in the part, although the decision couldn't have pleased hardworking director Hathaway.

Two anxious fathers-to-be, Gary Cooper and Frank Capra, walked the halls of Good Samaritan Hospital at the same time. The director's wife gave birth first, to a daughter named Lulu, their third child. On the following day, September 15, 1937, Maria Cooper was born. The infant would be raised in her mother's Catholic faith. Her godparents were Cedric Gibbons and Dolores del Rio.

Edie Goetz went to call on the mother and her new baby soon after they returned home. Rocky was out, and Cooper took Mrs. Goetz into the nursery. He tenderly pulled back the coverlet. "Look, Edie," he said, "she has slanty eyes just like you have."

From the moment of her birth, the girl with the almond-shaped eyes became the most important female in Gary Cooper's life. "Having a daughter is the thing I'm proudest of," he said toward the end of his life.

With the advent of Maria, it's understandable why Cooper may not have had his mind on his work. A bumbling Paramount could hardly plead the same excuse. The studio was blessed with two of the Top Ten box office stars that year, Bing Crosby and Gary Cooper, and the two actors should have been coddled and treasured. Through some incredible oversight, Cooper's contract with the studio had expired, and Paramount neglected to exercise its additional option period.

Goldwyn was aching for a chance to lure Cooper back to his studio. He came up with an offer of $100,000 a picture. Cooper's salary hadn't appreciably increased since he'd been raised to $6,000 a week nearly four years previously. If the projects at Goldwyn came in on scheduled time, he could be picking up twice that amount.

When Paramount brass discovered that Goldwyn had pulled a fast one, they were incensed. Cooper had "innocently" assumed the studio had lost interest in him, and consequently had accepted the Goldwyn deal. While the inevitable litigation was resolved—it took two years—Cooper commuted between the two studios.

Goldwyn geared up for the arrival of his semipermanent star, while Cooper agreed to make a picture first at Paramount, which had been in the works for some time. It would be supervised by Ernst Lubitsch, who by 1937 decided he was not cut out to be a studio executive and reverted to producing-directing. Its screenwriters were a pair of men who would be responsible for such future classics as *Ninotchka* and *Hold Back the Dawn*.

One of them, Billy Wilder, would break through as one of the great directors of the post-World War II period with such films as *The Lost Weekend, Sunset Boulevard, Some Like It Hot*, and *The Apartment*. He would continue the Lubitsch tradition of witty camera placement, brisk pace, and dialogue with a certain sardonic intelligence.

Wilder and his writing partner, Charles Brackett, complemented each other well, arguing and firing ideas back and forth through meals, massages, and manicures. Although the future director's work would evolve into a hard-edged and often hilarious look at contemptible aspects of existence, the attitudes of some of his early films with Brackett were merely contemptuous.

The picture they wrote, *Bluebeard's Eighth Wife*, was clever but couldn't overcome its queasy premise: an American millionaire, seven times divorced, is in pursuit of an eighth wife. Carole Lombard wanted the part, but Lubitsch had intended it to go to Claudette Colbert all along.

Cooper was more effective as a sophisticate than he'd been in *Design for Living*. He handled the Wilder-Brackett lines and the Lubitsch timing with authority and polish, bringing his accustomed naturalness to bear on a most unnatural style. In the public mind, it didn't work. The problem wasn't on the carefree, almost-innocent surface, but in the dark undercurrents felt about a man's divorcing so many wives in a row. It might have worked with another actor, although that is problematical, but it didn't work with a man many fans regarded as Mr. Deeds incarnate.

While Paramount tried to create a more enticing vehicle for him, Cooper reported to Goldwyn for his first assignment. Douglas Fairbanks had originally planned to produce a film on Marco Polo starring his namesake son. He went into partnership with Goldwyn, and when it didn't work out for Fairbanks, Jr., Cooper was offered the role.

Robert Sherwood's tongue-in-cheek script was first offered to René Clair. When the French director turned down *Marco Polo*, William Wyler was tapped. He refused utterly and unequivocally. John Cromwell took over the assignment, but quit five days into the shooting. That's when Archie Mayo, who'd scored a comic hit in 1936 with *Three Men on a Horse*, got the job almost by default. Mayo, however, didn't catch the subtle comic nuances and delivered a lead-footed opus.

He played it straight, and it came out unintentionally ludicrous. The Goldwyn Girls were used as dancers in the Chinese Court; he borrowed sequences from old Harold Lloyd movies; he had the ancient Chinese speak twentieth-century American.

Mayo and Goldwyn quickly developed a mutual antipathy. Despite a sumptuous production, the picture was a mess. The director walked out.

Jack Moss had been instrumental in bringing Stuart Heisler to Goldwyn, and his client would be required to direct many second units before he was given his own picture as director. With everything in a shambles, however, and director Mayo virtually exiled to Europe, it fell upon Heisler to rescue *Marco Polo*. He took Cooper to Mt. Whitney to reshoot some scenes, then to the desert at El Rancho on the edge of Owens Lake. Understandably, Cooper was bored with the project by this time. His famous ability to drop off to sleep was hampered by all the shouting going on around him.

"You couldn't tell the difference from the back between Coop and his double, Slim Talbot," Heisler said. "This guy used to do an awful lot of things for him . . . all the stunts and falls. In the long shots, riding for Coop, you couldn't tell the difference. We got away with so much that we didn't mind using him. Anything Coop didn't want to do in *Marco Polo*, we gave to Talbot. Slim liked to do it. He wanted to feel he was earning his pay."

Because of disinterest on all sides, the picture was the only one Cooper ever made at Goldwyn to lose money. "It needed a delicate something that would make it amusing," Heisler said. "If Lubitsch had done it, it would have been the most delightful thing you've ever seen."

Goldwyn next planned to star Cooper in *Graustark*, a costume drama which would also feature Merle Oberon and Sigrid Gurie, his highly touted Norwegian import, actually born in Brooklyn. Sigrid had appeared in the disastrous *Marco Polo*.

The day before production was to start, *Graustark* was abruptly canceled. Cooper was able to fulfill his commitment to Goldwyn when *The Cowboy and the Lady* opposite Merle Oberon was hurriedly substituted. Since there was no role for Miss Gurie, she was assigned to another picture.

The new project was a reworking of the spoiled heiress-simple Westerner romance Cooper had already filmed with Lombard in *I Take This Woman*. Leo McCarey had given an award-winning performance in a Goldwyn conference room and, on the basis of the passion and humor he engendered, was given $50,000 for his idea. There would be almost a dozen writers who would try to fashion a plot.

William Wyler was under contract to Goldwyn and, though he had little enthusiasm for the project, was assigned to direct. The second day of shooting, Wyler had an "attack."

Three doctors swore that Wyler was in very serious condition. "I don't know what kind of attack he had," Heisler, who was directing a second unit, said, "but he was sick. So they closed down the company the second day. He came back the following morning and had a real serious attack again. Five minutes from the time he got this attack, an ambulance came and they piled Willy into it. He never got out of bed until he was darned sure they had assigned a new director to do the picture."

H. C. Potter, a Broadway director, was brought in by Goldwyn to replace Wyler. "He was doing a really lousy job," Heisler said. "Not only that but he got so far behind schedule. When Goldwyn asked me about him, I said, 'I don't think he's doing a good job. He certainly doesn't know anything about staging for motion pictures. He's staging for the New York stage.'"

Goldwyn fired Potter and hired Heisler to finish the job. "I got to be very easy with Coop," Heisler said. "He got to have respect for me. Coop was a loner. When he took you into his confidence, that was something. I thought that if I ever got into real trouble, I could go to him . . . though I never did."

As close as he felt to Cooper, Heisler never met Rocky, nor would he even be invited to Cooper's home until the star lay dying. Cooper compartmentalized his life along class lines, perhaps at his wife's instigation. Distinguished acquaintances were acceptable socially, but Cooper's rough and rowdy pals were not. Ernest Hemingway was one of the few exceptions; as a celebrated author he was in a class by himself. In Cooper's films, the lady, in the end, always saw the light and came around to the cowboy's simple ways. This was not at all the case in Cooper's real life.

It took five months to put *The Cowboy and the Lady* in the can. Cooper walked through a role he'd played many times before, but his luster didn't dim. *Cowboy* was only a modest success.

The other studios were bidding for Cooper's services. If Goldwyn didn't know what to do with him, they surely did. Despite his turning down the Rhett Butler role two years ago, discussions were revived in March of 1938 when Louis B. Mayer became recalcitrant with his son-in-law, David Selznick, about loaning out Clark Gable for the role. Goldwyn wanted to distribute the picture through United Artists, and Selznick was adamant that this would never happen unless Cooper agreed to play Rhett Butler. Cooper backed off again, and, bowing to public clamor that only Clark Gable should play the part, Selznick signed away a large piece of the picture to Metro in order to get Gable, the popular choice.

Others were busy conceiving projects for Cooper. After Joan Crawford's *Chained* was released in December 1934, F. Scott Fitzgerald was assigned by Metro to write her next picture. The studio again wanted Cooper as her costar. Fitzgerald envisioned the protagonist of *Infidelity* as a white Othello in modern dress. His conception grew from his own experience, when his wife Zelda took a French aviator for a lover. Transposing the roles, he had the husband being unfaithful with his former secretary, whom the screenwriter-author thought should be played by Cooper's fellow Montanan, Myrna Loy. The script over the past four years had gone through several versions, the businessman-hero being changed into a drummer at one point. The Breen office, the industry's successor to the Hays office as official censor, ultimately refused to approve *Infidelity*. It fell apart just about the time that another great artist was creating a project expressly for Cooper.

Charlie Chaplin needed a vehicle to establish the stardom of his wife, Paulette Goddard. "It was a story of a young millionaire who takes a cruise to China and meets and falls in love with a beautiful White Russian employed in a dance hall," Charles Chaplin, Jr., wrote in his autobiography. "The picture was to be a comedy with social implications. Dad . . . was a great fan of Cooper's, not because he thought him a fine actor, but because Cooper didn't even try to act. He was always himself and thus completely believable. Dad was excited about this script."

Cooper didn't share the enthusiasm and turned down the offer. Chaplin would wait nearly thirty years to make the picture, *A Countess from Hong Kong,* with Marlon Brando and Sophia Loren. Perhaps Chaplin's assessment of Cooper's ability—or lack thereof—was insulting to the actor. A genius like Chaplin who made the difficult look easy should have known better.

"When I read somewhere that I am a natural-talent boy who never had an acting lesson in his life," Cooper said, "I wonder what all those thousands of hours add up to that I spent with Ronald Colman, Bill Powell, Henry King, Sam Goldwyn, Cecil B. DeMille, Charles Laughton, Thelma Todd, Claudette Colbert, Helen Hayes, Marlene Dietrich, Barbara Stanwyck—the list runs on and on. If those weren't lessons conducted under the most competitive of professional circumstances, then I wouldn't know a lesson if I saw one."

For his last contractual commitment to Paramount before becoming a free agent, Cooper decided to remake Ronald Colman's silent *Beau Geste,* with William Wellman directing.

The character Cooper played, Beau Geste, translates into English as "gallant gesture." Just what the gesture is, and why it's so gallant, takes the unraveling of the entire picture to reveal. And it helps to have read the book.

William Wellman's remake was modeled with disturbing closeness on its predecessor. At the same time it was terse and abrupt, the melodrama of brotherhood and the romance of self-sacrifice surprisingly downplayed for the sentimental era of the late thirties. The Major Henri de Beaujolais who appears in the first scene, played by James Stephenson, is the same character played by Cooper in *Beau Sabreur.* This was one of the few times an actor ever appeared opposite a character he'd portrayed in another film. Cooper was to perform this feat again in *Dallas,* opposite Reed Hadley's Wild Bill Hickok, in 1950.

Wellman took his company to the California desert west of Yuma, Arizona, to shoot the Sahara sequences. The area was generally known as Buttercup Valley, but the Board of Supervisors of Imperial County temporarily changed the name to Beau Geste Valley. A mile and a half of plank road was built to get camera equipment to the remote location. As in *Barbara Worth*, an entire tent city was built for the 1,000 men involved, with electricity, running water, and a movie theater. Paramount built two entire oases in the barren desert, and transported an array of palms to decorate them. *Beau Geste* would take only twenty-five shooting days.

Rocky and Maria waited out part of that time in sunny Phoenix. When word reached Cooper on location that his daughter was ill, he requisitioned a camel and rode through a violent sandstorm nineteen miles east to Yuma to the nearest telephone. Assured that Maria was coming along nicely, Cooper rode the nineteen miles back, in time for work the following morning.

Beau Geste was one of the first films to feature Susan Hayward. She and costar Robert Preston had emerged in Paramount's "Golden Circle," a showcase for young players with star potential, which also included William Holden.

Brian Donlevy stole a great portion of *Beau Geste* with his portrait of the evil Sgt. Markoff, changed in this version from a Frenchman to an expatriate Russian to avoid offending French audiences. The French foreign market was far more important than the Russian.

Cooper is fabulous in attempting to quell the post's insurgents with the quiet line, "I don't know much about mutinies, but I do know it isn't good form to plan them at the top of your voice."

"The men dote upon Mr. Cooper for his stature, his taciturnity, his gaunt countenance," said Bland Johaneson of *The New York Daily Mirror*. "The apotheosis of the manly, he is flawlessly fitted for the strong, silent, boyish heroics of *Beau Geste*. That he no longer looks quite boyish enough to play the grateful ward of a patrician lady is a captious criticism—and one the men will not tolerate."

Samuel Goldwyn wanted Cooper for *The Real Glory*. Working again with director Henry Hathaway, the $2 million film about the quelling of a Moro uprising in the Philippines during the Spanish-American War would take 200 days to film, longer than the actual happening on which it was based.

At the completion of one scene, a man happened to pass by the window of the office-set and cast a shadow through the shutters. As Cooper recalled, Henry Hathaway was struck by the visual effect created. "Quick, Gary! Get in back of your desk. I want a shot of you as you look up and see that shadow pass your window."

"Who is he?" the actor asked.

"I don't know, but it looks good. Let's go, before the sun moves around and spoils the effect."

"Is he a friend? An enemy? A spy?"

Hathaway assured Cooper they could figure it out later. "Now let's go before they tear down the set."

It was impossible for Cooper "to react to a situation that had not yet been created. I'd have to substitute acting for characterization, and I found I could no longer play that way."

The word he didn't use, since adopted by every serious actor, was "motivation." Such pretension wasn't expected of him in a whopping action film. Frank S. Nugent of *The New York Times* would find Hathaway's direction unfurled "with all the bugles blowing, the drums rolling, and a tall man like Gary Cooper on a parapet heaving sticks of dynamite down on the attackers."

The Real Glory built on the success of *Beau Geste*. Cooper, at year's end, became the first film actor to be the nation's top wage earner, receiving $482,819 in salary. He could be assured that the money wouldn't be frittered away. Paul Shields, Rocky's stepfather, was handling the family's investments.

Cooper stayed on at Goldwyn to work with William Wyler in *The Westerner*. Like John Ford's *Stagecoach* of the previous year, which made a star of John Wayne, Wyler's new film was an attempt by an intelligent director to get the shoot-'em-up genre off the "B" picture treadmill and into the more rarefied atmosphere of the national myth. *The Westerner* explored the conflict between encroaching law and order and backwoods savagery. In talking about his aspirations for the picture, Wyler was able to persuade Cooper to take the star, if not the leading, role. The lead was assumed by Walter Brennan as the cantankerous Judge Roy Bean. Cooper played a drifter who ultimately fought it out with the infamous "Law West of the Pecos" judge.

"I couldn't figure for the life of me why they needed me for this picture," Cooper said. "I had a very minor part. It didn't require any special effort. All the character had to do was exchange a few shots with the judge in the dramatic moment of the picture."

Wyler had additional casting problems. Because Merle Oberon was unable to reach an agreement with Goldwyn about playing the judge's adored Lily Langtry, the role was downgraded and given to a starlet named Lillian Bond.

Wyler, while directing *Wuthering Heights* for Goldwyn in 1939, had attempted to cast his wife, Margaret Tallichet, as Cooper's love interest in *The Westerner*. He was under pressure, however, to use a very limited actress named Doris Davenport. Wyler laboriously put together a test of the likable girl, but the effect was more a tribute to his technique than to the aspiring actress' ability, and it won her a studio contract.

"I've tried putting Doris Davenport with other directors," Goldwyn said to the director. "She's a *great* actress. I can see that from the test you made. You're the only one who can bring that out. I'm putting her in the picture."

Not only was Wyler hoisted by his own petard, he was sentenced to extracting an adequate performance from the girl.

The picture, shot outside Tucson, Arizona, at a

cost well over $1 million, hinged on the strange relationship that developed between Brennan's Bean and Cooper's Cole Hardin. The judge represents backward frontier justice and the drifter comes to represent a more advanced law and order.

Through it all, Cooper has some of his best moments. Waking up after a drunken binge with Bean, his leaden head and applesauce legs are a universally shared experience. His reaction to the commutation of his death penalty by Bean is an indecipherable murmur, a slight intake of breath, and a raising of the head—perhaps to heaven. To do more would be to turn a poem into a placard.

Brennan won his third Academy Award for Best Supporting Actor in the part. He also received the raves. "Gary Cooper is an exceedingly modest fellow," Bosley Crowther wrote in *The New York Times*, "too modest for his own good, perhaps . . . for in *The Westerner* . . . he casually permits the most important role in the picture to be taken away from him and bestowed upon capable Walter Brennan."

Cooper was often an uncommonly generous actor. Joel McCrea wanted to star in *Foreign Correspondent*, though he had a commitment to Cecil B. DeMille for *North West Mounted Police*. Cooper, the bigger star, agreed to take the part so that McCrea could do the picture he preferred.

Both Gary Cooper and Cecil B. DeMille were making their first color film. To guarantee best reproduction, many of the outdoor scenes were shot on light-controlled indoor soundstages. The extent of Cooper's sacrifice for friend Joel McCrea wouldn't be appreciated until years later, when a book entitled *The Fifty Worst Films of All Times* cited *North West Mounted Police* as a prime offender. Crowther of *The Times* said, "as usual in Mr. DeMille's pictures, the story is a heavy accumulation of dramatic clichés, while the action, the atmosphere, and spectacle are the things which count. . . . Only Mr. Cooper preserves his cool, dry, congenial personality. He is himself even in a DeMille film."

North West Mounted Police nonetheless was the sixth-biggest grosser of 1940. So much for the critics. The industry needed such hugely profitable pictures: like everything else, the industry was hit by the war in Europe. The foreign market was virtually eliminated. Legend has it that Greta Garbo ended her career as a result, since her pictures were greater successes abroad than in the United States. And when the war ended she was over forty, and felt her magic was lost.

Rocky, under her husband's tutelage, had become an expert markswoman, winning the 1939 California Women's Championship in skeet shooting. Cooper was such an avid marksman that he could occasionally be seen at a shooting gallery on the Boardwalk of Venice Beach taking shots at the moving targets.

The Coopers had gone to Sun Valley with Robert Taylor and Barbara Stanwyck, then married, to go pheasant hunting with Ernest Hemingway and his new wife Martha Gellhorn. Their host, as Cooper later recalled, assigned the Taylors to a slope a quarter-mile away, and told the Coopers to cover a blackberry patch across the field. He and his wife would stay uphill.

"Don't shoot if you flush a bird or two," Hemingway instructed. "In fact, don't shoot until you hear me holler."

As Taylor approached his patch, the air around him was suddenly thick with birds. The same thing happened with Cooper at his spot. Two flocks joined and headed toward Hemingway. "Fire!" he shouted, letting go with both barrels.

"It took a minute for the air to clear of feathers," Cooper recalled. "I looked down at Bob and he looked back at me. The Nebraska boy and the Montana boy, raised in pheasant country, had been took." At that point, Rocky, who disliked shooting living creatures anyway, resolved to stick with clay pigeons.

Hemingway's last wife and widow, Mary Welsh Hemingway, while not contradicting the story, since she was not involved, did say however that she and her husband subscribed to one of the cardinal rules of hunting protocol. "The polite thing, of course, is to aim at only one bird, and not splatter the sky with all kinds of shotgun pellets."

Of all Ernest Hemingway's friends, Gregory Hemingway liked Cooper most of all. "I'd seen a lot of his movies and he was not different in person than he was in them—unbelievably handsome, gentle, courteous, and innately noble." Gregory Hemingway said Cooper was an excellent shot, steady and deliberate and slow. Ernest Hemingway, because of poor vision, took a longer time to pick up a bird in his sights, and then had to shoot quickly.

Though Cooper and Hemingway had little in common intellectually, "a kindness and gentleness seemed to exist between them," Gregory Hemingway said. "And they really did enjoy each other—you could tell by the resonance of their voices and the way their eyes smiled. And there was nobody around to impress, that was the beauty of it, just their wives and kids. Maybe that seems like an unkind thing to say, but both of them were great actors—yes, my father was one [too]—who had forged, consciously or otherwise, two of the most successful hero images of this century. There was never rivalry between them, and there was no reason for any. They were both at their peak then."

It was the best of times for Cooper. He would get into old clothes as often as possible to cultivate his citrus grove with a small tractor and tend to the vegetable garden which put food on his table. He raised ducks and chickens. He could roll out of bed into his swimming pool, or play tennis on his own court. He hunted coyotes and bobcats in the mountains near Malibu in the springtime, and joined his friend Hemingway in Sun Valley in the fall. He'd at first endured Rocky's formal dinners, and the yearly pilgrimages to Southampton every summer. Now, he claimed to take as much pleasure in them as she. And he had his Maria. It was a good life.

Chapter 8

As he approached his fortieth year, Gary Cooper was on the threshold of even-greater renown. The earlier sensuality of his face was being displaced by a weathered, granitic appearance, and he was becoming an American symbol to be cherished almost as much as apple pie and motherhood. Soon, he would be the quintessential American Everyman courageously facing up to the challenges of his time.

Hollywood was mobilizing for war long before the American government did. It was in the self-interest of the motion picture industry, having lost a substantial portion of its European market, to be jingoistic and warmongering. By today's standards, as well as the more discerning current ones, these were not great films. Many weren't even good. They performed a vital service, however. First they anticipated a national mood. So hawkish were films of the period that the Interstate Commerce Committee of the United States Senate met in September of 1941 for the express purpose of investigating prowar and anti-Nazi propaganda in American films. Public sentiment had already turned interventionist and the committee was practically sneered out of existence. Three months later, with Pearl Harbor, the hearings were terminated, and films that had been denounced in Congress were now felt to be urgently needed to satisfy the national mood.

Cooper's pictures of the early forties would all be stamped by wartime fervor. Even *Ball of Fire,* which was released in January 1942 and was ostensibly about a professor and a burlesque queen, utilized the conflict between humane sensibility and irrational brute force which was then obsessing the Nazi-threatened world.

The first picture in this new phase of Cooper's career was Frank Capra's *Meet John Doe,* a protest film warning America against the dangers of Fascism from within. Capra recalled, "Seldom does a filmmaker ever assemble his dream cast. That rarity happened in *Meet John Doe.* For the [lead]—a lanky hobo, an ex-bush league pitcher with a glass arm—I had but one choice: Gary Cooper. I wouldn't have made the picture without him. But I had no script for him to read when I asked him to play the part. Surprisingly, he said, 'It's okay, Frank. I don't need a script.' His wife, Rocky, put it this way: 'John Ford sent Gary a script of *Stagecoach.* Gary was on the fence about it. I read it, and advised him to turn it down. *Stagecoach*? It made a star of John Wayne, but we turned it down.' "

Others rounding out Capra's dream cast were Barbara Stanwyck, Edward Arnold, Walter Brennan, and Gene Lockhart.

With this effort, Capra and screen writer Robert Riskin moved away from Columbia, putting up their own money to partially finance the picture at Warner Brothers.

The screenplay they prepared was about a fired newspaper columnist, played by Barbara Stanwyck, who prints a phony letter in her valedictory column from a "John Doe," stating he will commit suicide on Christmas Eve as a protest against misery and corruption. As a result of great public interest, the girl's job is saved. But when she is accused of perpetrating a hoax, she and her editor must find someone willing to admit he wrote the letter. He is Cooper, as the has-been pitcher with the bad arm. He so captures the public's imagination that John Doe clubs spring up everywhere. The newspaper's publisher, played by Edward Arnold, cynically sees this as an opportunity to create a power base for his own Presidential ambitions. When John Doe refuses to go along with the charade, the publisher denounces him as a fake. Disillusioned, John Doe can still commit suicide on Christmas Eve, as the original fake letter had indicated.

Production began on July 5, 1940, and would be completed in two months. Filming started without an ending in hand—would John Doe commit suicide or not?—because, Capra said, "I thought it would come during the making of the show." Capra and Riskin were taking few other chances with the film, other than with their reputations, for many would find their populist sentimentality as much a piece of populist demagoguery as the evil newspaper publisher's. A crowd of extras was paid a whole day's wages to respond as they chose to one of Cooper's speeches in the film. Capra also cut ten minutes from the picture, his decision made for him by the reaction of preview audiences in White Plains, New York.

Capra and Riskin painted themselves into a corner. They shot four different endings.

Gene Lockhart, playing the mayor in the film, came home complaining of the bitter cold they'd had to endure during the filming of the different versions of the suicide scene. "It was shot in a big ice house in downtown Los Angeles," his daughter, actress June Lockhart, said. "They had to work all night in this freezing building." The ice house had been converted to look like a modernistic city hall.

Movie audiences were equally frigid to the various endings. At one time three different endings were playing in Washington, New York, and San Francisco respectively.

The actions throughout the movie lead to the inevitable suicide of John Doe. The movement needs a dead martyr to continue to function. What was arrived at was a weak solution, one supplied by a "John Doe" among the moviegoing public. "The only way you can keep that man from jumping off that City Hall on Christmas

Eve is if the John Does themselves come and tell him he'd be of much more use walking around than dead."

In *Meet John Doe*, it's easy to see why Cooper attracted more attention as an actor in films that don't work well. He had to work twice as hard to make up for the deficiencies. When Capra's machinery breaks down, he taps the powers of Cooper's reactions again and again. Yet, the harder Cooper works, the more obvious is the director's audience manipulation. The film chokes on its own dishonesty.

Nevertheless, *Meet John Doe* was one of the year's top money makers. It was a pyrrhic victory for Capra. He would make more films in the future, but his popularity virtually ended with this picture. Increasingly sophisticated audiences began to regard his work as cornball simplistic, a great disservice to the man responsible for such acknowledged classics as *Mr. Deeds* and *Mr. Smith Goes to Washington*. Capra made the mistake of repeating himself once too often. As for Cooper, he came away from the picture with nearly unanimous raves for the quality of his acting.

Bosley Crowther of *The New York Times* analyzed the character Cooper had come to represent: "He is the honest and forthright fellow—confused, inconsistent, but always sincere—who believes in the basic goodness of people and has the courage to fight hard for principles. . . . Gary Cooper, of course, is 'John Doe' to the life and in the whole—shy, bewildered, nonaggressive, but a veritable tiger when aroused."

On May 22, 1919, Jesse L. Lasky took a brief pause from his duties as Vice-President in charge of production at Famous Players-Lasky in New York to look out his Fifth Avenue office window at an extravagant tickertape parade. Seizing on the idea that anybody worth that kind of fuss would make a good movie, he called for an assistant. "I want you to rush right out and contact that man. Don't come back until you have his signature on a contract to appear for us in a picture based on his own story." His secretaries burst into applause at the suggestion.

Two days later, his underling returned looking as if he hadn't slept in all that time. "It's hopeless, Mr. Lasky," he sighed. "But if it's any consolation, nobody else is going to get Sergeant York, either."

Alvin Cullum York was a hell-raiser from the Valley of the Three Forks of the Wolf, in the Cumberland Mountains of Tennessee, who put his prodigious skill at firearms to good use when he was drafted into service in World War I. Though he professed to be a conscientious objector, having been converted to a life of piety and good works, he was more opposed to the killing of his buddies by the enemy than he was to the killing of the enemy by himself. In the space of four hours, the body count was 25 Germans killed and 132 taken prisoner, just about singlehandedly. York was awarded the Congressional Medal of Honor, the Distinguished Service Cross, the French Croix de Guerre, and the Medaille Militaire. The United States Congress and Wall Street's Stock Exchange came to a total halt to cheer his deed. He accepted the awards and celebrations with humility. But when a gaggle of entrepreneurs descended on him waving contracts for endorsements totaling a quarter of a million dollars, he drew the line. "Uncle Sam's uniform," he stated flatly, "hit ain't for sale." And he went back to his previous life in the Tennessee hills, tending a farm that had been given to him by the people of Tennessee.

There the story had ended, for a time, despite repeated pleas from Lasky in the early days of the talkies. York was involved with his farm and with the people of the Valley, and wanted Satan behind him.

But in the spring of 1939, when war in Europe broke out again and American involvement seemed all but inevitable, the dream of making a film of York's life again obsessed Lasky. He hadn't found steady work in pictures since being forced out of Paramount in 1932. Lasky was now producing radio shows. It occurred to him that York could be sold on the idea that it was his patriotic duty to serve as an inspiration to a new generation of Americans at another point of national crisis.

When a telegram to this effect got no reply, Lasky went to Tennessee. The dirt roads through the mountain peaks got him as far as Jamestown, from which point he tried phoning. York, on the other end of the party line, replied that, twenty years after the fact, he was still thinking it over. In the meantime, he had been leading a private life, farming with his wife Gracie, and rearing his seven children. The most celebrated fighting man in American military history was now concerned with raising enough money to finish construction of a Bible school for the Valley. It took Lasky two more personal visits. Once he'd convinced York that the money would finish off that Bible school, the deal was cinched. Lasky and York signed a contract on March 21, 1940, in the Tennessee State House in Nashville, with Governor Prentiss Cooper as witness.

As proof of his honorable intentions, and in keeping with the ethical shortcuts of Hollywood, Lasky gave York a postdated rubber check in the amount of $25,-000, half of the total amount agreed on. He planned to borrow the money on his life insurance to cover it. The rest would be due in sixty days. Now the problem was getting the only man Lasky considered right for the part of Sergeant York: Gary Cooper. As he arrived in Nashville Airport, a possible solution came to Lasky. He sent a telegram to Cooper, who lived across the street from him in Brentwood: I HAVE JUST AGREED TO LET THE MOTION PICTURE PRODUCER JESSE L. LASKY FILM THE STORY OF MY LIFE, SUBJECT TO MY APPROVAL OF THE STAR. I HAVE GREAT ADMIRATION FOR YOU AS AN ACTOR AND AS A MAN, AND I WOULD BE HONORED, SIR, TO SEE YOU ON THE SCREEN AS MYSELF. SERGEANT ALVIN C. YORK.

Lasky's fabrication, over the next few months,

would be repeated so often that York himself came to believe that Cooper, too old for the part and clearly hostile to conscientious objectors, was the right man for the role.

Cooper professed that his first big struggle between public responsibility and private career goals came when he was offered *Sergeant York*. "In screen biographies, dealing with remote historical characters, some romantic leeway is permissible. But York happened to be very much alive, his exploits were real, and I felt that I couldn't do justice to him. York himself came to tell me I was his own choice for the role, but I still felt I couldn't handle it. Here was a pious, sincere man, a conscientious objector to war, who, when called, became a heroic fighter for his country. He was too big for me, he covered too much territory."

With Cooper vacillating, Lasky was frantically trying to persuade a major studio to underwrite the picture before the final payment to York came due. None was interested. There'd been no successful war pictures in years. In desperation, and at the suggestion of the head of publicity there, Lasky went to Warner Brothers. He'd been advised by publicist Charles Einfeld that Harry Warner's weak spot was patriotism.

Lasky said, "I told him the story of a simple mountaineer who was the best turkey shot in Tennessee and a rough character until he got religion and became an exemplary citizen. Then the same person who had accomplished his conversion and taught him 'Thou shall not kill' sat as head of the draft board in the grocery store in Jimtown and told him he was going to be conscripted in the Army."

Warner was so taken with the dilemma that he agreed to give the project serious consideration if all the pieces fell into place. This meant Cooper's remaining at Warner's to play the star role and the recruitment of an accomplished director in support of Lasky.

Director Howard Hawks agreed to take on the project, canceling his commitment to Howard Hughes to direct *The Outlaw,* which would introduce Jane Russell. His first responsibility was to talk Cooper into making *Sergeant York.*

Hawks told Cooper that the film was an ideal opportunity to create a screen biography without necessarily turning it into a success story. The narrative would unfold much as it actually happened, without a big buildup to the invention of the telephone or the digging of the Suez Canal. It would be the story of a man of peace who, after an interlude of violence he abhorred, would return to his former life uncorrupted.

Hawks reminded Cooper that it was Lasky who was partially responsible for signing Cooper to his first Hollywood contract. So Cooper agreed, and Lasky was back in the film business. Samuel Goldwyn, who had an option for Cooper's next picture, agreed to forego it if Warner Brothers would lend him Bette Davis for *The Little Foxes.*

John Huston (son of *The Virginian*'s Walter Huston and writer on *High Sierra*) and Howard Koch (best known as writer for Orson Welles's legendary *War of the Worlds* broadcast) were assigned to rewrite the script by Abem Finkel and Harry Chandlee. Hawks admitted that he had no idea what the final result was going to look like, since, he said, "it follows no patterns."

In 1963 Hawks told Peter Bogdanovich, "Huston and I wrote the script. We just kept ahead of shooting. We threw away the written script and did what Jesse Lasky told us about the real Sergeant York. Huston and I were very much in accord and it became very easy to tell the story simply."

It was anything but simple. The picture had an epic ninety-day shooting schedule, which began in early February 1941. There were more speaking parts than for any picture in history but *Anthony Adverse,* also a Warner epic. One hundred and twenty-three sets were needed, another record. Some of these included a recreation of the Valley of the Three Forks of the Wolf, on a Hollywood soundstage. The biggest stage in town (measuring 135 feet by 250 feet) was used, and a 40-foot mountain peak was made out of canvas and wood and mounted on a turntable. It was outfitted with removable crags and boulders to accommodate a wide variety of camera angles. Cameraman Sol Polito expressed his direct preference for the soundstage Valley over the real thing, allowing as it did for greater latitude in shooting.

It was originally felt that battlefield scenes prior to York's skirmish could be perfunctorily filmed, but as excitement mounted, nobody could resist going the explosive spectacular route. In the Simi hills about forty miles from Hollywood, location scouts found an eighty-acre barley farm with geographic configurations similar to those in the Argonne, scene of York's heroism. From 200 to 500 extras were used as soldiers each day of shooting.

Sergeant York set a precedent by filming the biography of a still-living man. It also set a record for the number of living characters being portrayed, necessitating a signed release form from each, for which the studio bargained anywhere from $250 to $1,500.

Donoho Hall, who hailed from a hollow about thirty miles from York's home valley, was hired as technical advisor on the Tennessee mountain sequences to coach the actors with their rustic dialogue. The result is something that strikes the untrained ear, at least, as remarkably authentic mountain speech. Distinguished stage actress Margaret Wycherly, as York's mother, was given magnificent dialogue which Hawks stripped away in the interest of simplicity. Finally he told her, "I know what we're after—I want somebody who doesn't talk." "That I can understand," she said. She graced the movie with a poignant, nearly silent portrayal.

Cooper wears his overalls and his soup-bowl haircut as comfortably as he wore evening clothes in *Bluebeard's Eighth Wife*. As far as directing him was concerned, Hawks had little to add to what directors had said about him since *Children of Divorce*: "You'd watch him do a scene. You'd wonder whether you had it. And I'd go home worrying about it. And come look the next day at the rushes—and there was more there than I wanted in the first place. I don't know why. Except that I think that he thought—and it registered . . . it's what the camera sees, not what *you* see."

As *Sergeant York* opens with the communal hymn-singing in the meeting house, our first thought is that someone must have switched John Ford's credits. But as the ensuing scenes unfold and we are afforded ample opportunity to stare at that reconstructed Valley, we know better. Ford had a strong feeling for the land and for man's relationship with his natural environment. He favored location shooting, and when he wasn't given permission to go on location, he became an artist at making painted flats and rear-screen projections fade into the background out of conspicuous, focused sight. Hawks's strongest feeling was for man's relationship with others, and with his chosen endeavor and destiny. When he holds on Sol Polito's beloved manmade canvas-and-wood backdrop, the "natural man" tone of the script rings hollow. Walter Brennan, as the local preacher, tells Cooper, "Take a look at that oak, yonder." We cut to an obvious painting of an oak tree. A scrim just doesn't photograph the way the sky does, and it's obvious the horizon is only ten feet away. When York goes up to the hill to ponder the question of his involvement with the war, it's not nature he communes with, but a painting of a valley, a technological re-creation of a sunrise, and Max Steiner's overpowering music. As commentator Don Willis pointed out, "You wonder how York could even think with that racket."

"I don't attempt to preach or prove anything," said Hawks of the approach his direction finally took. "I just figure out what I think was in the man and tell it." Many of the simple touches are pure and affecting. During York's quiet, determined quest for a piece of "bottom land," he gets a handful of the soil, brings it home, and pours it out on a plate in front of his mother: she knows what it is in an instant.

June Lockhart was cast as Cooper's younger sister in the picture. "He related to me, even though I was only fourteen," she recalled. "Let me tell you. Sometimes actors on a set treat the lesser character people . . . and the children . . . as something to be tolerated, rather than encouraged."

Because of technical problems, the "bottom land" scene had to be shot over several times. Cooper was sitting at a table in front of the fireplace, with Margaret Wycherly as his mother. In the far background, his little sister was lying in the dark.

"The scene was shot over and over again," June recalled. "It had to be filmed so often because it was a very important scene. They were shooting it in long shots and closeups and reverses. It took all day and through all that I was lying in bed with no dialogue. After many hours, just before they took another take, Coop turned around toward me and said, 'Are you ready, June?'"

If his remark tickled June and the others, she in turn amused Coop. She would fly her kite outside the soundstage whenever she wasn't on the set or in the studio classroom. "He found it funny, perhaps because it was rather audacious of me, especially when it got stuck on top of another soundstage and somebody had to go up and retrieve it. Cooper was very supportive of me. It gave one a feeling of affectionate nurturing. This was only the second or third film I'd done. He seemed centered . . . to have a nice inner calm about him."

June Lockhart and Joan Leslie had been at Immaculate Heart High School when they were cast in the film. Although the other girl, only sixteen, would be playing Cooper's child bride, June was two years younger and couldn't verbalize her impression of Cooper's magnetism.

One who could was the Warner school teacher, who after seeing a scene Cooper had filmed with Joan Leslie, remarked, "When he looks at you with those twinkling blue eyes, you never know what he's thinking."

Howard Hawks would host tea breaks every afternoon at four, and the young actresses were given a recess to join with the other cast and crew members. June Lockhart, in trying to look at him through adult eyes, agreed with her teacher. "Self-effacing he was, but very charming. He had a secret."

York himself was disturbed only by the fake note of the bolt of lightning that gives Cooper's York a sudden religious conversion in one fell swoop. "That weren't the rightdown facts of it. You see, I had met Miss Gracie. Miss Gracie said that she wouldn't let me come a-courting until I'd quit my mean drinking, fighting, and card-flipping. So you see I was struck down by the power of love and the Great God Almighty, all together. A bolt of lightning was the nearest to such a thing that Hollywood could think of." But Hawks claimed that York himself was his source. "I asked him how he got religion. 'I got it in the middle of the road,' he said. So my visualization of that was a mule, getting hit by lightning in the middle of the road."

The consistency in Hawks films—whether about backwater boys or city slickers, whether serious dramas or fast-paced comedies—is that they are about professionals who define themselves through their expertise. *Sergeant York*, like the rest of Hawks's movies, is about a man who knows his business, and that business is shooting. Not killing, necessarily, but shooting.

Shooting, in fact, formed the strongest bond between York and Cooper, when they finally met, and between Cooper and Hawks as they went through weeks of working together.

"Sergeant York and I had quite a few things in common even before I played him on the screen," Cooper said. "We both were raised in the mountains—Tennessee for him, Montana for me—and learned to ride and shoot as a natural part of growing up."

When asked what he thought of Cooper once he'd met him, York's reply was, "He's a good shot."

The paean to down-home simplicity opened in New York at the Astor on Broadway with an electric sign that was four stories high and half a block long, in the largest letters ever erected on a Broadway billboard, using half a million feet of wiring. Its 15,000 red-and-blue lights were ten times as many as were used by all the houses in Alvin York's home town. "The Lord sure does move in mysterious ways," as York put. it in the film.

Gary Cooper was rewarded with the greatest acclaim of his career. He was given the annual *Redbook* award "for the most distinguished contribution to the art of the motion picture" and was awarded the Veterans of Foreign Wars Distinguished Citizenship Medal "in recognition of your honest and sincere interpretation of the character of Sergeant Alvin C. York, which constitutes a powerful contribution to the promotion of patriotism and loyalty."

The film broke all existing records in its prerelease engagements, and didn't begin its regular run until July of 1942, and became the top moneymaking picture of the year. It received a score of laudatory notices, and was singled out by most of the critics in the nation as the Best Picture of 1941 and Gary Cooper as the Best Actor—in the film year of *Citizen Kane, How Green Was My Valley, They Died With Their Boots On, The Little Foxes, High Sierra, The Lady Eve, The Maltese Falcon,* and *Here Comes Mr. Jordan.* The Academy nominated it for Best Picture; Cooper for Best Actor; Walter Brennan for Best Supporting Actor; Margaret Wycherly for Best Supporting Actress; Howard Hawks for Best Director; Max Steiner for Best Musical Score; Chandlee, Finkel, Huston, and Koch for Best Original Screenplay; Sol Polito for Best Cinematography; John Hughes and Fred MacLean for Best Art Direction; Nathan Levinson for Best Sound Recording; and William Holmes for Best Film Editing. Gary and Rocky Cooper arrived at the Biltmore Hotel in downtown Los Angeles with their friends Robert Taylor and Barbara Stanwyck for the annual Academy Awards.

Cooper was competing in his category with Cary Grant, *Penny Serenade;* Walter Huston, *All that Money*

Can Buy; Robert Montgomery, *Here Comes Mr. Jordan*; and Orson Welles, *Citizen Kane*. When the winner for Best Actor was announced, Gary Cooper found himself standing before the crowd, accepting from presenter James Stewart, who was in uniform as an Air Corps Lieutenant.

His acceptance speech could have been uttered by Alvin York himself. "Shucks! I've been in this business sixteen years and sometimes dreamed I might get one of these things. That's all I can say. Funny, when I was dreaming, I always made a good speech!"

The long-range effects for everyone associated with *Sergeant York* were enormous. Jesse Lasky banked $2 million; writer John Huston was given a chance to direct and immediately turned out *The Maltese Falcon*; York received a total of $150,000 to underwrite his good works. There were some short-term losers. Only Cooper and Holmes won Oscars for the film.

Hawks lost to John Ford, who directed *How Green Was My Valley*. In later years, the two directors often saw each other in Palm Springs and would talk about a Hollywood that no longer existed. "I remember one time when I had a lousy picture and you had a real good one," Ford would say. "I got an Academy Award and you didn't."

The one who received the greatest benefit from the picture was, not surprisingly, Gary Cooper. He'd developed over the years an unearthly talent for being in the right place, in the right role, at the right time.

Hawks and Cooper continued their collaboration at Goldwyn in *Ball of Fire*. Brackett and Wilder, who'd written *Bluebeard's Eighth Wife* for Cooper and Claudette Colbert, were borrowed from Paramount to write the screenplay on the new comedy. They were traded to Goldwyn, with Bing Crosby and Bob Hope also thrown in for a future commitment, if Gary Cooper could be borrowed by Paramount to appear in *For Whom the Bell Tolls*. Wilder agreed to being shunted around this way if he was allowed to stay at Hawks's side during the filming, since he wanted to know how a master directed films.

Ball of Fire was based on a story Wilder wrote before coming to America entitled "The Professor and the Burlesque Queen." A dignified scholar, working on an encyclopedia, meets and falls in love with a stripper who's an expert on slang. Goldwyn, having learned his lesson from his misadventure with McCarey on *The Cowboy and the Lady*, paid $7,500 for the story, with the understanding that Wilder would get a $2,500 bonus if the picture became a hit.

Ball of Fire was a silly comedy. Brackett and Wilder, although nominated for an Academy Award for their story, had no feeling for or comprehension of college professors. For the role of the stripper, Goldwyn had originally wanted Ginger Rogers, but having won an Academy Award for Best Actress in *Kitty Foyle*, she now wanted to play only ladies. An incensed Goldwyn screamed at her agent, "You tell Ginger Rogers that ladies stink up the place!"

Barbara Stanwyck's performance as the stripper was recognized by the Academy with a nomination for Best Actress the same year that Cooper won for *Sergeant York*, but Stanwyck lost to Joan Fontaine for *Suspicion. Ball of Fire*, though small in scale and scope, was one of the top moneymakers of the year, the fourth Cooper picture in a row to hit the Top Twenty. Wilder said he had a devil of a time getting his bonus from Goldwyn.

Because of his age and various infirmities, not the least being the badly set hip that gave him his distinctive gait, Cooper was barred from military service in World War II. While other contemporaries like Clark Gable and James Stewart were off to war, he was at home becoming an American institution. John Doe enshrined is no longer John Doe, and the films in the following years were rarely the fresh, "simple yet far from simple" happenings his best films of the late thirties had been. They took on a stiff, formal air, and everyone acted as if his next utterance would ring through the ages.

Cooper's one film of 1942, Paul Gallico's *The Pride of the Yankees*, was the story of beloved baseball star Lou Gehrig, who rises to the top from obscure beginnings, and who tugs at our heartstrings when it's discovered that he's terminally ill.

Goldwyn had no interest in making a picture about just another ballplayer. Screenwriter Niven Busch saw the Gehrig story as an ideal vehicle for Cooper and Teresa Wright, whom he later married. Try as he might to persuade Goldwyn that Gehrig's life and death had inspired many people, Busch met unwavering resistance.

The writer decided to get newsreels of Lou Gehrig Day at Yankee Stadium, where the ballplayer was honored by his teammates and fans. The words of appreciation from the mortally ill Gehrig left Goldwyn in tears. That did it. The mogul ordered that the rights to the film biography be bought.

Goldwyn's publicists spread the story that an exhaustive talent search was under way, and that four actors—Eddie Albert, William Gargan, Dennis Morgan, and George Tobias—had offered to play the role for nothing but the glory. Actually, no one had ever been considered for the role but Cooper.

He was forty-one and he'd never played baseball in his life. Retired major leaguer Lefty O'Doul came down from San Francisco to coach Cooper in the rudiments of the game. "You throw a ball," he told the actor, "like an old woman tossing a hot biscuit." It took him weeks to train Cooper to throw the ball properly.

That winter, the Coopers went to Sun Valley, where he continued practicing by throwing snowballs, while five-year-old Maria took skiing lessons.

Once filming started, the numbers and letters of Cooper's uniform shirt were reversed. Because the actor was right-handed and Gehrig was a southpaw, the film had to be flopped so that Cooper would appear to be left-handed too. He also ran to third base instead of first in scenes where he connected with a hit.

Teresa Wright, only two years out of high school, was cast as Gehrig's wife. "I wasn't aware of learning anything from Coop particularly," she said, "but I recall certain specifics on the set. He prepared very quietly. He didn't make a point of working up an emotion. He did it, and when he was finished, it was finished. Although to the eye it wasn't right, he was instinctively right for film, which was something else again.

"He was very easy to work with. He knew his lines. He didn't like to rehearse a lot. He wasn't one to talk over the scene for its meaning.

"When he wasn't working, he liked to go off by himself. He used to whittle, making things out of light balsa wood, like airplanes . . . nothing intricate as far as I could see. He'd sometimes go off between takes and ride his bike around the lot.

"When he did talk, it wasn't inarticulate. He was very positive about his opinions. When he had something to say, he said it at great length, with great conviction. On politics, you couldn't call him right-wing. I would say he was conservative. Whether you thought that way or not, you respected his beliefs."

Certainly the highest power at the Goldwyn Studio did. Miss Wright never heard the argumentative Sam Goldwyn sparring with his major star. "If there were any disagreements, I imagine he let other people handle them. I wouldn't doubt a bit that Coop was often a guest in Mr. Goldwyn's house.

"I don't believe his mannerisms were what made him quintessentially American. I think the values of the characters he played were generally the values regarded as the American ideal. He played that character so much that it became identified with him.

"This was a paradox of a man. He could easily have gone back and forth in European society . . . not the typical American. He wasn't just a very sophisticated man with sophisticated values. He was a rather elegant man and liked very nice things. His wife was a very stylish woman. But he played the American ideal. Fundamentally, he cared very deeply about values that we've come to look on as old-fashioned.

"Gary was one of the biggest stars most of the time he was working. He made so many *classic* films. By the time I met him in 1942, he was certainly a great star and remained that, although some of his films were not that good. He had his pick and his say."

Miss Wright recalled the scene in the doctor's office where Gehrig learned of his terminal illness. "It was very understated, very quiet. He asks the doctor not to tell me, but I can tell by both their faces what has happened. He did almost nothing, but the audience was very moved by it."

Seen today, the scene doesn't hold up and the disturbing parallel to Cooper's last months doesn't register in retrospect, so flat and mechanical are the proceedings. The best that can be said of the parade of American truisms, as Miss Wright observed, is its understatement.

Director Sam Wood had worked his way up from assistant to Cecil B. DeMille. He inherited all of the venerable director's bad qualities and none of the redeeming ones. He was an avid Redbaiter during the notorious Hollywood witch-hunt, and was President of the Motion Picture Alliance for the Preservation of American Ideals. He was a solid craftsman nearing sixty who'd been directing films of every variety, in the traditional studio mold, since 1919. Wood seemed to have the capacity to bring a wide variety of topics to the screen competently, without establishing a style or point of view of his own.

What is missing in *The Pride of the Yankees* is the Ford or Capra touch that makes us feel this is an everyday guy and an American deity at the same time. Cooper has a characteristically wonderful moment when, half-uncomfortable and half-delirious, he's first forced out on a dance floor. In another memorable shot he takes a spectacular fall on a pile of baseball bats.

But his "spontaneous" scenes of horseplay with Teresa Wright are just as forced as the spontaneity that's *supposed* to feel forced after they've learned of his condition. And it's again hard to get past the contradiction in Gehrig's insistence that their private life is "something that belongs to just the two of us," while we're watching it on one of the most public forms of mass communication ever devised by man. Critics of the time found the drama subdued, its theme repetitious and lacking in basic conflict.

What the film had in large measure was sentimentality. When it was released in July 1942, it was a smashing success, among the Top Ten at the box office that year. Americans wanted to be moved and Cooper, in the midst of ersatz proceedings, delivered his usual naturalness. *The New York World-Telegram,* for one, felt he had "seldom been better than he is as Lou Gehrig. His performance grows, as the character grows, from shy gawky undergraduate to modest, unassuming hero of millions." For his performance, Cooper was nominated for a third Academy Award.

Soon after its 1940 publication and resultant critical and commercial success, a hot bidding war seemed to loom for the movie rights to Ernest Hemingway's *For Whom the Bell Tolls.* David O. Selznick was particularly interested in the novel, wanting to cast his new contract player, Ingrid Bergman, in the role of Maria. Having been through two recent exhausting experiences, the productions of *Gone With the Wind* and *Rebecca,* Selznick decided, however, that his energies weren't up to the job and reluctantly decided to pass. He continued to think that Bergman was totally right for the part, and planted newspaper items to the effect that she and Gary Cooper would make an explosive romantic team.

Perhaps taking their cue from Selznick's publicity campaign, Paramount paid $150,000 for the movie rights, with the express purpose of casting Gary Cooper as Robert Jordan.

Cecil B. DeMille was at first assigned to the project, and he'd worked for six months with Jeannie Mac-Pherson on a screenplay. During this period, Generalissimo Franco's American emissaries were making every effort to stop the picture's production. His ambassador asked the United States Department of State to suppress the film, but he was informed that censorship was not in the American tradition. Washington officially turned its back, one government official stating the situation was "too hot to talk about." The Spanish consul in San Francisco, after reading the MacPherson script, objected to a great deal of it. Paramount announced that the studio was ignoring the Spanish consul's objections to *For Whom the Bell Tolls*. Yet, in short order, DeMille was assigned to direct a picture with a Mexican theme—which was never produced—and Sam Wood was named to replace him as director, with Dudley Nichols brought in to write a new screenplay. Adolph Zukor protested that much ado was being made about nothing. "It is a great picture without social significance," he stated. "We are not for or against anybody." That much would soon be evident, the Fascists becoming "Nationalists" and the Loyalists being renamed "Republicans," giving critic James Agee the opportunity to saltily remark that the hero of the film "may easily give the impression he's simply fighting for the Republican Party in a place where the New Deal has got particularly out of hand."

It was never revealed to the public if the American government had been instrumental in blunting the passion of Hemingway's work. The Spanish Civil War was a past altercation and the United States was now involved in a global war with Franco's troops standing by in support.

It is possible that the studio policed itself without government intervention. Historically, Hollywood studios have acted insidiously with novels that are left-wing, populist, and humanistic. They make a worldwide show of their "courage" in bringing such controversial works to the screen, then turn them over to the most blatant right-wing conservative on the staff. Darryl F. Zanuck had previously done so with John Steinbeck's *Grapes of Wrath*, giving it to John Ford to direct. Yet, despite his extremely conservative politics, Ford had a feeling for the average man and the land he cultivated. There were compromises in his film, but it was nevertheless affecting. Sam Wood wasn't nearly as gifted an artist and lacked Ford's sensitivity. He would be turning universal brotherhood into commercial claptrap.

Hemingway must have been silently suffering over what was being done to his book, for it mirrored his zealous involvement in the Spanish Civil War. He'd gone to Spain in 1937 as a correspondent, and became involved with the Loyalist Army in its fight against Franco and the generals. Out of that devastating experience came a powerful novel about meaningless death in a meaningful fight, about courage in the face of death, and the reverberations that a single death can have in the universe. His antifascist novel, incorporating his hatred of politicians in general, was in many ways autobiographical. Its closest parallel to Hemingway's life was the suicide of Robert Jordan's father, just as the author's father had killed himself. It was a book he passionately believed in, telling of a cause about which he was equally passionate.

Yet, he didn't voice any misgivings about the mutilations being committed on his book. "Ernest sold his books to the movies," Mary Hemingway said, "then he paid absolutely no attention whatever to what they did with them. He made no effort to influence them in any way . . . his theory being that whatever he might try to do wouldn't be effective anyhow."

Consequently, and contrary to the popular conception, he had no voice about Gary Cooper's being cast in the film. The book was bought as a Cooper vehicle from the outset.

Cooper may not even have been Hemingway's first choice. The two men, according to Mary Hemingway, were "hunting friends and dining friends. But their politics were diametrically opposed. Cooper was conservative and rightish. Of course, we were leftish, so we simply never discussed politics."

Mrs. Hemingway didn't know if her husband felt Cooper understood the implications of the role he was playing. Nor was Cooper one to articulate them. "Ernest had intensive correspondence with *some* friends, but he and Coops didn't correspond at all. I can't imagine Coops writing much of a letter anyhow. He was not a voluble man. One of the things Ernest liked most was reading. Coops was bright after a fashion but he never read anything at all as far as I know . . . or certainly not much. So they didn't have any mutual interests in literature."

Paramount perversely ignored Selznick's suggestion and tested Paulette Goddard for the role of Maria. She was a touch too worldly, so ballerina Vera Zorina won the part. Filming started in the Sierra Nevada in late 1942. Three weeks after production, and having seen the rushes, studio executives found Zorina too inexperienced. They replaced her with Selznick's original recommendation, who'd just scored an enormous success opposite Humphrey Bogart in *Casablanca*.

"Ernest was pleased when they put Ingrid Bergman in it," Mrs. Hemingway said. "They'd dined once together, when Ernest and wife number three stopped off in California on their way to Hawaii. Ernest and I dined with Ingrid and her doctor husband another time. She was not only very pretty, but flirtatious and witty . . . an attractive woman. So it was quite natural that Ernest would like her."

That may have been the only thing Hemingway liked about the picture. It would prove to be synthetic from beginning to end. John Donne wrote in "Meditation XVII" that "any man's death diminishes me because I am involved in mankind, and therefore never send to know for whom the bell tolls, it tolls for thee." The lines were uncredited when used as an epigraph in the film, giving the impression they originated in "the celebrated novel of Ernest Hemingway," which *was* credited.

Cooper's profile is magnetically recognizable in the opening silhouette, and as he blows up a train and makes a dashing getaway, you get the idea the movie you're about to see is going to be terrifically enjoyable, whether it's faithful to the novel or not. But soon it ceases to be even that, degenerating into a series of talk scenes carried on by a band of gypsies somewhere in the Spanish mountains. Everything is discussed but what the fighting is all about, leading the viewer to believe these are simply a lot of disreputable people causing trouble.

Politics aside, Hemingway wrote his novel out of a genuine concern for people of the earth. The least Wood could have done was to have staged the mountain scenes on a real mountain somewhere. In some scenes the Paramount mountain is so blatantly false that one of the characters once casts a shadow on the sky. Standing against bare rock in the direct sunlight, people throw conspicuous multiple shadows which could only mean they are being lighted by a bank of Technicolor arc lights. A sunrise is suggested by a series of sunset shots and a lot of mid-shots of the actors with red light on their faces.

In Wood's defense, he may have been constrained by a government directive which *was* made public. As the war got underway, motion picture studios were instructed to eliminate the lavishness of their productions. They were entrusted with the duty of creating films to inspire the masses, as long as they were created without miles of gold braid and piles of spangles. Many picture companies were forced to move into studio soundstages instead of actual locales as a result.

Perhaps the worst effect in the whole picture was its garish use of color. It was disastrous in a film that sorely needed every bit of conviction it could find. James Agee accused it of resembling "the rankest kind of magazine-illustration and postcard art." There was a widespread belief until the mid-sixties that color was appropriate only for escapist fare, while anything realistic demanded black and white. A film like *For Whom the Bell Tolls* makes it clear why.

Cooper follows suit by turning in perhaps the most wooden performance of his career. He was looser and freer when fighting for imperialism in *The Lives of a Bengal Lancer* than he is here as a rebel struggling for the cause of freedom. Ingrid Bergman has no trouble stealing the show. Her love scenes with Cooper are the most genuine scenes in the film. Maria's lifelong concern, expressed at the moment of her first kiss, is, "Where do the noses go?" To her tremendous relief, after it's over, she finds, "They're not in the way, are they?" It is one of the few incidents to touch us from the other side of the screen.

Once again a complex Hemingway novel was used as an excuse for another boy-meets-girl story. Somehow that was more forgivable in *A Farewell to Arms*, when part of the point of the original was that the war had no real meaning. Dismissing the war altogether is a conceivable extension of that position.

For Whom the Bell Tolls proves totally inarticulate when the war is an intrinsic part of the story and has deep meaning. Days and nights of death-defying sacrifice were explained away with Robert Jordan's simple statement: "A man fights for what he believes in." What *did* he believe in? Paramount and Sam Wood weren't letting us in on the secret.

If there was any justice—and Hemingway was always the first to say there wasn't—the film version of his book should have been consigned to the cinematic scrap heap. It was the studio's most profitable film of the year. The masses may have bought it, but a diehard group of intellectuals looked on it with enduring contempt. Not the least of them was Hemingway himself. René Jordan wrote in *Gary Cooper*, "for two decades one of the sure ways to test Hemingway's awesome gift for profanity was to mention director Sam Wood."

Bergman and Cooper were immediately teamed again with Wood in *Saratoga Trunk*, based on the Edna Ferber novel. Bergman's role of a courtesan was wickedly comic, while Cooper's card-playing rogue fared less well in the basically tedious film. The players reportedly were having more fun off the set than before the cameras.

Where Bergman had been a tragic wounded fawn in the Hemingway film, she was now the eternal coquette. She lived her role, and where she'd been protected by Cooper in the Hemingway picture, she was now toying with him in real life.

For the first time since his marriage, Cooper was leaving the set with his costar and was being seen with her in public.

"On that picture," he told columnist James Bacon, "Ingrid loved me more than any woman in my life loved me. The day after the picture ended, I couldn't get her on the phone."

Their association received enough public notice that a nervous Paramount decided to hold up domestic release of the picture. American servicemen were dying in action, and civilians at home wouldn't look kindly on the brazen capers of the two spoiled movie stars. This didn't deter the studio from letting the servicemen see the picture, and it played for two years abroad before Americans at home were finally given a chance to see it three months after the end of the war. It was one of Paramount's top moneymakers that year.

The entire country was involved in the war effort, and the Hollywood of the early forties was no exception. Rocky overcame her reserve to do volunteer work at the Hollywood Canteen. It was the thing to do for stars and their wives to entertain servicemen going off to battle.

Hedda Hopper had been trying to persuade Cooper to come along also.

"Those guys don't want to see me," he said. "They want some pretty girls. What in the world can *I* do?"

"Now, Coop," she lectured, "leave it to me. I'll just ask a few questions and you follow my lead. They'll love it."

Against his better judgment, he consented.

Standing before a microphone, Hedda sensed that Cooper was squirming uncomfortably behind her. She began asking him questions, which he answered in a mumble. The audience laughed uproariously. Puzzled by the explosive response to the innocuous words, she nevertheless continued. The wave of laughter resumed as Cooper mumbled another reply. Curious, Hedda turned around to see Cooper spit out a mouthful of feathers. He'd been eating the plumage on her hat.

So gratifying was the response of the servicemen that Cooper returned often to the Canteen. In October of 1943, he also undertook a 23,000-mile tour of the Southwest Pacific, in a troupe which also included actresses Phyllis Brooks and Una Merkel.

The usual procedure was to give a matinee show, then visit base hospitals, to be followed by an evening show. Cooper took along a batch of scripts given him by his friend Jack Benny, and he was delighted that they went over so well. "Those boys weren't just starved for entertainment," he recalled, "they were plumb out of their minds." The entire troupe would close the show with a rousing rendition of "Pistol Packin' Mama."

A cloudburst hit one of the camps one evening, and the stars thought the show would be called off. Cooper was napping in his tent when an officer informed him that 15,000 servicemen were sitting in the rain and mud waiting for the show to go on.

When he and the actresses arrived at the open-air stage, they found it had been covered with makeshift canvas. They did their show, yet the audience wouldn't let them get off the stage.

"Hey, Coop," one of the young men yelled out, "how about the Lou Gehrig farewell speech to the Yankees?" The rest of the young men broke into applause.

"Give me a minute to get it straight," Cooper replied. While the actress filled in the time, he committed the words again to his memory. He rose and quietly spoke them into the microphone:

"I've been walking on ballfields for sixteen years, and I've never received anything but kindness and encouragement from you fans. I've had the great honor to have played with these great veteran ballplayers on my left—Murderer's Row—our championship team of 1927. I've had the further honor of living with and playing with these men on my right—the Bronx Bombers—the Yankees of today.

I have been given fame and undeserved praise by the boys up there behind the wire in the pressbox—my friends—the sportswriters. I've worked under the two greatest managers of all time—Miller Huggins and Joe McCarthy.

I have a mother and father who fought to give me health and a solid background in my youth. I have a wife—a companion for life—who has shown me more courage than I ever knew.

People all say that I've had a bad break, but—today—today I consider myself the luckiest man on the face of the earth.

All about him, Cooper saw young boys crying. They, who were facing possible death, were stunned by Gehrig's simple words and the way an insulated and well-protected movie star had interpreted them. It was a humbling experience. Never before had Cooper felt the magical effect his presence could have on a live audience. He continued giving the farewell speech at every show, invariably receiving the same reaction.

Cooper returned from the six-week tour to start work on a new film with Cecil B. DeMille. To rumors that he would next be portraying flying ace Eddie Rickenbacker, he replied, "The next picture I hope to do is about a wholly fictional character—Casanova Q. Brown."

First, however, he would star for DeMille in *The Story of Dr. Wassell*, an account of a Naval doctor who rescued a group of wounded sailors from Java in 1942 after they'd been abandoned there to the Japanese.

While the picture was being filmed, Cooper took time off to celebrate a family anniversary. Mrs. Alice Cooper belonged to the Mothers Club, an organization consisting of members whose offspring were all Hollywood stars. Hedda Hopper, because of actor-son Bill, also belonged. When Judge and Mrs. Cooper celebrated their golden wedding anniversary, all the members of the club were invited to their home for a reception.

"Gary was busy with a picture and about the last person I expected to see there," Hedda said. "But in the midst of the gathering he stalked shyly in, greeting all the mothers separately, shaking their hands to make them glow, and kissing his own mom warmly as he handed over his golden roses and gold gifts of all kinds for the golden wedding day."

The critics were especially cruel to *Dr. Wassell*, attacking DeMille for turning historical truth into technicolor sherbert. The casting of Cooper in the role of the elderly doctor was also attacked. So was the introduction of an extraneous romance. How much more stirring it would have been to show a man past the peak of his physical powers accomplishing the physically impossible.

With that commitment ended, he could start working with his friend at International Pictures, paying a debt of gratitude for the way Bill Goetz and his wife had accepted Rocky years before.

Goetz, in describing the fledgling operation he'd founded with former RKO President Leo Spitz and screenwriter Nunnally Johnson, said, "We have a new company. The only people we have signed are a chef and Gary Cooper." Walls were knocked out of a bungalow and the chief, who wanted to slow down after years of work in the world's greatest restaurants, was installed therein. He'd been transferred from the Goetz home to work for International, a sacrifice Bill and Edie Goetz made to get the company off the ground.

"The studio was run by 'Applecake Hans Meyer,'" Edie Goetz recalled. The bungalow became so popular that Meyer soon was supervising three or four sittings of various business associates every day. Cooper was his most constant, most ravenous guest. One day, Meyer prepared marinated herring. Cooper had never eaten any. After his dessert of applecake, the actor said, "I think I'll have a little more of that fish."

Goetz and Johnson, being noted wits, brought a delicious premise to the two pictures Cooper would be making for International. Why not work against his stalwart image for comic effect? Why not satirize yourself? Cooper was not noted for being quick with the repartee, but he appreciated a good joke. By agreeing to do the unpretentious pictures written by Johnson, he was showing his willingness to laugh at himself. It was not yet proven that the public would appreciate his self-deprecation, or the modest scale of these projects which were in such contrast to the blare and the bombast of his previous pictures.

Teresa Wright was his costar in *Casanova Brown*. "I wasn't really secure yet as an actress," she said. "The film wasn't good, and it should have been. It was a very funny script. I blame Sam Wood. He was an old-time director who directed in an old-time way. Wood needed lightness of touch, but he was back to an old form. In a crowd scene, he would take a master shot, then get reactions of the same line on every face . . . in long, medium, and close shots. By that time nothing was left."

Miss Wright recalled that "I sort of slumped the way kids do. Gary spoke to me very seriously about my posture. He'd obviously given it some thought. He said, 'It's important for an actor to know and use his body well.' You don't associate that idea with a natural actor, yet Gary knew actors had to know how to use their bodies."

Cooper also chastised her in one scene. She played his aristocratic wife who, after their divorce, discovers she's pregnant and decides to give the baby up for adoption. Cooper insisted she use the word "Mama" instead of "Mommy" in a scene they were shooting. It didn't make much difference to Miss Wright, who continued to use the "Mommy" in the script. "Gary was very firm about wanting 'Mama,'" she said. "This meant something. It was an old-fashioned and important term to him. His talking about it convinced me."

In his character of Casanova Brown, Cooper was required to call at the mansion of his new wife. Her parents are straitlaced and allow no drinking or smoking. His wife leaves him alone in the drawing room to fetch her parents. Nervously, he lights a cigarette. When he hears approaching footsteps, he tries to put it out, only to discover there are no ashtrays in the room. He snuffs the cigarette out in his coat pocket. The introductions are made, as the coat starts to smoulder. Taking his smoking coat off, he sticks it under a sofa cushion. The sofa catches fire, as does everything else in the room. The house is burned to the ground. It was wonderfully accomplished comedy, a far cry from his days in *Children of Divorce* when he couldn't walk through a crowded room without flubbing the scene.

"The role is a boon to Gary Cooper," Alton Cook wrote in *The New York World-Telegram*, "rescuing him from his recent strong dynamic characters in which he is so ineffectual. The very lack of these qualities is the foundation of his great talent. His work in this picture belongs with his best, right up with *Mr. Deeds.*"

The audience thought enough of the picture to make it one of the top grossers of the year, though Cecil B. DeMille had great reservations about Cooper in such a role. "You can let down your public once, Gary, and be forgiven," he warned. "But don't try it a second time."

Cooper may have taken DeMille's advice seriously, but he proceeded with business as usual at International on his second picture there, *Along Came*

Jones, which he also produced. In it he played a meek cowpoke mistaken for a dangerous highwayman, and his every whim is the townspeople's command. His reading of one line is classic in its timing: "I ain't hardly said ten words in this town, and already I got a certain . . . standin'!"

With this film, Cooper put Stuart Heisler—who'd just returned from World War II duty with the Signal Corps—under personal contract as a director. That was to be Cooper's only effective contribution as the picture's producer. When it was discovered that costar Loretta Young had commissioned a costume designer to create a $750 housedress for her, which could be bought for less than ten dollars in the budget section of any department store, Cooper was informed it was his responsibility to tell Miss Young that this wouldn't be permissible. His decision, rather than to risk a confrontation with the willful Miss Young, was to give in and let her have the custom-designed dress. Hardly the sign of a great producer.

The film was based on *Useless Cowboy*, an Alan LeMay novel. Its title, from among six suggested by International Pictures employees, was selected by film critics across the country. It was Bill Goetz's suggestion to call the picture *Along Came Jones*.

Cooper tried to stay removed from the personality conflict between Nunnally Johnson and Heisler which made it impossible for the men to work together, particularly when Stuart Heisler inserted ungrammatical words into the brilliant lunacy of Johnson's dialogue.

It was of course impossible for producer Cooper to avoid the contretemps indefinitely, and eventually he had to make peace on the set. Cooper simply wasn't cut out to be a Thalberg or a Selznick. "I hate the desk work," he complained. "Here the hunting season is on and I'm missing everything."

Along Came Jones was also among the top box office pictures of 1945, proving Cooper's considerable drawing power. Of the nine pictures he made during the period coinciding with the World War II years, only one—*The Story of Dr. Wassell*—was not an unqualified success.

DeMille was right in his assessment, however, for the long-term effect of the two pictures on Cooper's career was negative. The public wasn't ready for self-parody, such as John Wayne successfully achieved years later in *True Grit*.

"Those pictures really didn't have anything to do with Gary," Teresa Wright said, "because he wasn't a bumbler.. It *is* funny. But it's also limiting to play the caricature of the original."

Many, conversely, felt that Cooper was indeed a bumbler and that he proved it during the Presidential election of 1944. He had every right to campaign for Thomas Dewey for President, but when he made a speech criticizing President Roosevelt because of the "company he keeps," explaining that the country had to be saved from "foreigners," his public image was badly tarnished. Everyman does not talk like that, particularly when the unnamed "foreigners" were believed to be such Jews as Bernard Baruch and Felix Frankfurter. It was a blunder to speak that way in the middle of a war in which many of the Jews were being killed, and Cooper would be more careful with his utterances as a private citizen in the future.

Chapter 9

It seemed as if every great motion picture of the war years had starred Gary Cooper. How long could he continue his naturalistic acting before he was dismissed as mannered and self-conscious? How much longer could a middle-aged man continue to play convincingly the naive bumpkin?

Now, in the postwar era, the paucity of male stars had ended, and the public was eager to see Gable, Stewart, and Fonda return to the films they'd forsaken for the duration. That Cooper retained considerable appeal was proven by his remaining fourth at the box office in the three years from 1946 to 1948, even though he made only one picture each year and only one of them, *Unconquered* in 1947, was a blockbuster. His older pictures, still playing, kept him in the Top Ten.

In his youth, Gary Cooper's nose was pressed at the windows of the world of glamour. Now he was inside, looking out. Did that give him any great satisfaction? His daughter, Maria, yet to reach her tenth birthday, was the sole undisputed joy of his life.

But what about Rocky? A proud woman, she had ample reason to resent her husband's womanizing. With the exception of Ingrid Bergman, however, his affairs were conducted with discretion, outside of the glare of publicity. Perhaps from a sense of guilt, Cooper yielded to his wife in virtually every aspect of their life together.

Also, as in his affair with Dorothy di Frasso, Rocky had led him into an exclusive enclave, introducing him to society. He was flattered to be considered one of them and if he wasn't exactly comfortable in their company, by and large he kept his own counsel.

Hedda Hopper knew better, but she persisted in painting his marriage to Rocky as idyllic. In a profile she wrote, she didn't mention Cooper's well-known peccadillos, but she did reveal her ambivalence toward his wife: "Rocky has a fine chiseled profile, big dark eyes, a queenly air. She's Gary's queen and he loves pleasing her slightest whim. It's a marriage that's been perfect from the start. . . .

"Gary has fitted himself into the life his wife likes—the topdrawer, smart Hollywood life of unending parties and quiet luxury living. Rocky's a social sparkplug. . . .

"This sort of high life is not really Gary Cooper's natural style. He's not a party boy or greeter: he's shy, built for open skies and a saddle, not drawing rooms and Hepplewhite chairs. Gary has never cared about cocktails. He hates like fury to dance. Small talk and clever conversation aren't his strong points. Fluttery, flirtatious society girls scare him to death. Yet he likes it—because Rocky does . . ."

The Hollywood columnist said Cooper actually suffered physically to please his wife, citing an instance when all were at a beach party at the home of Merle Oberon and her then husband, Lucian Ballard. The sky was overcast and the water freezing. Rocky wanted to go into the surf and, though Cooper would have preferred to sit by the warmth of the fireplace, he was inveigled into joining her. It was a simple enough gesture for Cooper to leave the comfort of the hearth to please Rocky, yet the tone of Rocky's voice left Hedda with the impression that his wife was the undisputed domestic boss of the family.

Jack and Ann Warner started seeing the Coopers socially after they hosted a party honoring the actor when *Sergeant York* opened.

On a later occasion, Cooper arrived at a big house party alone. Rocky was visiting in the East. He sat in a corner, an observer, not taking interest in any particular woman nor participating in the clusters of conversation around the room. Ann Warner went over to sit with him.

"I have to report everything to Rocky," Cooper explained. "She'll want to know who wore what and what we had for dinner."

Mrs. Warner was astounded. "I couldn't imagine Jack or other men I've known doing the same thing. It was very cute, like a little boy going home to mother. I sat the rest of the evening with him, and saw a sweet and unusual side to Gary I'd never noticed before."

Many women were attracted to Cooper in a non-sexual way. His manners were innately impeccable, transcending the knowledge of which fork to use and the ability to exchange informed conversation with a restaurant's sommelier. He gladly acknowledged the personal dignity of every individual, no matter what his station in life. He astounded people with his memory for names and faces, no matter how obscure, recalling the circumstances of their last meeting.

"I've seen them all come and go," Edie Goetz said about movie stars she's known over the years, "and they all get spoiled. Many begin to believe their image. Gary was never spoiled. He was a natural person with no temper that I ever heard of or saw. It's a little thing, but indicative of the man that I never received a thank you note from him that wasn't handwritten (instead of typed up—and often signed—by a secretary). Jimmy Stewart is the same way."

Cooper was one of only five men in Hollywood whom Hedda Hopper could trust to be always truthful to her. The others were Mario Lanza, William Holden, Alan Ladd, and Clark Gable. Conversely, Hedda Hopper—of all the columnists and correspondents covering the Hollywood scene—could be trusted not to betray any of Cooper's confidences. She knew that his relationship with Rocky was often strained, but that wasn't something her readers would be told. "You know," he told Hedda, "it seems to me whenever I've come home from the studio someone has been underfoot. I wonder sometimes if those people realize how much they've cashed in on my name. I'm tired after a day's work. . . It is really work for me, you know. I'm not a quick study. Nor am I the greatest actor in the world."

Perhaps the death of Judge Cooper that year at the age of eighty contributed to his son's vague discontent. His father had never fully recovered from an automobile accident in 1934, in which he'd suffered back and knee injuries. He'd retired the following year, opening an "office" in Hollywood, where Bing Crosby's father also hung out. Cooper had sent his parents on a round-the-world tour in 1939. Wherever Judge Cooper went, he called on theater managers to urge them to show more Gary Cooper and Bing Crosby pictures. The judge had grown increasingly frail over the years, and was permanently bedridden when he caught pneumonia and died. After a parent's passing, a son often remonstrates with himself, thinking he should have done more for the parent.

Cooper's first postwar film, *Cloak and Dagger*, was also Lilli Palmer's first American film. The Warner Brothers picture was directed by Fritz Lang, and the espionage story was already dated when the picture was released. Few found it notable. Some found it contemptible. Miss Palmer, however, was entranced by Cooper:

"Naturally I never took my eyes off him during the first few weeks of shooting. He was the ideal movie actor. . . . Trained actors work out their screen roles down to the last detail, sentence by sentence, word by word, just as they do their stage roles. The personality actor doesn't work out anything. He knows his lines, and that's it; for everything else he relies on personal magnetism and improvisation. This type has no nerves, while the trained actor strained his to the limit. Cooper could deliver a long speech on camera while rummaging in his pocket for a cigarette, continue talking while he fussed with the matches, pause for a moment of what looked like intense concentration, pick up where he left off, put the matches away, rub his nose, and go on talking as if the camera didn't exist. . . .

"He was exactly as I'd always imagined him, only older, with iron gray hair. He moved slowly, spoke deliberately, tired quickly, and would then pull his hat down over his face and fall asleep wherever he happened to be sitting. There was something unassailable about him, a dignity which he never lost even in the most commonplace pictures."

Of which *Cloak and Dagger* was definitely one. Miss Palmer, enacting the archetypal smoldering, beckoning foreign lady, found more in Cooper's performance than the critics did. Many found him predictable, a danger sign in every actor's career. It was an inauspicious start for a new era in films.

By 1946, Cooper had been in films twenty years, a star for sixteen, and among the Top Ten box office attractions for ten. He'd been a "Yup" and "Nope" character since his first talkie in 1929, an image further strengthened with his one-word guest starring roles on the Edgar Bergen radio shows of the late thirties, which he'd satirized in his last two pictures at International.

"Most of what makes them great stars," Teresa Wright said, "is that they are identifiable. You're apt to see the person they are more than the character they're playing. The great ones made you aware of them and somehow made you believe the character. But I think as stars got bigger they began to imitate themselves more and more. They became caricatures—the Gary Cooper cookie cutter and the James Stewart cookie cutter. You stamp it into the dough and there you have it. It's entirely their own manner. Today, an awful lot of actors won't repeat the same roles."

The Coopers took Clark Gable with them for their annual summer visit to Southampton in 1946. Socialite

Millicent Rogers made up the foursome as Gable's friend for the summer, which extended into the fall.

With a commitment to Cecil B. DeMille at Paramount that fall, Rocky and Cooper weren't able to spend as much time in the Sun Valley area as he would have liked, even though there was a new person for them to meet. Ernest Hemingway had married his fourth wife, Mary Welsh, the previous March, and she would be a highly visible member of the parties going out on pheasant hunts. Rocky, by this time, had retired to the Sun Valley Lodge, choosing not to go on the daily expeditions.

Mrs. Hemingway was impressed that Cooper observed the protocol of hunting. "Walking across the field, abreast, the proper thing is for the hunter not to get ahead of the others as you cut through the fields. It's the polite thing. . . . Coops had longer legs and could have easily gone ahead, but he held back and stayed with the party.

"When we used to go bird hunting, we would drive twenty or thirty miles south of here [Ketchum, Idaho]. Rocky would say, 'Coop, I want you to be back at the lodge by six.' Well, this time of the year, with the ducks or pheasants or whatever, it bored us to have to quit shooting that early. But she had Coops intimidated. So we'd have to leave earlier than we wished to so he could be back at the time she announced."

Mrs. Hemingway didn't volunteer an opinion, but when asked how she felt about Rocky, she said, "She was just a very domineering woman." She also conceded that she never got to know Cooper's wife very well.

Back in southern California, however, a woman from Cooper's past was making herself very public all over again. Dorothy di Frasso, having divorced the Count, but retaining the title she'd paid for, was back in America to stay. The social scene was considerably enlivened by her presence.

When the Jack Warners had a dinner party and found themselves one male short, the Countess asked if she could invite a houseguest. The man who arrived, as Ann Warner described him, "was as handsome as Paul Newman."

Her husband eyed him suspiciously. "What did you say your name was?" he asked the newcomer.

"Ben Siegel."

Toward the end of the evening, Warner realized who his guest was: the notorious Bugsy Siegel of Murder, Incorporated. He would be, Ann Warner said, "the love of Dorothy's life."

Meanwhile, a past obsession of hers was busy at work on his new picture. Cooper's last film with De Mille was *Unconquered*, which James Agee, a severe critic of DeMille, rather liked, referring to it as, "Cecil Blount DeMille's florid $5 million Technicolored celebration of Gary Cooper's virility, Paulette Goddard's femininity, and the American Frontier Spirit. . . . It is, to be sure, a huge, high-colored chunk of hokum; but the most old-fashioned thing about it is its exuberance, a quality which sixty-six-year-old Director De-Mille preserves almost single-handedly from the old days when even the people who laughed at movies couldn't help liking them. . . . Mixed with all the nineteenth-century theatricalism, the early twentieth-century talent for making movies move, and the overall impression of utter falsity, *Unconquered* has some authentic flavor of the period."

The picture would be Cooper's last unqualified box office success until *High Noon* in 1952. It was released the same month that a most unlikely witness would be appearing before the House Un-American Activities Committee, which convened in Hollywood in October of 1947. Such conservative friends as Robert Taylor and Adolphe Menjou would be testifying about the infiltration of Communist elements into Hollywood life and the scripts that were being prepared for mass consumption.

The virtually apolitical Cooper, who'd been subpoenaed by the committee, couldn't recall the names of any scripts he'd read which he considered to incorporate Communist dogma, but he did remember one in which "its leading character was a man whose ambition was to organize an army in the United States that wouldn't fight to defend the country."

In answer to the question from the committee, Cooper guessed it would be a good idea to outlaw the Communist party in the United States, "although I have never read Karl Marx and I don't know the basis of Communism, beyond what I have picked up from hearsay. From what I hear, I don't like it because it isn't on the level. So I couldn't possibly answer that question."

If his testimony didn't have the unifying effect on the public that any of the Capra films did, Cooper could at least return to work on his new film with the satisfaction that he'd performed his patriotic duty. The picture was aptly named: *Good Sam*.

The following month, under heavy pressure from their Wall Street financiers, motion picture producers issued a declaration in which they promised not to knowingly employ any suspected subversive in their films.

As for Cooper's work in *Good Sam*, there were further indications that he was repeating himself and his appeal was finally wearing thin. A typical summing-up came from *Cue* Magazine: "It may be unkind to quote vital statistics to make a point, but Mr. Cooper is now a grown man, and his boyish bashfulness, sheepish grins, trembling lip and fluttering eyelids are actor's tricks he can surely do without."

He licked his wounds in the doghouse at his Brentwood estate, which had been transformed into an artist's studio. Cooper was a dabbler at painting, but his young daughter was already beginning to show a decided talent.

A new category of female star was emerging in the postwar period: sultry, spoiled, and neurotic. She had a throaty voice and was as direct about satisfying her desires as any man. The style was originated by Lauren Bacall, Lizabeth Scott, and Gloria Grahame.

"These women were absolute individualists," director King Vidor said. "They were selected because they looked different. They dared to be unconventional. They picked their own clothes and made themselves up. Patricia Neal was like that. There was a percentage of masculinity about her, with her deep voice and capability. She was a real woman and didn't go in for the weak feminine stuff. Whether it was a facade or not, it was part of the image."

Pat Neal was a dedicated, trained actress. She'd taken two years of drama courses at Northwestern University before moving on to New York to study with Elia Kazan and Robert Lewis, two of Broadway's foremost directors. Her fellow students included Marlon Brando, Montgomery Clift, and Karl Malden.

She'd auditioned for Eugene O'Neill, who was casting his *Moon for the Misbegotten*. Although she didn't get the part, the playwright was impressed enough with her talent to suggest she be cast in the Theatre Guild's summer production of *Devil Take the Whistler*. It was there that playwright Lillian Hellman spotted her and thought she would be ideal for a role in her next play.

When it was offered to her, Pat was understudying the lead in *The Voice of the Turtle*.

She made her first great impact in the 1947 production of Hellman's *Another Part of the Forest*. In the opening scene, she burst onto the stage, a tall, beautiful, and willful presence. She was in a passionate rage because she suspected that her aristocratic antebellum fiancé planned to break off their engagement because of her family's disreputable background. Her dazzling performance won her the Donaldson, Drama Critics, Antoinette Perry, *Look* Magazine, and Ward Morehouse *Pic* Magazine awards, as well as a Warner Brothers contract.

Patricia Neal turned down the stage role in *John Loves Mary* to perform in the Hellman play. When the romantic comedy was made into a film in 1949, she was cast in the role, closer to her own conventional,

Kentucky-bred background. In real life, she was as youthful and girlish as her first film suggested. But the studio, seeing the twenty-three-year-old girl as a cross between Bette Davis and Rita Hayworth, started looking for roles both semipsychotic and sexy for their budding star.

In that same year, Warner Brothers bought Ayn Rand's *The Fountainhead*. Though it was not general public knowledge, the author of one of the twentieth century's greatest publishing phenomena was a professional product of Hollywood. When Ayn Rand emigrated from her native Russia, it was at the Cecil B. DeMille studio that she found her first work in America in 1926, as a junior screenwriter and an extra in *King of Kings*. She went on to work at several major studios as filing clerk, wardrobe department head, script reader, and screenwriter. Two of her scripts, *Love Letters* and *You Came Along*, were produced by Paramount in 1945.

Her first impression of America, however, as she sailed into Manhattan, was "one skyscraper that stood out ablaze like the finger of God, and it seemed to me the greatest symbol of free men. . . . I made a mental note that some day I would write a novel with the skyscraper as the theme." New York's tallest edifice at the time was the Gothic Woolworth Building.

She began research for *Second-Hand Lives* in 1934, when she worked without pay in the office of architect Eli Jacques Kahn. She was one-third finished when Bobbs-Merrill agreed in 1940 to publish it. The book emerged on May 8, 1943, as *The Fountainhead*. At 754 pages, the novel was 75,000 words shorter than she had originally written it.

It chronicles the career of Howard Roark, generally thought to be a Frank Lloyd Wright clone but actually inspired by Wright's mentor, Louis Henri Sullivan. His was a struggle to achieve individualism in a society "cluttered" with altruism, public welfare, social concern, and other crimes against humanity.

Ayn Rand's concept of objectivism was the crux of

The Fountainhead, "that man is an end in himself, not a means to the ends of others; he must live for his own sake, neither sacrificing himself to others nor others to himself; that no man has the right to seek values from others by the initiation of physical force; that the politico-economic expression of these principles is laissez-faire capitalism, a system based on the inviolate supremacy of individual rights." It is an unattractive philosophy and it did not attract a general following, despite the novel's immense popularity.

Pushing for modern architecture in a world dominated by the Gothic, Roark the objectivist eventually blows up a multimillion-dollar housing project he has designed because his plans were tampered with and its integrity damaged beyond repair. Roark is tried and acquitted after he makes a marathon speech about the rights of man to his own fulfillment.

The book sold three million copies in hard and soft cover. With those sales figures, it was hard for the studios to resist, for its theme was just the kind of troubled self-examination that was hot in the postwar market. Other notable films of the genre were: *Gentlemen's Agreement, Pinky, The Snake Pit, Intruder in the Dust,* and *All the King's Men.*

Weekly movie attendance had, in two years, dropped from eighty to sixty million. Studios were in great trouble. They'd been forced to divest themselves of their theater divisions by a 1948 government edict, and pictures would have to be sold on their own merits in the future. They would also be competing with the new medium of television.

Frank Capra, who with a handful of other prestigious directors was trying to establish Liberty Films as an independent entity, was forced to return to work as a studio contract director at Paramount. These weren't propitious times for breaking away.

Capra, while at MGM, suggested Gary Cooper as the lead for MGM's *State of the Union.* Cooper was forced to leave the project, which would star Spencer Tracy, when Capra moved over to Paramount.

He had another project in mind for Cooper there, a large-scale opus, *Westward, the Women*. But MGM bought the property for director William Wellman.

Cooper, in the meantime, signed a six-picture deal at Warner Brothers, calling for an estimated $500,000 per film. Rocky thought he would be well cast in *The Fountainhead*, which the studio also envisioned as a good vehicle for Barbara Stanwyck.

King Vidor doesn't recall if he turned Miss Stanwyck down, as rumor had it, but he well remembers that Cooper was already cast for the part of the architect. The actor wasn't his ideal choice, for Vidor saw a more aggressive type like Humphrey Bogart or James Cagney in the part.

Ayn Rand had her own ideas. She thought Greta Garbo would be ideal as Dominique, the spoiled heiress turned architecture critic.

Vidor, an old friend, sent the script to Garbo. She came to his house to return it in person. "Do you really think I should come back with this part?" she asked.

Vidor knew there wasn't a chance she would do it, and he tended to feel it wasn't right for her, no matter how commercial her return to the screen would be. "As a friend, I don't think you should," he told her.

Ayn Rand was to have no further say about the production. When the two screenwriters turned in their first draft, however, Vidor found it unacceptable. He went to studio brass. "Why don't we get the woman who wrote the book?" he asked. "She lives around here. I'll work with her. I'll guide her."

The novelist agreed to write the screenplay free of charge with the proviso that not one word of it was to be changed without her approval. Both Warner's and Vidor agreed. She retired to her house in the San Fernando Valley, designed by another great architect, Richard Neutra, to write her third solo screenplay, her first in four years, and her first based on her own work.

Next, Vidor would have to find a leading lady. He was informed that there was a girl under studio contract who might work out. "Well, Patricia Neal was tall,"

Vidor said, "and she seemed to be right, opposite Gary. I said I'd talk to her. The first time I saw her, she was riding her bicycle on the lot, and I hailed her. She read the script and liked it. And I liked her. She had a lot of strength and vitality."

One of the first scenes in the picture was to take place at a rock quarry. The sexual imagery was overpowering, Howard Roark stripped to the waist and manning a drill which battered the side of the cliff in an obvious symbol of his virility. Vidor decided to film that scene first, and found a location for filming near Fresno, California.

The two stars would meet for the first time on location. The director and Pat Neal took a studio limousine together, while Cooper drove up alone. It was a risk to be in a car with Cooper. "He talked a lot about automobiles," Vidor said, "about going to Sun Valley and how fast he could get there. I think he was once trying to set a record for driving to Sun Valley and back."

All the principals arrived in Fresno on a Sunday, and Vidor invited his stars to join him for dinner at a Basque restaurant he'd heard about. Cooper and Pat Neal anticipated their first scene, where she would be riding by the quarry on her horse and notice the manly architect at work. "They fell immediately in love with each other," Vidor said. "It was a big, terrific romance. Outside of work, I hardly saw either of them again."

Cooper had been through many on-set romances in the past. They'd usually ended with his work on the picture. He was now a not particularly well-preserved forty-eight—in the dangerous years—and it was immensely flattering that a beautiful girl twenty-five years his junior should have so irrevocably fallen in love with not just the movie star but also the lonesome man.

Pat's father, a coal miner, had a sign hanging in his office, an adage she lived by: "If you call upon a thoroughbred, he gives you all the blood, sinew, and heart in him. If you call upon a jackass, he kicks." No one ever disputed that Patricia Neal was a thoroughbred.

"He was the most gorgeously attractive man," she said about Cooper. "Bright, too, though some people didn't think so."

When the company returned to shoot interiors in Hollywood, many people in town knew about the affair. "His wife visited the set a couple of times," Vidor said. "I think she was aware of what was going on, though I'm not sure. It was uncomfortable for all of us."

Vidor and his associates didn't need such awkward scenes, since they were dangerously close to creating some of their own. Roark's architectural designs were integral to the concept of the story. He was described on the screen as possessing "brilliance" and "genius." Yet the designs his individualism was protecting are considered today supersleek instant urban blight. Critics of the period also noticed that Roark's was a quixotic fight, judging from the quality of his work.

Unlike other film adaptations of previous novels, *The Fountainhead* fell into the pitfall of being too faithful to its source, too literal a rendition of an overly literal novel. "Artistic value is achieved collectively," as one line went, "by each man subordinating himself to the standards of the majority."

Both the visuals and the dialogue are bald, stark, and overstated. When Cooper balked at speaking awkward lines, Vidor reminded him of the agreement with the author.

"If you're really sincere, we'll have to get Ayn Rand in," King Vidor said. "She's an hour away. It'll probably take her another hour to get dressed."

"Oh, to hell with it," Cooper said. "I'll read the line."

The film culminated with an extraordinarily long courtroom scene in which the Roark character, over a ten-minute period, explains why he destroyed his altered design.

Vidor, to begin with, was opposed to the blowing-up of the building's facade. He said to Jack Warner, "If you make some changes in the picture after I've fin-

ished it, and if I blow up the vault and burn the negative, you're going to forgive me. Right?"

Warner replied, "Well, I wouldn't, but a judge
might." Vidor shot the script as written.

Cooper's culminating speech covered six script
pages. "God, I don't know whether I'll ever be able to
say that," he told Vidor.

"Well, we'll cut it up, get a few cuts," Vidor replied. He was hoping Cooper could get through at least
a page at a time. A phonograph record of the lines was
made, and Cooper took it home. He played it over and
over again until all the lines were committed to memory. When the scene was shot, Cooper delivered his
lines perfectly. It was the actor's quiet conviction rather
than the ideals enunciated that saved the scene.

Vidor found Pat Neal's performance splendid as
well.

Critics didn't agree with his assessment. "Garry
[sic] Cooper seems slightly pathetic with his candor
and modesty in the midst of such pretension," Bosley
Crowther wrote in *The New York Times*. "As the
idealistic architect he is Mr. Deeds out of his element
and considerably unsure of himself. His lengthy appeal
to the jury is timid and wooden indeed. . . . Patricia
Neal is almost funny, so affected is she as the girl."

Had the picture been an unqualified success,
Cooper and Pat Neal might have gone on together to
separate triumphs. Although they did go off on different
projects, they took time to comfort each other over
their mutual failure.

Cooper almost immediately began work on *Task
Force*, a film about aircraft-carrier warfare. It was the
first major postwar production made with large-scale
military assistance. The United States Navy supplied
Technicolor newsreel footage of World War II action,
and it turned out to be one of Cooper's most popular
films of this period of comparative career limbo.

Much of the location shooting was done at Coronado Beach, and the company stayed at the gingerbready

Coronado Hotel. In his spare time, Cooper again took up painting.

Director Delmer Daves's wife often observed him in front of an easel. "Since I've been painting, I see everything with a different eye," he told her. "You look at a nasturtium and think it's just one color. Then you paint it and you discover that it's made up of so many colors."

"He was so excited," Mary Lou Daves said. "He talked like a very naive young child. He never realized what painting could be."

Cooper returned to Hollywood for *Bright Leaf*, a picture with Lauren Bacall and Pat Neal. The torpid romantic melodrama was set in the tobacco-growing lands of North Carolina. He portrayed an entrepreneur financed by a sporting house lady (Bacall) and virtually destroyed by a haughty, faithless woman (Neal).

Cooper's face had aged dramatically and it was more essential than ever before in his career for him to be cosmeticized by flattering cinematography. But in *Bright Leaf*, he looked troubled and older than his years in the opening scenes. By the end of the story, attention seemed deliberately to be drawn to his haggard face. Oddly, he was filmed in direct light; the sockets of his sunken eyes disturbed 1950's moviegoers.

It was not a good film, and Pat was savaged by the critics. "Patricia Neal plays his female tormentor as though she were some sort of vagrant lunatic," Bosley Crowther wrote. "Her eyes pop and gleam in crazy fashion, her face wreathes in idiotic grins and she drawls with a Southern accent that sounds like dimwit travesty."

Warner's was paying her a star's salary, but still didn't know how to channel her talents. Michael Curtiz's direction, or lack thereof, left her vulnerable and unprotected.

Cooper and Pat Neal were having as much difficulty registering as a team with the movie audience as they were experiencing in their efforts to be accepted by the people of Hollywood. They continued to see each other, drawn together by the shared adversity coming at them from all sides.

Phyllis Thaxter recalled that Cooper often came into the makeup department to visit Patricia Neal when the two actresses were filming *The Breaking Point* in mid-1950. "I didn't know how involved she and Gary were. Patricia was a working friend . . . marvelously funny . . . a good person. I liked her tremendously. In the picture, she's having an affair with my husband. She was sultry, a mold they tried to fit her into. But it wasn't her. She was awfully good anyway, for Patricia was a very fine actress."

Other contemporaries found her the brightest and the best.

Teresa Wright came to know Patricia Neal later. "I didn't know her during the affair. I just knew what I read. It seemed nice that two such lovely people got together for a while."

June Lockhart found her to be "a true class act. Pat's a totally lovely woman, intelligent and well educated and elegant in ways so-called fashionable women don't even know about. There's compassion and humor about her, and absolutely no self-pity."

She was torn by her love for Cooper and her respectable upbringing. She wasn't one to settle for a back-street affair, nor did she want to separate Cooper from the daughter he deeply loved. She detested the shame that burned within her. Yet she couldn't give him up. Nor did he want her to.

They were seen at out-of-the-way places, having a hamburger at a drive-in or a cup of coffee at a greasy spoon. Occasionally, Cooper joined her at the acting classes conducted by Michael Chekhov.

He didn't want to humiliate his wife, from whom he hadn't actually separated, and whenever he accepted an invitation from people who'd entertained them as a couple, he came alone. Yet, to one of these hostesses, he described part of Pat's enormous appeal. "I can stretch my legs and put on slippers and relax. We don't need parties."

It was a difficult time for many of their friends. "I knew them all," Ann Warner said, "and felt sorry for all of them. Rocky was very smart. During that period, she wasn't nasty, she looked good, and she made her own life. She went out with a few boys, and she acted very cleverly. She was fighting a woman like Pat Neal who happened to be a decent woman . . . a truly lovely girl . . . I used to study Dianetics with her. If Pat were conniving, she might have been able to break up the marriage. Pat was so in love with him, and Gary with her. She satisfied him a great deal. There was an intellectual quality to her, and she was a real woman."

The affair had been going on for two years, and it was going nowhere. Pat tried to develop an interest in men closer to her own age. One of her closest friends at the time was actress Jean Hagen, who was then married to an agent named Tom Sidell. They arranged for her to go out with another William Morris agent, but they only saw each other a couple of times.

"She struck me, in the little I saw of her," the agent said, "as being elegant . . . very kindly and nice. But there was a kind of sadness about her, and it had to be about Cooper.

"I knew him too, and I can see why her loving him compounded her problems. If he was a bastard, her good sense would tell her to get away from him as soon as possible. But Coop was a likable man, a very nice man. That made it even worse, and more difficult for her to break it up."

Just before Christmas of 1950, Rocky took Maria to New York and set up residence at the River Club. When Louella Parsons called to ask if she and her husband had separated, Rocky replied, "Well, I'm here and he's there. It's true we've had some trouble. But if you're asking me about a divorce, I'll tell you right now the answer is—no! I am a Catholic and I have no intention of ever getting a divorce."

Now that the estrangement was in the open, Hollywood observers began to analyze the reasons for the rift. Elsa Maxwell, a close friend of Dorothy di Frasso, was among the first: "As for the Coopers," she wrote in April 1951, "I must say I suspected Gary had a new interest long before I read the first rumors about him and Pat Neal. Always when Gary gets a romantic gleam in his eye, he sees his tailor . . . and now his grooming, having picked up again, is more casual in tone."

Just where the romance could lead, with his wife adamantly refusing to grant him a divorce, was the unhappy quandary Cooper and Pat were caught up in. Then, surprisingly, a move on Rocky's part suggested a resolution might be imminently in the offing.

In mid-May, while Cooper was on location in Naples, Florida, making *Distant Drums* with director Raoul Walsh, Rocky's attorney announced that the Coopers had separated. Graham Sterling said he didn't know if there were any plans for a divorce, but negotiations for a property settlement were under way.

Hedda Hopper telephoned Cooper from Hollywood. "Don't let her get all your money," she cautioned.

"She's not like that, really," Cooper protested.

"Oh, no," Hopper sarcastically replied. "She'll have a hard time finding another one like you. There aren't any men."

"It's all my own fault," Cooper said. "Too many things during our long marriage were taken for granted. It's all my doing, but I do want to be free."

"Don't you think you deserve some happiness?"

"Listen," Cooper said, "after twenty-five years [in pictures] I've had a helluva lot of happiness and many things that have been good . . . many more than most people get and many more than I deserve. Picture stars are spoiled. They get a little hoggish. They think they're the best things in the world. They're not."

Hedda asked, "If she doesn't get a divorce, will you?"

He didn't reply.

Cooper, in his *Saturday Evening Post* memoirs, glided over the reasons for the breakup. "I didn't feel satisfied with anything at all, and least of all with myself. Rocky and I talked it over. She understood me better than anyone else in the world, and she knew, probably better than I did, that the time had come for me to take another long walk alone.

"We agreed that the separation should be legal, and I shoved off. I would try Europe for a while. Well it didn't work. My take-a-walk formula that had worked so well in the past was a bust from the very start." He didn't mention Patricia Neal.

Now that the estrangement was formally confirmed, the press descended on Pat, casting her in the role of the "other woman." "Am I in love with him? Could be. But I'd be silly to go around advertising it, wouldn't I? After all, he's a married man."

After casting her in eight films in two years, Warner's did not renew her contract, to the delight of several Hollywood wives. Patricia Neal and her "kind" represented a threat to their privileged, celebrated existences.

"Knowing Rocky," Ann Warner said, "I'm sure she knew a lot of women who were afraid they'd lose their own husbands. My mother always said, 'What's yours, no one can take from you, and what's not yours, you do not want.' This group, not too attractive, stuck together. They built up a barrier. They wanted to make the woman pay so that the next woman wouldn't have a chance."

Pat Neal tried to overlook the obvious resentments she'd engendered, yet she conceded they were there in a November 1952 interview with Howard Thompson of *The New York Times*. "I don't understand how anybody gets ahead in Hollywood," she said. "No one gets in. They say knowing the right people is so important. But those walls!"

When Warner Brothers dropped Pat's contract, these wives felt they were instrumental in driving her out of town. "It's so untrue," Mrs. Warner continued. "Jack Warner ran his business and no one ran a studio like him. He was a man who, if a person had talent and made money for the company, would keep them on.

Jack loved good actors. He wouldn't run anyone out of town. Pat was a fine actress . . . a character actress, actually . . . and she'd been given many important roles. A lot of money was spent on her, but she belonged to another category of star."

Pat understood this. "They dropped me," she said about Warner's. "I never had a box office hit, although some of the films I made were critical successes. I came in there at a big salary which kept growing. That salary was one of the reasons we parted company." Her salary hit $3,000 a week, yet she hadn't made one big commercial hit, including the two films she made with Cooper. Now she was free to join him on his travels. One of their first was a hop over to Cuba to visit the Hemingways.

"Gary Cooper came for a night in which we talked until near dawn, mostly about his problems," Mary Hemingway wrote in *How It Was*, "and went on talking about them the next day."

What she didn't say, but confirmed to me later, was that Patricia Neal was with him. Nor was the visit as filled with the tension and drama she suggested in her book, but did not amplify on. "I guess Coops thought it would be fun to take her over there."

Hemingway, in principle, didn't approve of extramarital wanderings. He recognized the polygamous nature in many men, including himself. To Harvey Breit, a columnist for *The New York Times Book Review*, he wrote, "I am very faithful. But I can be faithful easier to four good wives than to one." The contradiction between the two men was that the fire-breathing liberal subscribed to convention, while the dyed-in-the-wool conservative in this case did not.

To publicly flaunt a new love, when Hemingway and his wife were, if not overly fond of Rocky, at least civil to her, was bad form.

If Cooper had come to Cuba to get the writer's blessing, he was disappointed. "He may in some way have disapproved," Mary Hemingway said about her husband. "He was, of course, a good host and polite to the girl."

Mrs. Hemingway found Patricia Neal "flattered to death . . . pleased . . . that Coops gave her his attention. He was a famous film star. She was a pleasant, giggly girl . . . agreeable . . . that was about it."

When the pair returned to southern California and Pat reported to Twentieth-Century Fox for her one picture a year commitment, at a considerably lower salary than she'd received at Warner Brothers, she was again bombarded by reporters' queries. Cooper somehow evaded commenting on the situation altogether. She didn't know how to be coy with her inquisitors, yet she tried to hold back, only to realize that they'd succeeded in gradually wresting several implicit admissions from her.

"I'm very fond of him," she replied to one query. "He's quite wonderful. But I absolutely had nothing to do with the breaking-up of their marriage."

To another questioner, she said, "We're very good friends. He's a wonderful guy and I love working with him. But I had nothing to do with his marriage trouble. I'm sure most intelligent people agree with me that no such thing could happen—that no one could break up a happy marriage."

Questions insidiously continued. At one point, poor Pat Neal cried out in exasperation, "Please! I'm from a pretty conventional family background and I don't like this kind of thing at all. I hope this talk will die down, that people will find something else to talk about. I wish that everyone would just ignore this."

But the talk wouldn't go away. For a brief period, the couple thought they would brazen it out. They were seen at big gatherings. Inevitably, they arrived at a party where Rocky was also present.

"It was at the big party that Charles Feldman gave for Dolly O'Brien," Hedda Hopper recalled, "that I saw the break coming for Coop and Pat. It was one of their first party appearances. When they came in they went directly to the end of the bar. There they remained until dinner was announced. Rocky, on the other hand, arrived with Peter Lawford, went immediately to the table assigned her. I was sorry Pat didn't look prettier that night. She wore flowers in her hair, like an ingenue. They didn't become her. Rocky, in contrast, being a sophisticated woman of the world and having all the cards in her hand, was very gay, danced every dance, and never took the smile off her face. At about midnight—when Pat was dancing—Coop got up and, for a few minutes, visited Rocky's table. Everyone held his breath. I would not be surprised if it was then and there that Pat accepted the fact that things would not work out, and so—stepped out."

Cooper was suffering silently. The strain he was feeling manifested itself in a common way. While visiting New York in early December, he was hospitalized at Roosevelt Hospital for treatment of a duodenal ulcer. He'd been planning to go to Korea to entertain American troops, but the trip had to be canceled.

He wanted to marry Pat, but not if it sacrificed the respect of an adolescent daughter who worshiped him. Rocky had yet to agree to a divorce. Pat was caught in the middle of the impasse, bearing the brunt of outraged opinion. The American public was at its most sanctimonious at this time. Ingrid Bergman, because of her affair with Roberto Rossellini, the Italian director, was in danger of not being readmitted to the United States. After the birth of her love child, she chose to stay on in Europe.

Cooper, by his inaction, was throwing Pat to the vengeful moralists. If this diminished her respect for him, she never said so. Someone would have to make his mind up for him.

Pat Neal traveled north to Sonora, California, while Cooper was filming *High Noon* there in the fall of 1951. The crew viewed the lovers curiously. When Pat returned to Hollywood, she was resigned to the inevitable, although it would take her some time to act on her decision.

"I was very much in love with him," she said about their affair. "But I got myself into a sticky mess which couldn't work, didn't work, and never should have worked. I lived this secret life for several years. I was so ashamed . . . yet there was the fact of it. I had made few close friends. All I had, there in Hollywood, was that one love. I'm sorry for any damage that was done—and I'm sure there was. You always think no one is going to get hurt, but someone always does—lots of people."

Pat, in writing about the affair years later to a friend, said she and Cooper were sorry above all that they'd hurt Maria, but that was a message that could never be sent home. It was one Maria herself didn't grasp, if the reaction Pat described the one time they came face to face was true. She said that once at El Morocco, Maria had spent the entire evening glaring at her across the room. Cooper's daughter, by that time, was older than Pat had been during the affair with the actor.

Patricia Neal walked out of Gary Cooper's life on Christmas Eve of 1951. They never saw each other again.

Even then the press wanted a final word. "My feelings are still the same as they were," Pat said. "I don't say this will last for ten years, but that's the way it is now."

Chapter 10

His films were artistically mediocre and not the commercial blockbusters of the past. His aging features were being reviewed as often as his performances. Nevertheless, the popularity of Gary Cooper as he reached the mid-century point was unabated. From 1941 until 1957, he was among the box office Top Ten. The one broken link in the golden chain came in 1950 with the failure of *Bright Leaf*, Cooper's sole release that year.

Hollywood cognoscenti theorize that major stardom lasts an average of seven years. Cooper's, by 1951, had endured three times that long. In a period when the movie and its theme emerged as the true star, it was a tribute to his durability that his fans still went to see a Gary Cooper picture. Their devotion was often above and beyond the call. No one realized it more than the star himself. He was coasting on past triumphs, and wasn't sure there would be any more in his future. Jack Moss was no longer the steward of his career. His well-known leftist politics perhaps made him a casualty of the paranoia of the times. Also, because of their estrangement, Cooper couldn't turn to Rocky either for counsel.

He'd thought a renewed association with Stuart Heisler, whom he'd always liked, might prove the solution. The director, four years previously, had begged Cooper to release him from his personal contract to accept an offer from Howard Hughes. "Gary," he wrote, "this is my big chance, and I need it desperately." Cooper wouldn't stand in the way.

Just one abortive picture with Hughes, *Vendetta*, convinced Heisler he'd made the wrong decision. He wriggled out of the contract to return to Warner Brothers as a contract director. He would be able to work with Cooper in *Dallas*. Heisler was an uneven director, creating magnificent sequences often leading up to hollow climaxes. *Dallas* turned out to be a routine Western, neither harming nor enhancing Cooper's image.

Henry Hathaway directed Cooper in his next project, *U. S. S. Teakettle* (later released as *You're in the Navy Now*), an engaging comedy about a bunch of greenhorns taking over the command of a ship, led by a "ninety-day wonder" played by Cooper. The actor was a generation too old for the part, but the film was a delight. Yet it was a small picture. As winning as Cooper was in the role, it didn't liberate him from his limbo.

While he marked time, he appeared in a couple of all-star pictures, *Starlift* and *It's a Big Country*, before taking on another Western, *Distant Drums*. There was still no appreciable upgrading of his career. Perhaps it was a combination of ego, greed, and rapidly onsetting middle age that required a breakthrough for him. During much of this time, he'd been involved with Patricia Neal, and he may have had to prove something to her as well.

Two factors—the advent of television and the forced divestiture of studio-owned theaters—were leading to the end of the contract system which created and nurtured careers. Virtually every star, no matter how luminous, became a free agent, selling his appeal on the open market.

Some—Robert Mitchum, Kirk Douglas, Burt Lancaster—would soon be forming their own production companies. Cooper thought he might do the same, buying two novels in which he planned to star: Alfred Hayes's *The Girl on the Via Flaminia* and A. B. Guthrie's

The Way West. Having acted as producer on *Along Came Jones*, however, he wasn't enthused about resuming front office duties. He eventually sold both properties.

Other actors were negotiating profit participation deals. James Stewart pioneered the concept with Bill Goetz, who'd merged his International Pictures with Universal, and needed big names to get the new studio—Universal-International—off the ground. Stewart on his fifty-fifty deal, made $750,000 on just one film, *Winchester 73*, and would be receiving millions more for pictures made later at U-I. Stanley Kramer offered a similar deal to Gregory Peck for *High Noon*, but was turned down. Peck felt the role was too similar to *The Gunfighter*, the serious Western he made in 1950 for director Henry King at Twentieth-Century Fox. It was the first of the Western genre to be classified a "problem picture," in that it explored social issues.

High Noon, however, gave birth to the term, "adult Western," though Cooper didn't know this would happen when he was persuaded to follow his friend Stewart's example. He would make the picture, agreeing to a lower salary against a percentage of the profits. This enabled Kramer to budget the picture at $750,-000. If Cooper had taken his usual salary, it would have cost nearly twice that much.

The actor found himself involved with a group of Young Turks. Kramer had been producing serious alternatives to standard escapist fare, and had already made *The Men, Champion,* and *Home of the Brave.* The distributing organization, United Artists, was also an iconoclast, known for offering haven to such lone-wolf filmmakers.

Vienna-born Fred Zinnemann, assigned to the picture, directed dramatic short subjects before turning exclusively to features in 1942. He supervised the debut film performances of two of the postwar era's greatest actors, Montgomery Clift in the 1948 production of *The Search*, and Marlon Brando in *The Men* in 1950. His reputation was that of an intelligent and realistic artist. His concerns usually reflected man's struggles with his conscience. Zinnemann and Gary Cooper as the White Knight were made for each other. This they discovered as they worked on the story of a man fighting to maintain his human dignity.

Zinnemann considered Cooper's participation a coup. He was the "personification of the honor-bound man," he told Diana Dreiman. "He was, in himself, a very noble figure, very humble at the same time and very inarticulate . . . and very unsure of himself. . . . Cooper just being there made all the contribution in the world . . . he made the difference between an average movie and a much better than average movie."

Zinnemann described the picture's theme as "the conscience of one man who felt he couldn't walk away from a situation. . . . it just happened to be in a Western background. . . . It could have taken place anywhere a man is faced with that decision. It's a timeless situation."

The story of a man whose friends and countrymen desert him one by one, while his conscience tells him he can't avoid the oncoming battle, had topical references of which Cooper, given his conservative leanings, must have been ignorant.

Because of them, the most controversial person involved in the production would be screenwriter Carl Foreman, who saw the plot as "the investigation of the anatomy of fear." In the midst of his work, he was the one dissected, being called before the House Un-American Activities Committee to talk about his alleged Communist ties. From that point on, Foreman changed the emphasis, making *High Noon* an allegory about the hysteria engendered by McCarthyism, and a far greater commentary on contemporary America than the prosaic John Cunningham short story, "The Tin Star," on which it was based. The script constructed by Foreman was short and terse, rapidly cutting from one scene to another, relentlessly creating tension throughout.

About this script, Foreman said, "So much of it is

comparable to what was happening. . . . There are scenes taken from life . . . [one] is a distillation of meetings I had with partners, associates, and lawyers. And, there's the scene with the man who offers to help and comes back with his gun and asks, 'Where are the others?' and Cooper says, 'There are no others.' "

Zinnemann and Kramer, aware of the controversy such an approach would cause, disclaimed any connection with the current political climate. But it was Foreman who gave the script its form and structure. Contrary to the popular conception that the film was extensively revised, it remains exactly as it was written in the 110-page final shooting script. Minor cuts were made to tighten the film, and only two major sequences were excised. One had the retiring marshal, played by Cooper, contemplating suicide as the showdown neared between him and Frank Miller, whom he'd sent off to prison five years previously. The pardoned convict is on his way on the noon train to the prairie town of Hadleyville to exact revenge, with three members of his old gang awaiting his arrival. Suicide would not only weaken the film, but also the character of Will Kane. He couldn't conceivably consider such an act. It would be cowardly and negate the questioning conscience of the film.

The second involved a scene outside of town with several other characters, including a second deputy. It proved extraneous, slowing the buildup of tension.

There were two major female characters in the picture. One, played by Katy Jurado, had been the marshal's "friend," as well as Miller's. The heart-of-gold character tries to impress on the marshal's new wife the importance of standing by her man. But Amy is strong-willed and idealistic, a Quaker by conversion after her father and brother were killed in a gunfight. She refuses to stand by her husband, but not through fear. To fight goes against her convictions.

Cast as the wife was a novice to pictures named Grace Kelly. Zinnemann said she was the only actress ever to apply to him for a job wearing white gloves. He was taken with her. Columnist James Bacon claimed that some of Zinnemann's later editing problems involved his having to cut out the many loving close-ups he'd shot of Grace Kelly.

Though he was still involved with Patricia Neal during the making of the film, Cooper was also getting strong sexual emanations from the cool and beautiful Kelly. She would become a major star in a very brief period. Hedda Hopper asked Cooper if he recognized Grace Kelly's potential during the time they worked together.

"I knew this," Cooper said. "She was very serious about her work . . . had her eyes and ears open. She was trying to learn, you could see that. You can tell if a person really wants to be an actress. She was one of those people you could get that feeling about, and she was very pretty. It didn't surprise me when she was a big success. . . .

"I also feel she fills a much needed gap in motion pictures. It's been quite a few years since we had a girl in pictures that looked like she was born on the right side of Park Avenue. Looks like she could be a cold dish with a man until you got her pants down and then she'd explode." Since this was the precise quality another director sought in his leading ladies, she made the ideal Alfred Hitchcock heroine.

Miss Kelly had to work hard to keep up with Cooper. "When I look into his face I can see everything he is thinking," she said. "But when I look into my own face I see absolutely nothing. I know what I am thinking, but it just doesn't show."

Roberta Haynes, a stage-trained actress who would be Cooper's costar the following year in *Return to Paradise,* had a small role of a sensuous Mexican girl who waylays the second deputy, in one of the major scenes cut from the picture. She worked a week at the Sonora, California, location. She said several townspeople recalled some of the earliest pictures Cooper had shot there, and had seen his development from the cowboy who was one of them to a star who belonged to the world.

The entire crew stayed at a local lodge, and spent their free time at the gaming tables, for gambling was legal in Sonora.

"One night, I was sitting at the table having dinner with Carl Foreman and some other people," Roberta said. "I hadn't talked much to Cooper at that point. He came up to me, very nice, and said, 'Do you like to gamble?' I said yes. 'Well, here,' he said, 'Gamble for me.' He handed me thirty-five dollars. I thought it was very strange."

She'd never rolled dice before, but she wound up winning seventy dollars. Side bettors won even more. She later saw Cooper on the set, but no mention was made of his staking her at the craps table.

Cooper's low-key performance was his best in years. He would later joke that the ulcer he'd come down with created the racking pain that photographed as self-doubt. The tenor of his performance was established in the first scene, in which he marries Grace Kelly. Aged just enough for weathered grandeur, and photographed looking ten years younger than he did in *Bright Leaf*, Cooper is visibly trying to assume the mantle of dignity to mask his childlike delight. He's the abashed boy and the responsible marshal all at once. He chuckles irrepressibly as he tells his new bride, "It seems like people oughta be alone when they get married." He sobers immediately by promising he'll do his best by her. This scene created audience identity with Cooper's character, and at the same time evinced the picture's only playful mood.

The levity ends with word of Miller's impending arrival, setting up the dilemma, similar to the one Cooper's character played in *The Virginian* more than twenty years before.

Amy must choose between the two things she feels most strongly about. When, in the defense of her husband, she kills someone, the action goes against everything she's believed in.

"It doesn't negate the value at all," Zinnemann said. "It just says that she's not capable of living up to [her values] at that particular time, because those values are absolutes, and a human being can't possibly live up to an absolute . . . everybody falls short, no matter how good, no matter how honest. . . . I don't think one should be blamed for that as long as they're trying to live up to it; it's in the trying."

All of the action takes place within less than the two hours that it takes to tell the story. It begins just a few minutes before 10:33 A.M. and ends about 12:15. The actual running time of the film was eighty-five minutes, twenty minutes shorter than the elapsed time in the picture.

Clocks were used throughout the picture, heightening the mood of desperation at time's inexorable passing.

Floyd Crosby's cinematography achieved the mood of a newsreel of the period. Zinnemann and Crosby studied Matthew Brady photographs of the Civil War. They noted the sky was always white and that the lighting was very flat.

"We decided *not* to correct the skies," Crosby said, "to have hot skies because we thought it would give the feeling of heat. And, the last thing we wanted to do was to make this little town look pretty or attractive or beautiful in any way. We wanted it to look like a crummy Western town. So we didn't correct skies, and I think it did give the feeling of heat and of a dusty little cow-town."

Crosby used many close-ups in the film, tightly framing two or three people in most shots. His long shots were memorable. One started with a close-up of Cooper, the camera on a crane drawing back until the whole town could be seen. Once the camera reached its highest elevation, it encompassed three anachronistic telephone poles, but the overall composition was so dynamic that nobody except cinematographer Crosby later noticed it.

At picture's end, after Kane with the help of his

new wife has dispatched the four villains, the townspeople gather around him to offer their congratulations. Cooper deliberately unhooks his badge and drops it in the dirt. With neither a word nor a backward glance, he shows his contempt for those who didn't want to get involved. He and Amy drive off in their wagon. The gesture was also Foreman's, his protest against the "law and order" which fostered the patriotic hysteria of the McCarthy era.

Cooper, after finishing work on the production in October 1951, went on a hunting and fishing trip to Idaho. Before his departure, he agreed to buy stock in a new independent production company being formed by Carl Foreman, who'd severed his association with Stanley Kramer.

Both Louella Parsons and Hedda Hopper chided Cooper in print for going into business with an "unfriendly" witness during the HUAC hearings on Communist infiltration of Hollywood. An act of defiant courage might have reinforced the message so eloquently and simply delivered in *High Noon*. Cooper was not to be the man of the season.

He issued a statement through his attorney, I. H. Prinzmetal: "When I indicated my willingness to purchase stock in the Foreman company, I was convinced of Foreman's loyalty and Americanism and of his ability as a picturemaker. My opinion of Foreman has not changed. However, since the announcement was made that I intended to become a stockholder, I have received notice of considerable reaction and I now feel it best for all concerned that I should not purchase this stock."

Foreman tried not to show his bitter disappointment. "Gary Cooper is the finest kind of American and one of the most decent men I have ever met," he stated. "I regret to lose him as a business associate, but I hope to keep him always as a friend."

Unexpectedly, Cooper's withdrawal created a backlash among some liberal quarters. Because many of the "unfriendly" witnesses were Jews, word spread that he was anti-Semitic. His activities in the 1944 Presidential election had already planted the seed of doubt. He'd had little exposure to Jews in his youth, and the Southampton circles he and Rocky moved in were composed of White Anglo-Saxon Protestants. Yet, the man he'd entrusted his career to, Jack Moss, was a Jew, as were four of his closest friends, Jack Benny, Charles Feldman, Bill Goetz, and Jerry Wald, who would serve as pallbearers at his funeral. He wasn't directly accused of harboring such ill will. Consequently, he didn't have the opportunity to disavow the talk, if he was of a mind to. What survived was a consensus with no tangible basis in fact. McCarthyism could also work in reverse.

With Patricia Neal walking out of his life, it was generally assumed that Cooper and Rocky would reconcile in short order. Now that divorce wasn't necessarily inevitable, Rocky, in late January 1952, said to the press that Cooper could have a divorce any time he wanted. She confirmed that neither had such plans at present. About being seen around town with aviation executive Robert Six, she commented, "He's an awfully nice fellow, but we are just having dates, that's all."

Hedda Hopper called Pat Neal in New York. She wanted to know, since Cooper obviously hadn't reconciled with his wife, if the affair with the actor might be resumed. "I will not see him when I go back to Hollywood," Pat said. "I have been very much in love with him. And I am sure he has loved me. But I saw that it wouldn't work. So I've stepped out. I have a lot of life ahead of me. And I want to live it with someone who is fun and unentangled, someone with whom I can have a relationship that will be good—and permanent.

"Coop is wonderful. I never knew anybody like him. But he's a very complex person, as you well know. . . . It is, I assure you, over and ended forever. Wouldn't you know it would be just my luck to fall in love with a married man?"

Hedda asked, "How many times have you been in love, Pat?"

"Only once."

Her early return to working at Twentieth was not to be. It took her some time to get over the affair. "When we broke up," she told Rex Reed, "I went to a woman psychiatrist in Philadelphia and nearly had a nervous breakdown. Then I ended up in Atlanta and hid out there for six months in my sister's house and went to a wonderful psychiatrist who saved my sanity and got me in shape to go back to work."

Along the way she developed a resilience and strength to face the horrendous traumas of her future: a taxi running down her infant son in his carriage, and the multiple operations needed for his recovery; a daughter's death from brain inflammation following measles; and her own series of near-fatal strokes which temporarily paralyzed her left side, leaving her with a permanent speech problem—Olympian retribution for the sin of falling in love.

Cooper returned to Warner Brothers in the spring of 1952 to star in another Western opposite Phyllis Thaxter and David Brian. It would not fare well, being unfavorably compared to *High Noon*. Also, the picture's producers would be accused of giving the picture a title, *Springfield Rifle,* which had nothing to do with the proceedings, but might have had a lot to do with the success of *Winchester 73*.

Miss Thaxter and her husband, James Aubrey, were Brentwood neighbors of the Coopers, and she was delighted to be assigned to the Cooper picture.

Their first scene together called for Miss Thaxter, as his wife, to pay him a surprise visit at his army base. He enters a hotel room, where he finds her changing her dress behind a screen. "We went on kissing forever," Miss Thaxter said. "The director, André de Toth, never said cut. We were both blushing about it.

"I was pregnant at the time, but I didn't want the studio to know. It wasn't a tremendously big part, and I had only four scenes with Gary. I wanted to complete the picture before they discovered I was expecting.

"I was eating soda crackers because I had morning sickness. When I told Gary why, he was very protective and sweet with me. He called me Sparkle Plenty, because he said my eyes were always dancing."

The Aubreys didn't socialize often with the Coopers, according to Miss Thaxter, "only at the big parties. I didn't know either one of them well. I felt Gary was a very shy, simple man. I didn't know him any other way, because the international set wasn't in my life at all."

Neither did she know Rocky well, although Cooper's wife and daughter Maria briefly visited the set. The visit was a friendly one, but it didn't lead to a reconciliation.

As the production on the picture continued, *High Noon* was being prepared for a sneak preview in Riverside, California. It was a disaster. Each participant had a varying version of how the picture was "saved."

Columnist James Bacon, who wasn't directly involved, said, "half of the picture was close-ups of Grace." Everyone feared it would be a dismal failure.

Its commercial potential also seemed dim to United Artists. They urged that the action be tightened. Several claimed credit for the final version. Film editor Elmo Williams said he and Zinnemann worked on the first cut for some time. Kramer was due to edit further after Zinnemann left the project. He was called out of town for a few days, and Williams edited further.

"I knew I had a good movie," he told James Bacon. "I also had a short movie. There was no exposition of the plot. I hit upon the idea of putting a song in front and over the titles."

What resulted was "The Ballad of High Noon," composed by Dmitri Tiomkin with lyrics by Ned Washington, and sung by Tex Ritter. The song told the story of the movie, supplementing Cooper's fundamental inarticulation. It would be difficult for him to ask his woman, "Do not forsake me, oh my darling, on this our wedding day." Yet the words perfectly reflected his feelings.

There would be enough credit to go around, for this was a notable team effort which, after trial and error, created a hugely successful motion picture.

Like many of the "message" pictures of the period, *High Noon* has lost much of its initial impact now that films with serious content are commonplace. Though heralded at the time as an instant classic in the Western genre, it looks today more archly self-conscious than more basic Westerns like *Rio Bravo, The Searchers,* and *Buchanan Rides Alone.* With the McCarthy era theoretically over, much of the tension in the movie is gone, just as the vital undercurrent in *Sergeant York* is missing once Hitler is defeated. Few variations are made on the basic theme, and few ideas are explored besides the fairly predictable main current. One new wrinkle is introduced. The previous marshal talks about the thankless, risky job of catching killers so that juries can turn them loose again to come back for your blood. Once again a deliberate imposition of timely social concern occurs in a supposedly timeless bit of mythmaking.

The story had traveled a long way since its first appearance in *The Virginian.* Most of its progress was etched on the face of its tired, aging pilgrim. *High Noon* propelled Cooper to number two at the box office that year, on which he built to become the top box office star of 1953. It was the first time Cooper reached the zenith, an unprecedented feat that a star would soar to the top after more than a quarter-century in the business. From that point on, he would be taking a percentage of every picture he made, in addition to his reinstated $500,000 minimum salary.

With his career so dramatically revived, these should have been the best of times for Cooper. He was, however, a desperately sick and unhappy man when he reported to the Samoan location for the filming of *Return to Paradise.*

Mark Robson had directed *Champion,* the 1949 picture which made a star out of Kirk Douglas, and he was assigned to helm the film based on the James Michener book. He and Roberta Haynes, cast as the native girl to Cooper's beachbum, were stuck at the location a full three months before the bulk of production started. A shipping strike had delayed the arrival of much of the equipment needed for filming.

Perhaps because of fraying nerves, the director and his female star didn't get along. "Coming from New York," Roberta said, "I felt that anyone who could direct a picture must obviously be very knowledgeable and very good. It's not that Robson was a bad director. He just wasn't the great director I thought he was."

Nor was he considerate. The actress complained about her treatment. "If you were Greta Garbo," Robson told her, "and I were paying you a lot of money, I'd treat you nicer."

The island was plagued by persistent mosquitoes, and Roberta requested that screens be put on the windows of her room. Her request was ignored. When two bites became infected, she went to the island hospital and asked the attending physician to put a bandage on every mosquito bite, not just the infected ones. She returned to the dining room.

"What's the matter with you?" Robson asked.

"Oh, nothing," she replied, "just some infected mosquito bites."

The screens were installed on her windows that same day.

When Cooper arrived, she was surprised to see that a star of his stature was treated with the same contempt. "He could have demanded a lot of things but didn't," Roberta said. "His dressing room was absolutely minuscule. There wasn't even a chair, much less a bed to lie down on. Cooper needed rest more than ever, as his ulcers were bleeding.

"It's rather crazy to take a risk with your health like that," the actress said. "I don't think he realized how dangerous it really was until he got down there. I think he wanted to get away, where nobody could reach him. You couldn't telephone there. Mail took two weeks."

When Cooper was subjected to mistreatment, he rationalized by saying his lawyer would take care of it after he returned to the United States. "He meant financially, I suppose," Roberta said. What upset her was his refusal to speak up for anybody else's benefit. He could have used his influence to make the work easier for others.

"By Cooper allowing them to treat him the way they did, they treated us even worse. In those days I was terribly shy. It was hard for me to stand up for my own rights, and when I did I just got clobbered. Cooper could have done something. I was his leading lady in the film, but he just didn't want to be bothered. That was his way. I don't think it was because he didn't care, because he obviously did."

From the start, the largely platonic nature of their relationship was established. "Don't be upset if I don't make a pass at you," Cooper told Roberta. The medication he was taking, he explained, was making him impotent.

"That was a strange remark," she said; "because I never expected him to make a pass at me. We became nice friends. He never talked about anything very personal . . . just about everyday things. Sometimes we would talk about the script, but not much. He would say he didn't know it very well, but he knew it backwards and forwards. Yet I never saw him pick up his script and study it. I would sometimes look at him on the set, off in a corner, practicing hand movements and gestures. I'd later see him using them. He knew *exactly* what he was doing. He knew what lens was on the camera. He was a master, a consummate film actor. I had great respect for him after doing that film.

"He was very good to me. He'd explain to me what lens was on, how close up it was. He'd turn me around so that my face was in better view. He was incredible . . . giving. He knew I couldn't steal a scene from him, so he would throw the scene to me, many a time. But I would see him with Barry Jones, who had about as many years of experience, and there was a great rivalry about who was going to steal the scene."

Among the valuable lessons Roberta learned from Cooper was the handling of awkward dialogue. They were going over a scene one day, which involved a long speech for the Cooper character.

"It's terrible!" she said. "What are you going to do about it?" She thought the logical thing was to go to the director and complain.

"No, no," Cooper said. "You don't do that. You just say it so badly that when they get in the cutting room they'll cut it out." It must have worked; the scene in question did not appear in the film.

As their work continued, Cooper's health remained poor. Roberta found him to "drink quite a bit," usually spiking coconuts with vodka; he shouldn't have been drinking at all. In addition to the ulcer, he had a throat infection. But he persisted in reporting to the set, perhaps in the hope that he would be sent home.

Roberta went first to the assistant director. "Cooper's sick," she said. "Why don't you send him home?"

"Not yet," she was told. The cast wasn't dismissed until five that afternoon. When he returned to his quarters, Cooper was so ill that he was kept in bed for a week. Roberta took over his recuperation.

"I think women wanted to take care of him. Why else would I bother to go around finding somebody to look after him? It wasn't *my* problem. If I hadn't done it for him, somebody would have. I'm sure there was always somebody like me to do it for him, but somehow it was all right, and he was so nice about it."

She understood why Rocky had interceded for him for so many years, making herself unpopular with many in the process, and why Cooper allowed his wife to dominate him.

"I realize now that people get what they want. I'm sure he didn't want to run his own life, and he was happier giving over the power to somebody else. But, then, doing that didn't make him very happy, either. It's a lot harder to go out and run your own life, and it's a lot easier to let somebody else take the blame . . . to sit back and be the nice guy. That's what he did, essentially. He wanted to be the nice guy. It's very normal, and I think if he hadn't been so nice, people wouldn't have been so willing to do things for him."

Cooper rarely talked about personal matters, other than to discuss his daughter. "I think he cared a great deal about what people thought of him . . . particularly Maria. He didn't do a lot of things because he didn't want to hurt her. I think for that reason he wasn't living fully at all. . . . He did most of his chasing out of the country, where people wouldn't see a lot. He liked going over to Paris."

Roberta said Cooper, although he had many reservations, had decided to return to Rocky. "When he came to the islands, he'd made the decision to go back. He was doing it because of his daughter. I don't think it was a happy decision for him. He was not a joyful man . . . not an outgoing man . . . not an aggressive man. I think that . . . came about because of his own inhibitions. Cooper must have been fifty-one or fifty-two when he did the picture with me. I thought he was older. He wasn't basically a very happy man. When I heard the people in Sonora talk about his chasing Lupe Velez up and down the stairs, those seemed the happiest times. When you look at his earlier pictures, there's a light in his eyes. He began to look very careworn. I don't think people who get ulcers are terribly happy."

In March 1953, when the annual Academy Award ceremonies were held, Cooper was on location in Cuernavaca, filming *Blowing Wild* with Barbara Stanwyck and Anthony Quinn, a potboiler which Bosley Crowther characterized as "a loose miscellany of random actions."

John Wayne accepted Gary Cooper's Oscar for Best Actor, chiding his agent for not getting him the part in *High Noon*. "First time in the history of the

Academy that an ulcer ever won an Oscar," Cooper said to Jim Bacon. *High Noon* also won the film-editing award for Elmo Williams and Harry Gerstad, a best musical score citation for Dmitri Tiomkin, and best song for Tiomkin and Washington. It was also nominated for best picture but lost to DeMille's *The Greatest Show on Earth*. The Western was the most honored of all of Cooper's motion pictures.

Blowing Wild wouldn't be nearly as distinguished, and would be mostly remembered by Cooper as the picture in which he suffered severe bruises and contusions when struck in the right shoulder by fragments of a dynamited bridge. Why, at his age and with his star standing, would he be performing his own stunts, as he did in *Return to Paradise*?

In May, he went to the Cannes Film Festival, and took up with French actress Gisele Pascal, who'd been a passing interest of Prince Rainier III of Monaco. He denied any long-range plans with the beautiful brunette, stating he was already married. To prove the point, Maria and Rocky joined him in Paris the following month. The Coopers were inching their way toward a reconciliation. One of the most sanguine indications was the fulfilling of Maria's lifelong ambition when the three had a private audience with Pope Pius XII.

In July, after scoring a Broadway success in *The Children's Hour*, Patricia Neal was married to British writer Roald Dahl, whom she'd met at a Sunday evening dinner party given by Lillian Hellman.

The Coopers continued their European holiday by joining other celebrities on a junket to Madrid for the grand opening of the Hilton Hotel. Radie Harris informed the actor of Pat's wedding. "Gary's face whitened, and suddenly there was no light in his eyes, as if a switch had been turned off," Miss Harris wrote. "Then very quietly he said, 'I hope he's a helluva guy. She deserves nothing but the best.' "

Cooper stayed on in Europe, while Rocky and

Maria returned to California. In November, he returned from Paris and moved back into the family home.

When Harrison Carroll of the *Los Angeles Herald Express* called Rocky for a statement, she responded, "We don't like announcements. What we have decided to do in our minds is our personal business, we feel. Gary is staying home. You can put any interpretation on it that you like."

If this was a reconciliation, it was short-lived, for Cooper left within a week to start filming his next picture, *Garden of Evil*, in Mexico. His wife and daughter planned to join him at Christmas.

Uruapan, Mexico, was the site of the location shooting, as well as an early donnybrook. Cooper was involved in a movie fight with costars Richard Widmark and Cameron Mitchell. The simulated battle turned into a real fight, leaving the two other actors nursing assorted cuts and bruises, and Cooper the worst off with a sprained wrist, black eye, and cut lip. Combined with the volatile Susan Hayward's redheaded temper, odds were against maintaining a happy set. There were other ways for Cooper to fritter away his time.

When a fan magazine columnist noticed the conspicuous wedding band on his finger, Cooper explained, "Just spent some time at home." He wouldn't confirm that a reconciliation had actually taken place. The nature of his arrangement with Rocky was explained away by a laconic, "We get along."

His name was linked a few days later with San Antonio model Lorraine Chanel, working as an extra in the picture. Cooper denied any plans to divorce his wife and marry the girl.

He told International News Service, "Yes, I take Lorraine out . . . among others." When asked if he and his wife would reconcile, Cooper almost in self-defense answered, "Yes."

The making of the picture with Henry Hathaway, after so much extracurricular activity, seemed anticli-

mactic. Cooper's eighty-first film, his first in Cinema-
Scope and his second for Twentieth-Century Fox,
starred the spectacular Mexican scenery.

Cooper's third film to be shot in Mexico during
this two-year period had its origins during the making
of *Return to Paradise* when Roberta Haynes took him
over to an adjoining Pacific island to introduce him to
Burt Lancaster, then starring in *His Majesty O'Keefe*.

Vera Cruz was greeted with vilification and loath-
ing when it first appeared in 1954, as if in depicting
amorality it were itself tainted. Bosley Crowther snorted
in *The New York Times*, "What we have is a wild and
endless scramble of cheaters on one hand and hijackers
on the other, shooting, stabbing, fighting for the
money—and occasionally for a girl. . . . There is
nothing to redeem this film . . . loaded with meaningless violence . . . the whole picture appears to be designed as a mere exhibition of how wicked and vicious
men can be."

What Crowther didn't grasp was that in director
Robert Aldrich's films meaningless violence is never
meaningless. It mingles with bizarre camera angles and
harsh transitions to form a picture of a decadent, disor-
dered world. Aldrich continues to be criticized for amorality and sensationalism, whatever the context.

Cooper, while leading a charge of 500 extras up a
hill, continued to be accident-prone, being hit in the left
shoulder when an extra's Winchester fired accidentally
and discharged the wadding from a blank shell. Lancaster, the villain of the piece, but also the picture's producer, gave his costar the rest of the day off.

The general tone of *Vera Cruz*, while it appalled
many of the critics of the time, anticipates Italian director Sergio Leone's "spaghetti Westerns" starring Clint
Eastwood. It's also a major influence on Sam Peckin-
pah's notorious *The Wild Bunch,* down to identical
scenes, shots, and the casting of Ernest Borgnine.

The film made in the neighborhood of $5 million
domestically, which was extremely good business in

1954. The public, as Adolph Zukor maintained, is never wrong.

After being separated for nearly four years, Cooper and Rocky officially reconciled when he returned from filming in Mexico. The entire family spent the summer in Southampton, as they had in years past, and returned to Brentwood in the fall.

"If all women had the good sense of Mrs. Gary Cooper," Louella Parsons wrote, "fewer marriages would end in the divorce courts. Rocky was sure Gary would come back to her even when he moved into a hotel and was in Mexico so long, and she waited until he decided that home was the place he wanted most to be."

The actor was able to spend considerable time at home during the making of his next picture, *The Court Martial of Billy Mitchell*, which crackled during the courtroom scenes but otherwise fizzled. This would be his last enactment of a real-life character.

He remained close to hearth and home in every respect as he made his next picture early in 1956. *Friendly Persuasion,* based on the Jessamyn West novel, had been planned by Frank Capra as a Paramount picture starring Bing Crosby and Jean Arthur. It would be shot in the novel's southern Indiana setting at a cost of $1.5 million. The project passed on to William Wyler, who took it with him to Allied Artists. The picture, completed at a cost of $3 million, was mostly shot in the San Fernando Valley.

Working again with Wyler, Cooper has one of his best latter-day parts in a family picture saturated with quality. The book was based on the experiences of an actual Quaker family during the Civil War. Cooper is excellent as a family man threatened anew with the violation of his principles, handling the coy comedy and the somber intensity of his role with equal skill. Dorothy McGuire as his wife counterpoints Cooper's delivery in this Quaker household. When compelled to explain to a neighbor about a family quarrel, he announces, with all the dignity possible, "Eliza has taken up residence in the barn."

In a bit of inspired casting, Anthony Perkins was given the role of Cooper's son. His lanky frame, spindly stance, and tentative, fleeting facial expressions made him a natural for the part of a blood relative of Cooper's.

The picture's gentle values slowly caught on, so that by 1960, its worldwide gross exceeded $8 million.

Its star was not proving to be as oriented to the domestic life as the Quaker father of the piece. Cooper was filming the picture when he met a Scandinavian actress at a social gathering, and whisked her away for the rest of the night. A correspondent for an exposé magazine of the period followed them and, shortly thereafter, an article about the encounter was published, giving a minute-by-minute account from their meeting to when the lights were turned off at their point of assignation.

"They must have followed me with a stopwatch," Cooper said, off the record, to columnist James Bacon. He'd also had a brief fling with Barbara Payton, a supporting player in *Dallas*, in the midst of his affair with Patricia Neal. Among certain friends, the quickest way to prove he was a man's man was to show he was a devil with the ladies. That these were no ladies, and that Cooper seemed to be indulging himself in a final burst of sexual excess, was a disturbing sign to at least one of his socialite friends.

"What I didn't like," she said, "is that he was associating with a different class of women . . . the broads. That says something to me. There was still a tremendous sex drive in him which couldn't be satisfied with just one woman. That he no longer used discretion to protect his family seems very sad."

Chapter 11

In the late fifties and well into the sixties, several men, middle-aged and beyond, remained great film stars and retained their romantic appeal. Their durable popularity resulted in their being cast in love stories opposite actresses young enough to be their daughters.

Gary Cooper hadn't played such roles as yet, but a film project being dangled before him sounded intriguing. It was *Love in the Afternoon*. He would be working with Billy Wilder, the screenwriter of two of his past pictures, who would be directing this romantic comedy based on *Ariane* by Claude Anet.

Cooper knew he wasn't Wilder's first choice for the role opposite the ethereal Audrey Hepburn. But Wilder's perception of the picture had been drastically changed as he and writer I. A. L. Diamond worked on the screenplay.

Wilder at first wanted Cary Grant to play the international playboy who became romantically involved with a young music student. When he was unavailable, Wilder and Diamond began thinking of Yul Brynner in the part and Aly Khan, the playboy prince, as its real-life inspiration.

Doris Vidor, a leading hostess of Hollywood who often entertained Aly Khan, agreed to offer Wilder and Diamond her impressions. When she met with Diamond, she said that Aly Khan was "charming." Pressed further, she said he was charming in "many ways." He knew about Paris styles, horses, and . . . "To tell you the truth," Mrs. Vidor concluded, "Aly Khan is a fucking bore!"

Wilder and Diamond promptly switched to Howard Hughes as the model for the character—and that is when they decided to go after Gary Cooper. Cooper was available, and the part would be a nice change of pace. He was also attracted to the project because it was to be filmed in Paris, one of his favorite cities.

On the face of it, his casting did not come from out of left field. Cooper affected many of the trappings in his private life one would associate with a wolfish roué. His wardrobe bore such labels as Brioni, Gucci, Charvet, and Turnbull and Asser; his casual infidelities were real-life credentials he could bring to the enterprise.

Once again Cooper was to sally forth into seamy Billy Wilder territory, playing another Bluebeard hotly pursuing the fair heroine. But he was too old for such capers, and made the audience uncomfortable. Once again he was subjugated by the wiles of a scheming, determined female.

At the outset, Wilder realized he was going to have problems. One scene called on Cooper to perform a ballroom dance routine. The director, an old Viennese tea dancer, personally put the actor through his paces before the cameras rolled. Cooper proved to have two left feet. He was graceless and self-conscious. "Old Hopalong Nijinsky," Wilder fondly called him.

Of greater concern was Cooper's aging face. The director tried several types of subterfuge. Gauzy filters, usually used with aging movie queens, were brought in. Cooper's face was often shot in shadow. Scenes were shot with the camera behind his shoulder. Fortunately, much of the action took place at an apartment in the Ritz Hotel, and shooting through gauze created a consistent photographic style.

The most jarring aspect of Cooper's performance,

however, was that he was straining to feel comfortable in the part, instead of trying to fit it, and he gave the impression that his shirt collar was too tight. The rare time when the casting seems appropriate comes when he is described as having an American face "like a cowboy or Abraham Lincoln."

Nevertheless, Cooper brought an educated flair to the role, nimbly handling the witty lines of Wilder and his new coscenarist I. A. L. Diamond, a partnership which continued with *Some Like It Hot, The Apartment, Irma La Douce,* and *The Fortune Cookie.*

Bosley Crowther raved about the picture's gossamer charm, stating that a new pedestal alongside that of Lubitsch should be erected for Billy Wilder. A more typical reaction came in an unsigned review in *Cue* magazine. Wilder was accused of miscasting "long, lanky, lethargic, leathery, and (let's be frank about it) no longer youthful Gary Cooper as a gay young dog, an international Don Juan, a prowling libertine of the boulevards, a gal-chasing gent with a sweetheart in every hotel in Europe and in ports most sailors never even heard of. Neither in appearance nor performance is Gary the type. Let's face it!"

Wilder, in retrospect, agreed. "But there was more to it than that. The role of the playboy tarnished Cooper's image. In most people's eyes, he was still thought of as the virtuous sheriff and they didn't relish seeing him messing around with a young girl."

The negative reviews didn't reflect so much on Cooper as an actor but as a man. To be dismissed as a man of fading appeal and waning sexuality, when this was not yet the case, was grossly inaccurate. The picture was successful enough, however, to place Cooper on the Top Ten list of box office stars for the eighteenth time. No other star could match that record.

More accurately reflecting his actual life was the picture he would next star in.

With his and Rocky's reconciliation, the rebellious, prodigal husband had returned to his wife's all-encompassing fold. Now, more than ever, the family would do Rocky's bidding. If he subjugated himself, it was a sacrifice he made for Maria's happiness.

Husband, wife, and daughter became a familiar, inseparable threesome at social events and public affairs. Cooper totally catered to his pretty daughter, yet she remained curiously unspoiled. He was delighted that he could take her, Rocky, and Mrs. Shields to Europe in 1956 to meet Pablo Picasso, an acquaintance of Hemingway's. As a gift to his host, the actor took Picasso a Western six-shooter and cowboy hat.

Maria, having inherited the looks of both parents, had grown into a beautiful young woman. In the midst of a hedonistic world, she was a devout and reserved anachronism. Young men who came calling felt she was too much in love with her father, and they paled by comparison.

Cooper wanted an active social life for Maria, he informed Hedda Hopper, but the movie colony didn't seem the proper place in which to have it. "Actually, this is a real square town when it comes to going to parties," he said. "That's the reason I like to take Maria East where they mix a bit. At school parties here these little knotheads dance only with their own dates all night long. There's no such thing as a stag line or cutting in. It's stupid."

Cooper preferred the young men at Southampton as escorts for his daughter. "They come from families who've been coming there for years. You see kids of all sizes from toddlers on up . . . very nice families. Seem to have more family life there than you get anywhere out here."

He also didn't mix well with the old California society of Los Angeles which predated the movie industry. "The only time you ever hear from them is when they're raising funds. They say, 'You're wonderful! Why don't we see more of you picture people?' Frankly, most of them are a pretty dull bunch. . . . Truth is they don't really like picture people, and I don't think that picture crowds like to have much to do with them. I remember when I first came out here, I was invited to a socialite's house in Pasadena, and before the evening was over I got loaded in self-defense."

When Rocky decided that the Brentwood house was too large for the family to handle, Cooper agreed they could build in Holmby Hills, next door to the Bill Goetzes. His wife traded her Georgian house with its period interiors for contemporary architecture and furnishings.

Cooper, in describing the reasons for moving from the Brentwood house, said, "Rocky . . . has always liked modern architecture. From start to finish our new house . . . is almost all her own idea. One story high, with Palo Verde stone walls, and so advanced in outline that we sometimes wonder if we're in the year 2000. But it sure is designed for living."

"It was funny seeing him in that house," Tab Hunter said. "The house was very chic and modern, with marble floors and Picasso paintings, and Rocky was so pulled together. You'd see Coop maybe sitting there in a robe and slippers. He looked like he didn't belong."

Cooper claimed that he did, and that his chasing days were over. "Girls don't go on the make for me," he admitted to Hedda Hopper, "and I don't go on the make for girls. I live a quiet life now . . . spend my evenings reading." He wasn't painting much, since it was no longer a joint family hobby. Rocky had quit altogether. Only Maria persisted. After graduation from Marymount, she began serious study at the Chouinard Art Institute. Maria developed into a notable painter of still lifes and seascapes.

Cooper's domestic situation was reflected in *Ten North Frederick*, his next film. Director Philip Dunne, who also wrote the screenplay, took out the elements of John O'Hara's novel and inserted some that bore disturbing resemblances to Cooper, Rocky, and Patricia Neal.

The wife in the novel didn't encourage her husband's Presidential ambitions, yet she went along with them. The girl was a one-night stand.

Dunne changed the emphasis to make the ambitious, pushing wife a total shrew, played by Geraldine Fitzgerald. Cooper falls in love with a girl played by Suzy Parker, but they separate because of the great difference in their ages. The promiscuous daughter was turned into a confused girl with ambivalent feelings about her father.

Spencer Tracy turned down the Twentieth-Century Fox picture, and Cooper stepped into the role. One wonders why.

Stuart Whitman, a newcomer to films, had a featured role in *Ten North Frederick*. He recalled how closely Cooper worked with Suzy Parker, an inexperienced actress, who would be delivering the best performance of her brief career.

Whitman was also impressed with the solicitous way Cooper treated him. Cooper asked Whitman if the producers were treating him right. "I'd been running into cutthroats all my life," Whitman said. "I'd had experiences with other actors who even resent it if you're taller. This guy was completely different. Cooper had no hostility toward another attractive man."

As for the real-life parallels to Cooper in the script, Whitman observed, "As actors we all do those kinds of things. We fill our wells one way or another. Then it's right there at the tip of our emotions."

Whitman said Cooper's ability to be totally natural is the most difficult thing for an actor to accomplish, "It's much easier to hide behind a mask. To play oneself is very difficult, and I don't feel comfortable just playing myself. It's more exciting to hide behind a character. That's the training I had."

When he was under contract at Twentieth, a studio executive advised him, "Get closer to you." Buddy Adler, who headed the studio, advised him to do the same. "You've got a lovely personality," he told Whitman. "If you could just bring that across instead of hiding behind these characters like you're doing."

"That's what I see when I read these roles," Whitman said. "I see they're characters. They're not me."

"Well," Adler concluded, "you'll be a bigger star if you do."

Whitman felt Cooper's ability to project his own personality was a form of great acting he could never master. "Cooper was a great one. He was spellbinding . . . a big personality. I admire that ability. I can't do it. It requires a total lack of inhibition."

The picture slops off on the wrong soap-operatic foot early on, as we open on Cooper's funeral and listen to his son and daughter discuss his character. The rest of the film is an extended flashback, with Cooper maintaining his powerful but unprepossessing presence, as the character he plays is walked on and ignored beyond all reason. He manages to bring to some of the scenes the only depth and feeling they contain, as in his half-hearted excuse to get away from his wife to dally with Suzy Parker. He conveys both relief and disappointment at the ease with which his ruse works. Other than the scenes delineating the affair, the film was tedious.

Bosley Crowther wrote, "As an isolated observation of a middle-aged man's pathetic try to get a little love from a sensitive young woman of a sort that he has evidently never known, this major component of the picture has considerable warmth and sympathy. It shows us an emotional experience in simple, clean, and generally credible terms. And because it is tastefully written and also intelligently played by Gary Cooper and Suzy Parker, it makes a happy episode in a hapless film."

According to the *Times* critic, when the romance is played out, "the hero is allowed to die, with a passing indication that his life has been one towering irony.

"The point is weak and unsatisfactory. Mr. Cooper makes too gracious an old boy to be knocked about so unkindly by what appears nothing more than the long arm of coincidence. . . .

"As for the lovely Miss Parker, she is remarkably good in the role of the girl who is strongly attracted to the lonely middle-aged man. . . . She is a subtle, intelligent, sensitive soul. Miss Parker underplays her neatly. She's the one character you begin to understand. . . . Geraldine Fitzgerald is bloodless and bitchy as the wife whom some odd fury eats upon."

It was a movie that wouldn't presume to succeed and a role Cooper wouldn't dare to play well. The parallels were too close to his own life. Its message, though melodramatic, was unnerving. If you can't have the woman you love, you get sick and then you die.

Man of the West is generally considered Cooper's last great film. Though less well known than *High Noon, Friendly Persuasion*, and *Love in the Afternoon,* it establishes basic integrity and skillful intelligence in a distinguished, unspectacular way. Wrtten by Reginald Rose, author of *Twelve Angry Men,* it was based on a novel by Will C. Brown.

Coming to Hollywood by way of Broadway, director Anthony Mann made an abundance of cult favorites which are studied today as classics of the genre of the sophisticated Western. Many were made at Universal. He turned to superspectacles in the early sixties with *El Cid* and *The Fall of the Roman Empire.* Mann is noted for brilliant exterior shooting and for creating characters of prodigious strengths who extend themselves even beyond their natural reach. Driven by divine force or by insanity, they reject the pull of a settled life to satisfy the powerful urges churning inside of them. The conflict between passion and duty was the basis for many of his better pictures.

Cooper's one film with Mann is one of his best, and one of that director's best as well. *Man of the West* tells about a man who tries to reject his vicious, violent past, but finds it not easy to smother what he once was.

Cooper is ideal as the supposedly good man on a journey of civic virtue who suddenly turns out to be an ex-member of Lee J. Cobb's gang. The ambiguity inherent in the script is reflected in the look Cooper gives Cobb on seeing him for the first time in years—admiration, regret, and utter hatred all manage to appear on his face in the same look. We know before

Cobb has entered the story that Cooper is reluctant to talk about something in his past, by his expression and the things he *doesn't* say. Only late in the picture do we find out it's an inescapable tension that dominates his life.

As in many of Mann's films, the villain represents an aspect of the hero's own psyche which he wishes to purge. Purging it and indulging it are the same thing. To perform the act he must awaken the instincts he least wants to awaken.

The conflict suffuses all the action in the movie. As Cooper stalks Cobb and one of Cobb's men, and is in turn stalked by them through the empty streets of a ghost town, it is part of Cooper's inner struggle to avoid any tactics but the honorable ones. He is burdened by the traditional baggage of the Western hero, while the two weasels he's up against are free of any such scruples. Mann ends the showdown with a characteristically magnificent use of landscape in CinemaScope vistas. Cobb refuses to surrender to Cooper and taunts him with the necessity of killing him. They are just beyond the ghost town, and at the point where Cobb begins to look like a ghost, Cooper tells him he is one.

"A Western is a wonderful thing to do," Mann has said, "because you take a group of actors who have acted on the stage or who have acted in rooms and now you take them out into the elements, and you throw them against the elements and the elements make them much greater as actors than if they were in a room. Because they have to shout above the winds, they have to suffer, they have to climb mountains."

Time Magazine, reviewing *Ten North Frederick,* pointed out, "1) Suzy Parker is a charming young actress and 2) Gary Cooper is getting a little old (fifty-seven) for love scenes."

In mid-April 1958, Gary Cooper checked into Manhattan Eye, Ear and Throat Hospital, registered as Frank James. The surgeon performing the cosmetic surgery was Dr. John Converse.

Cooper, noted for his leathery, weather-beaten looks, decided to transform himself into a more youthful Marlboro man. He'd exposed himself to the elements for years, and the resultant appearance was an intrinsic part of his appeal. So why alter that?

"Toward the end of his life," Tab Hunter said, "maybe he was regretting his choices. Free will is very important. Your wants are going to make you fat, physically and spiritually. Coop didn't seem like he wanted a great deal out of life. Maybe Cooper had an aggressiveness about his career at the beginning. Once you do it so long, you actually become that character, and sometimes you lose your identity in that character. And once you have it, now what? Perhaps it wasn't really all worth it. Once he got there, he realized this wasn't what he really wanted."

Roberta Haynes observed, "A lot of reviewers said that he was an old man in *Love in the Afternoon*. I don't know if it's actor ego or not. I think it's just people ego. That was very early. A lot of men now are doing it. As an actor it was probably a good thing to do. I think he cared very much about his appearance. He was always thin. He never let himself get heavy. It was very hard to be suddenly told you're an old man, when you're not even sixty."

Some press reports had it that Cooper had actually been treated for a stomach ulcer, but an eye, ear, and throat hospital was an unlikely place to go for relief.

If one didn't look too closely, Cooper was actually looking very fit, having dropped his weight from 206 to 180.

He had suffered many injuries on movie sets, including the impairment of hearing in his left ear because of a too-close dynamite blast. His last serious incapacity was for a fourth hernia operation, caused by lifting a heavy teakwood bench while on location in Samoa.

Cooper was sufficiently recovered to take the family to the Bahamas that summer, where they took up skin diving. Joining them were Mr. and Mrs. Henry

Ford II. The industrialist's wife, Anne, had gone to school with Rocky in the East, and they'd remained close friends.

When the family returned to California, Cooper admitted to Hedda Hopper that he was largely disinterested in the offers he'd recently received.

"I've taken acting seriously," he said. "I'm not very good. You've got to have a fire under you. When you're new, a beginner, you've got a fire under you all the time. Now when I read stories I think I've read these same lines before. And when I read them I try to keep in mind whether or not it would sell at the box office. Pictures run in cycles. I like to do something different but not to startle the world with an artistic floperoo. I just want to do something that isn't running in every other theater."

The Hanging Tree, though designed as a psychological Western with Cooper playing a doctor, was substantially below the standards set by his recent Westerns. The film was the first for his own independent company, Baroda Productions, named after the street on which Cooper lived. The location in Yakima, Washington, took on the look of an infirmary. Cooper's bad hip caused him great pain, and he couldn't film several riding scenes. Delmer Daves was felled by an ulcer in the last week of shooting, and Karl Malden—playing the villain—filled in for the director.

Cooper resumed his professional association with Bill Goetz in *They Came to Cordura*, which was filmed by Columbia. Shooting took place in and around St. George, Utah.

While many critics found Cooper too old to play the cowardly officer who takes charge of a band of social outcasts, costar Tab Hunter found Cooper to be totally admirable.

"What impressed me about Coop," Hunter said, "was the way he would go off by himself. There was a lot of confusion, and for a star to be able to detach himself from all that was something. Robert Rossen was the director. It wasn't his type of film, really. He had more on his mind. His next project was *The Hustler,* which turned out to be sensational."

Occasionally, while waiting for bad weather to clear, the cast and crew would play cards. Late one afternoon, as Hunter recalled, Cooper stood up and slowly stretched.

"Okay," the director called out. "Wrap it up."

Driving back to their hotel together, Cooper asked Hunter, "Why did we wrap up so early? I can't believe it."

"Well, you did it, Coop. You're the one who did the wrapping."

"*I* did that?"

"Sure," Hunter said. "All you did was stand up and stretch, and they figured you were ready to quit for the day."

Unlike his experience with Mark Robson in *Return to Paradise,* his every word—and gesture—was law.

They Came to Cordura, a $5 million production, was not a successful film. Edie Goetz said it was twenty years ahead of its time.

"I feel Rossen wasn't the right director for that," Hunter said. "This was about men who were going to receive medals, but they were all despicable. We never really delved into the characters enough. It was all too surface. The first fifteen minutes, with a cavalry charge, was really done well. You think you're going to see something. Then it fell apart. Bill Goetz produced much finer films than that.

"Coop was a lovely guy. His sense of humor was kind of within. He'd do something he knew was funny. He laughed inwardly. It was a delight! He'd say things, then chuckle within himself. He was wonderful, low-key, like Fred Astaire, an absolute gentleman. These are quality, quality people. They have their own atmosphere about them. Coop's was very laid back and easy. Sure he was a study. He probably had a lot of honey to spread around."

Hunter felt Cooper retained "that down-home

quality which is so sensational. When people have been in Hollywood too long they get kind of jaded. They dazzle you with their footwork. Coop was Coop . . . a wonderful presence. It was felt although he never asserted any kind of authority.

"Coop as an actor was so natural, so easy. But I know he had tensions. Today, when you're getting ready to go on in a play, they ask you, 'How can you be so relaxed?' You say, 'Do you want to see the X-rays of my ulcer?'"

Hunter escorted Cooper's daughter about town for a short time. "When you took Maria out on a date, she was very held back and suppressed. Maria was a very pretty girl. She needed to give vent. She was a late-bloomer. Some colts take longer to develop. Her mother wanted so much for her, only the best. I don't think she ever allowed Maria her freedom. Maria was always walking on egg shells, afraid to make a mistake. Coop went along with it. I'm sure he felt this was what one should do."

Hunter ran into the two women in Rome after Maria's marriage to concert pianist Byron Janis. "She blossomed. She was *entirely* different."

Tab Hunter admits his relationship with Rocky wasn't smooth. "I like ballsy women, but when they get to be too aggressive, it bothers me. I used to find myself saying, 'Yes, you're right.' It finally went against my grain, because I knew it wasn't true. One day, I said to Rocky, 'That's a bunch of shit!' She stopped and looked at me. She said, 'Well, maybe you're right.' We had an entirely different rapport after that."

On April 9, 1959, Cooper further yielded to the desires of his wife and daughter by converting to Catholicism at the Church of the Good Shepherd in Beverly Hills. He'd been taking instruction there from the Reverend Harold Ford. His conversion was announced by Radio Vatican.

Mrs. Alice Cooper wasn't pleased. "Gary will always be a Protestant," she stated, "no matter what other religious influences enter in his life."

Even without her publicized opinion, Cooper had great doubts about his decision, which he confessed to Ernest Hemingway. Hemingway himself was a "miserable, failed Catholic," yet he'd taken no official steps to sever his relationship with the church and would ultimately have a Catholic funeral.

"It'll probably turn out all right," Hemingway told Cooper. "I believe in belief."

Chapter 12

The fifties, with the exception of the singular *High Noon*, had largely consisted of middling successes for Gary Cooper. His last picture of the decade, *The Wreck of the Mary Deare*, would follow the norm. It was a verbose tale of an aging ship's captain improbably involved in underwater combat. Vigorous Charlton Heston was more believable in the story about the recovery of a sunken treasure. Much of the action took place in a courtroom conducting an inquiry into the affair. Directed by Michael Anderson, it was an uneven film, but did well at the box office, largely due to the popularity of the two stars.

In November 1959, the Coopers went to Russia on a six-day tour of Moscow and Leningrad. When Russian Premier Nikita Khrushchev had visited Hollywood in September, he'd personally invited the Coopers to visit Russia.

Such a trip was unthinkable five years before. Gregori Alexandrov, the great Soviet film director, had wanted Cooper to make a movie in Russia. The State Department urged Cooper to do so. The actor refused. "The whole thing is a wild dream and impossible with the government that now exists in Russia," he stated. "They say they like us today; maybe they won't tomorrow. I certainly would not want to be associated with

241

anything that would be used for Communist propaganda."

Now, however, the political climate had changed, and it was innocuous enough to accept an invitation for the premiere of an American film, *Marty*, in a Russian theater.

Cooper was slowing down, and while he'd always conserved his energies on the set, he was taking life easier than ever. He hadn't been feeling sick, but he was easily enervated. He wasn't as interested in pursuing social life with Rocky when they returned from Russia, and it was even difficult for him to indulge his most enduring passion—outdoor life.

Cooper, physicians said later, suffered all his life from a "weak ring" in the lining of his intestines. His great physical exertions, either before the cameras or during the hunting and fishing he loved, were directly responsible for his many hernias. It wasn't out of the ordinary for him to be feeling similar pain in April 1960. Rocky and Maria were with him when he underwent prostate gland surgery at Massachusetts General Hospital in Boston. They were also by his side in Los Angeles a short time later when part of his colon was removed.

His health had declined precipitously, but he and his family didn't confirm to each other the gnawing fear in their minds.

His ailments forced Cooper to turn down Fred Zinnemann's offer to star opposite Deborah Kerr in *The Sundowners*, to be filmed in Australia. Robert Mitchum took over the part and got the best acting notices of his career.

The weeks of recuperation gave Cooper plenty of time to think. All was quiet on the domestic front. He and his wife had gone through many turmoils, together and apart, and after these crises, they were still together after twenty-seven years of marriage. What he could change was the roles he would accept in the future. With very few exceptions, his films of the last several years were uninspired and he was uninspiring. That might change with his next picture.

Before starting it, Cooper worked with Leonard Slater on an article for *McCall's* magazine, which would be published the following January. "Nothing I've done lately, the past eight years or so, has been especially worthwhile," he said. "I've been coasting along. Some of the pictures I've made recently I'm genuinely sorry about. Either I did a sloppy job in them, or the story wasn't right. I can't blame anybody else for the stories that didn't come off. If I don't get fired up about a story, why should the audience? I have to take a personal interest in my work to make it believable. And yet I can't force an interest in a character if the story has holes in it that make it illogical or unsound. When I get talked into the project I don't believe in, I'm the one who's wrong—not the fellow who does the talking. . . .

"I intend to take care of myself from now on, so that I can be around a while. As an actor, I want to do something better than I've ever done."

He'd had a long run of stardom. His financial picture, thanks to his father-in-law Paul Shields, was so sound that he could have retired years ago with an impressive body of work to look back on. Gary Cooper, arguably, starred in more classic films and more popular heart-stirring pictures than any other major star in the history of films—*The Winning of Barbara Worth, Wings, The Virginian, Morocco, City Streets, A Farewell to Arms, The Lives of a Bengal Lancer, Mr. Deeds Goes to Town, Sergeant York, The Pride of the Yankees, High Noon, Friendly Persuasion,* and *Man of the West.*

True, his recent films weren't as good, but neither they nor their star deserved the contempt Cooper was heaping on them. He'd said he wasn't an actor so many times that he began to believe it. But an actor he was, and he was as ambitious now to show the product of a lifetime of professional training as he'd been to get into films as a raw and gangling recruit. Cooper yearned to continue his career, and it was the actor himself as the producer who talked him into the new project.

Cooper went to London in the fall to star with Deborah Kerr in *The Naked Edge,* a project for his own Baroda Productions, in which Cooper halved his usual acting fee to $275,000. He would in addition share half of the picture's profits with Pennebaker Productions. Because Marlon Brando was a substantial owner of the latter company's stock, Marlon Brando, Sr., was installed as executive producer. Walter Boxer and George Glass were hired to actually supervise production activity. In this way, Cooper was freed from the onerous business dealings he detested.

Based on Max Ehrlich's novel, *First Train to Babylon,* the plot was roughly similar to Alfred Hitchcock's *Suspicion*: a wife suspects her American businessman husband of being a murderer on the loose. The film could have been the change of pace Cooper thought would lead to greater acting triumphs, but no matter how accomplished an actor he'd become, the public still would not accept Cooper as a sinister figure.

Cooper didn't know this would be the posthumous reaction to his performance, but he was nevertheless looking ahead to portraying a role more in the heroic mold.

A. E. Hotchner went to London as Hemingway's representative to negotiate the film sale of *Across the River and into the Trees.* During the 1958 hunting season in Ketchum, the possibility of Cooper's starring in the picture was broached. Hemingway told Cooper, "Good idea. You'd just be playing Robert Jordan ten years older."

There were now some reservations. First, Hemingway had never heard of Cooper's suggested costar, Sophia Loren. Then there was the matter of Cooper himself. "Coops sounds fine," Hemingway told Hotchner about a recent telephone conversation. "From what he says, I don't think they tipped him [about] the black spot on the prostate. Do you think he's too old to play Colonel Cangwell?"

If Hotchner felt Cooper wouldn't be able to undergo the strain of another film, he didn't let on. He came to an agreement, with contracts to be drawn up in Hollywood upon Cooper's return.

The Coopers, Maria included, spent nine weeks at London's Savoy Hotel while the movie, to be distributed by United Artists, was filmed at Elstree Studios. They took as much free time as possible, his duties on the picture and his health notwithstanding, to go to the theater and visit friends in the estate country. Mostly, Cooper had to conserve his strength for the film. He worked five days a week from 8:15 in the morning until six every night. In photographs taken on the set, the haunted look on Rocky's face showed the great strain she was under. It wasn't lessened when her husband began complaining about a pain in his neck.

He finished the picture, however, and returned to California in December with plans for several projects. In addition to the Hemingway film, he'd signed a three-picture deal with United Artists, the first a story about Madison Avenue and the magazine world, based on Theodore White's *The View from the Fortieth Floor*. He also wanted to narrate a television special on the West.

Joe Hyams interviewed him in London. Cooper conceded he would probably never star in another Western, but there were many misconceptions that should be corrected in the plethora of outdoor series cluttering the television airwaves. Even his past successes were lacking, for "the public has been fed a false concept of the West for so long I don't think they'll accept anything authentic.

"This worries me because kids around the world are growing up thinking one man will always ride into town to fight their battles while the rest of the community sits on its collective hands.

"In most of the television shows and Western movies I've done, the hero is a kind of father-figure who fights alone for justice against the entire commu-

245

nity. Humanity and decent human nature are always on the short end. . . .

"It also gives them the wrong picture of violence which should only be the last extreme of settling a problem rather than the first and only way. The fact is the real West was actually populated by pioneers with guts—many of them with brains, too—and the gunmen were parasites. . . .

"What's happened now is that movies and TV have made a uniform out of the cowboy's colorful character and put him in a background of Chicago and New York gangsterism. Only the costumes are Western.

"I know I've contributed my share to the false picture. . . . What we tried to do was glamorize the period but that didn't give us the dramatic license to knock down humanity. There was no excuse for that and I don't like it."

As if to contradict everything the White Knight of the West found distasteful, the Board of Supervisors declared December 13 "Gary Cooper Day" in Los Angeles County. The actor was a visual contradiction himself, advocating realism while eschewing it in the nips, tucks, and tints on his remodeled head.

Pete Martin of *The Saturday Evening Post* called on Cooper during this period. "His face was seamed and lined," he wrote about the precosmeticized actor. "When he walked in, a piece of the West walked in with him. I liked those seams and lines . . . [now] the seams were gone. Somebody—perhaps a plastic surgeon, although he denied it—had ironed them out. And his hair was a kind of orangy light brown. It wasn't a good dye job. But the voice that came out of that unseamed face was the same voice that had said, 'Nobody wants to read about me.' It gave me a weird feeling."

That same distinctive, hesitant voice was effectively deployed in "The Real West," a documentary for the National Broadcasting Company's *Project 20* series. Cooper narrated a script about a time before the West was glamorized by dime novels, Hollywood, and television.

Because of the persisting pains in his neck, Cooper was put into traction. Then the news came from Dr. Rexford Kennamer that cancer had spread throughout his body.

How long it took Cooper to discover his disease was terminal is open to conjecture. Adela Rogers St. Johns, in writing about the Friars Club testimonial which honored Cooper in early January, said only three members of the audience knew: Rocky, Maria, and Dr. Kennamer.

Yet, Cooper's words of thanks poignantly echoed those of Lou Gehrig in *The Pride of the Yankees*. They suggested what he sensed even though it may not have been as yet confirmed. "I want to thank each and every one of you for coming here tonight. Never has so much fuss been made by so many over so little. The only achievement I am really proud of is the friends I have made in the community."

Young Dr. Kennamer had never been required to tell a patient that he was dying. His agitation was obvious as he told Cooper. The actor remained composed. Then he said comfortingly, "It must be terrible for you to have to tell someone that."

Cooper called him later at his office. "Young fellow," he said. "I know you were a little nervous about telling me the news. I just want you to know that I appreciate it."

Cooper signed his last will and testament on February 27, 1961. The bulk of the estate, later to be valued in excess of $3.5 million, would go to his wife and daughter. To his mother, he left life-time use of the house in which his parents had lived for many years, as well as $600 a month for ordinary living expenses. Executors would have discretionary powers to adjust that income if it was needed.

Other bequests were modest. His brother, Arthur, and his two children were left $5,000 each, and the Motion Picture Country House and Hospital was willed $10,000.

Rocky, as one of the executors, was excluded from

discretionary powers involving Mrs. Alice Cooper, but attorney Deane F. Johnson, a member of one of Los Angeles' most prestigious Old Guard law firms, was not.

The Coopers went to Miami for the March 13 heavyweight championship fight between Floyd Patterson and Ingemar Johansson. Cobalt therapy had begun when announcement of his honorary Oscar was made. This was followed by his final performance on March 29 with the television airing of *The Real West*. Cooper's simple, sincere delivery was singled out for praise by television critics. They weren't aware of the pain he'd undergone to leave one last legacy. He was only able to work on the project a few hours at a time before the pain forced him to go home and rest.

Hedda Hopper called to congratulate him on the show. "He didn't return the call for two days," she said. "I later learned he was too ill to talk. When he did he was delighted at the way I felt about the show and said he'd dreamed of doing it for many years."

Whenever he was able, the Coopers continued to go out among their friends. Bill and Edie Goetz asked them to dinner one night. Cooper showed no indication of the pain he was suffering. He started sweating profusely and put his hand to his neck, excusing himself early to go home to bed.

Easter Sunday fell on April 2 that year, and the Coopers were seen at Mass. Although he was scheduled to promote *The Naked Edge* on Dinah Shore's television variety show the following Sunday and was due to accept his Oscar the week following that, this was the last time Gary Cooper was seen in public.

Ernest Hemingway was at the Mayo Clinic, his ailment being diagnosed for the press as high blood pressure and "incipient diabetes." Delusions and fears, however, had led to a deteriorating mental condition, which would lead to his suicide on July 2. Hemingway called Cooper to tell him he was sick. Gary Cooper in turn informed Ernest Hemingway of his own death sentence.

They tried to buoy each other's spirits, trading empty talk about going hunting in the fall. "We'll get our butts wet again," Hemingway said.

Cooper knew that wasn't to be. "Papa, I bet I beat you back to the barn."

By the time the world was told of Cooper's condition, he was confined to his separate bedroom suite in the house on Baroda Drive.

President Kennedy called with words of appreciation and encouragement. From the Pope came a message through Cardinal Tardini, Secretary of State of the Vatican: "The Holy Father, fondly recalling the visit of Gary Cooper and his family, is grieved to learn of his illness and lovingly imparts a special apostolic blessing, the pledge of abundant comfort, and divine grace and favors."

Friends were still allowed to call.

Edie Goetz knew that the best medication is often laughter. She called Danny Kaye.

"Danny," she said, "dress crazy."

"I *am* dressed crazy," he replied. "Just came in from the baseball game."

"Then please get to the Coopers right away," she requested. When the comedian arrived, Mrs. Goetz was already there with the Coopers. Kaye improvised a comic routine, and Cooper *did* laugh.

Under the abnormal circumstances, he tried living as normally as possible. Cooper had never been an eloquent man, but there was something that still had to be said.

Rocky told writer Richard Gehman, "You know, Gary and I had a little trouble, ten years ago. It invariably comes up in articles, and I certainly have no plans to deny it. He left the house . . . but I don't think you could say we really were separated. During his last few weeks, Gary would say that the only thing he resented about his life was that year and a half of trouble. But by the same token, we both felt it made a much better marriage, better than it ever had been before."

Early in May, Fred Zinnemann returned from

Cannes. The French government had honored Cooper, and Zinnemann delivered the medal he had accepted in Cooper's behalf. Cooper could only smile his gratitude.

A. E. Hotchner was among Cooper's last visitors. Hemingway's friend found Cooper to be a wasted and immobile figure lying in a darkened room on a bed from which he would never again rise.

It was painful for Cooper to speak. He had to pause between words. He seemed to take pleasure in Hotchner's description of the previous hunting season in Ketchum, and his gossip about their mutual Idaho friends.

Cooper contorted in pain, and sweat poured out of him. When it eased, he reached over to the bedside table and picked up a crucifix. He placed it beside his head on the pillow.

"Please give Papa a message," he torturously said. "It's important and you mustn't forget because I'll not be talking to him again. Tell him, that time I wondered if I made the right decision—" He brought the crucifix to his cheek. "Tell him it was the best thing I ever did." Cooper was referring to his conversion to Catholicism.

At the end, only the women in his life were allowed to see him. Mrs. Alice Cooper joined Rocky and Maria every day for the vigil, bringing a rose from her garden. Two nurses watched over Cooper round the clock.

On Friday, May 12, Gary Cooper received the last rites of his church. He was heavily sedated when he quietly died at 12:27 P.M. on the following day, six days before his sixtieth birthday.

His friends had been sitting by their radios for days. The moment news of his passing was flashed, they gathered to comfort Rocky. Among the first were the Goetzes and James Stewart's wife, Gloria.

Dr. Kennamer, who'd been with the family when death came, told Mrs. Goetz, "Rocky has earned his place in heaven."

Within minutes, it seemed, before the press could congregate about the house, the body was carried by police out the rear of the house and to Cunningham and O'Connor Mortuary.

The world's newspapers on Sunday, May 14, bannered the death of Gary Cooper. Many of his films in the past had taken artistic license with the facts. Gary Cooper wouldn't have bridled at the inaccuracy of a headline in the *Sunday News*: HE LIVED AND DIED . . . AT HIGH NOON.

Epilogue

Every year since 1957 had been marked by the death of a great star . . . Humphrey Bogart, Tyrone Power, Errol Flynn, Clark Gable. Now, in 1961, Gary Cooper too had died. His widow, Veronica, did not want her husband's funeral to degenerate into the circus that had marked the other funerals. She asked the public to let her husband go to his rest with dignity and quiet.

Twenty of Cooper's closest friends gathered for a Monday night rosary at the mortuary chapel. Admission to the funeral on the following day was by printed invitation.

A solemn high requiem mass was offered before the sealed casket at the Church of the Good Shepherd by the Right Reverend Monsignor Daniel Sullivan, who attended the actor in his final illness and was present with the family when he died.

Active pallbearers at the funeral were Jack Benny, Charles Feldman, William Goetz, Henry Hathaway, James Stewart, and Jerry Wald. The honorary pallbearers named by Rocky were the most prominent people of Hollywood and the world. They were Ernest Hemingway (his illness barring his attending), Deane Johnson, John Wayne, Henry Ford II, Bing Crosby, Burt Lancaster, Peter Lawford, Tony Curtis, Dick Powell, Walter Brennan, William Wyler, David O. Selznick, Irving

Lazar, William Winans, Kirk Douglas, Pat di Cicco, Danny Kaye, Samuel Goldwyn, and Fred Zinnemann.

In lieu of flowers, the family asked that contributions in Gary Cooper's name be made to the Sloan Kettering Institute for Cancer Research in New York.

Fans kept their respectful distance as an all-star cast of mourners arrived at the church in Beverly Hills. Two of the less familiar people there were an eighty-six-year-old lady and her sixty-five-year-old son: Mrs. Alice Cooper and her son Arthur.

During the mass, Jack Benny sat beside Bill Goetz in the front pew reserved for the pallbearers. Toward the end of the service, a mass movement of humanity came toward the altar to receive Holy Communion.

Benny had never been in a Catholic church before. Quizzically, he turned to Goetz. Before he could ask, Goetz replied, "I don't know, Jack."

The comedian, who could break up quicker than any of his fans, tried to hold back the laughter. As the cortege left the church for burial at Holy Cross Cemetery, he was still trying to control himself. To spectators, he was racked by silent sobs, tears streaming down his face, holding on to Edie Goetz for support.

With the finality of Gary Cooper's death, family and friends went about reorganizing their lives. One woman who had desperately loved him could no longer grieve. Patricia Neal had mourned his passing almost ten years ago.

One of Rocky's first acts in the next few weeks was to call in interior designer Jimmy Pendleton. She wanted to refurbish her dead husband's spartan suite, to remove the smell of sickness that permeated the air. The memory of Cooper's last days still lingered, and, not surprisingly, she moved back to New York to start a new life there.

In June 1964, Veronica Balfe Cooper married Dr. John Converse, the doctor who performed her first husband's cosmetic surgery. Maria Cooper was twenty-eight when she married concert pianist Byron Janis in April 1966. In October 1967, Mrs. Alice Cooper died at the California Convalescent Hospital at the age of ninety-three. After her son's death, she had moved to Palm Desert to live with her firstborn son, Arthur, a retired savings and loan company executive.

The body of Gary Cooper was removed from its grave at Holy Cross Cemetery in May 1974, and was reburied at Southampton, Long Island, closer to his two surviving women.

He survives, of course, as an American folk image, the tentative, questioning man who rose to the occasion to do the right thing. The very human, very flawed Gary Cooper and his stalwart, upstanding roles merged into one composite being. He was the same as the fictional characters he portrayed. He could have been, as students of film describe him, Tom Sawyer grown up or a stoical Abraham Lincoln. But it's not which one of these figures Gary Cooper in some way resembles, but that he has joined their ranks and will go down in history as one of them. Shakespeare wrote in *Henry VI,* "In thy face I see the map of honor, truth and loyalty." No roll call of American twentieth-century folk heroes would be complete without the man who was called by many names, and who represented those sterling qualities, and who was billed above the title as Gary Cooper.

Bibliography

Of special note in my research on the life of Gary Cooper is the voluminous Hedda Hopper Collection, which includes recorded but unpublished conversations the syndicated columnist held with the actor.

Agee, James. *Agee on Film*. New York: McDowell, Obolensky, 1958.

Anger, Kenneth. *Hollywood Babylon*. Phoenix, Ariz.: Associated Professional Services, 1965.

Bacon, James. *Hollywood is a Four-Letter Town*. Chicago: Henry Regnery Co., 1976.

Bankhead, Tallulah. *Tallulah*. New York: Harper & Brothers, 1952.

Behlmer, Rudy, editor. *Memo from David O. Selznick*. New York: The Viking Press, 1972.

Bogdanovich, Peter. *The Cinema of Howard Hawks*. New York: The Film Library of the Museum of Modern Art, 1962.

Brownlow, Kevin. *The Parade's Gone By*. Berkeley: University of California Press, 1968.

Capra, Frank. *The Name Above the Title*. New York: The Macmillan Co., 1971.

Carpozi, George. *The Gary Cooper Story*. New Rochelle, N. Y.: Arlington House, 1970.

Chaplin, Charles, Jr., with N. and M. Rau. *My*

Father, Charlie Chaplin. New York: Random House, 1960.

Cooper, Gary, as told to George Scullin. "Well, It Was This Way," *The Saturday Evening Post*, February and March 1956, eight-part series.

Corliss, Richard. *Talking Pictures.* Woodstock, N. Y.: The Overlook Press, 1974.

Crowther, Bosley. *Hollywood Rajah.* New York: Henry Holt and Co., 1960.

Dardis, Tom. *Some Time in the Sun.* New York: Charles Scribner's Sons, 1976.

Davies, Marion. Edited by Pamela Pfau and Kenneth S. Marx. *The Times We Had.* Indianapolis: Bobbs-Merrill Co., 1975.

DeMille, Cecil B. Edited by Donald Hayne. *The Autobiography of Cecil B. DeMille.* New York: Prentice-Hall, 1959.

Dempsey, Jack with Barbara Piattelli Dempsey. *Dempsey.* New York: Harper & Row, 1977.

Dickens, Homer. *The Films of Gary Cooper.* New York: Citadel Press, 1970.

Donaldson, Scott. *By Force of Will. The Life and Art of Ernest Hemingway.* New York: The Viking Press, 1977.

Dreiman, Diana S. *The Films of Fred Zinnemann: An Analysis.* Los Angeles: UCLA Master of Arts Thesis (unpublished), 1971.

Easton, Carol. *The Search for Samuel Goldwyn.* New York: William Morrow and Co., 1976.

Eells, George. *Ginger, Loretta and Irene Who?* New York: G. P. Putnam's Sons, 1976.

Federal Writers' Project of the Work Projects Administration for the State of Montana. *Montana.* New York: Hastings House, 1939.

Fenn, George N. and William K. Everson. *The Western* (expanded edition). New York: Grossman, 1973.

Franklin, Joe. *Classics of the Silent Screen.* New York: The Citadel Press, 1959.

Geduld, Harry M., editor. *Film Makers on Film Making*. Bloomington: Indiana University Press, 1967.

Harris, Radie. *Radie's World*. New York: G. P. Putnam's Sons, 1975.

Hart, William S. *My Life East and West*. Boston, New York: Houghton Mifflin Co., 1929.

Hecht, Ben. *A Child of the Century*. New York: Simon and Schuster, 1954.

Hemingway, Gregory. *Papa. A Personal Memoir*. Boston: Houghton Mifflin Co., 1976.

Hemingway, Mary. *How It Was*. New York: Ballantine Books, 1977.

Higham, Charles. *Marlene*. New York: W. W. Norton & Co., 1977.

————. *Warner Brothers*. New York: Charles Scribner's Sons, 1975.

Hotchner, A. E. *Papa Hemingway*. New York: Random House, 1966.

Jordan, René. *Gary Cooper*. New York: Pyramid, 1974.

Kanin, Garson. *Hollywood*. New York: The Viking Press, 1974.

Kitses, Jim. *Horizons West*. Bloomington: Indiana University Press, 1970.

Lasky, Jesse. *I Blow My Own Horn*. Garden City, N. Y.: Doubleday and Co., 1957.

Lasky, Jesse L., Jr., *Whatever Happened to Hollywood?* New York: Funk and Wagnalls, 1975.

Latham, Aaron. *Crazy Sundays. F. Scott Fitzgerald in Hollywood*. New York: The Viking Press, 1971.

Madsen, Axel. *William Wyler*. New York: Thomas Y. Crowell Co., 1973.

Manvell, Dr. Roger, Editor. *The International Encyclopedia of Film*. London: Crown, 1972.

Marion, Frances. *Off With Their Heads*. New York: The Macmillan Co., 1972.

Marx, Arthur. *Goldwyn*. New York: W. W. Norton and Co., 1976.

Marx, Samuel. *Mayer and Thalberg*. New York: Random House, 1975.

Mast, Gerald. *The Comic Mind*. New York: Bobbs-Merrill Co., 1973.

Maxwell, Elsa. *R. S. V. P.* Boston: Little, Brown & Co., 1954.

Medved, Harry, with Randy Dreyfuss. *The Fifty Worst Films of All Time*. New York: Popular Library, 1978.

Milestone, Lewis. *Autobiography*. (unpublished).

Morella, Joe and Edward Z. Epstein. *The "It" Girl*. New York: Dell, 1977.

O'Hara, John. *Ten North Frederick*. New York: Random House, 1955.

Palmer, Lilli. *Change Lobsters and Dance*. New York: The Macmillan Co., 1975.

Parish, James Robert and Don E. Stanke. *The Glamour Girls*. New Rochelle, N. Y.: Arlington House, 1975.

——— with Steven Whitney. *The George Raft File*. New York: Drake, 1973.

——— and Michael R. Pitts. *The Great Western Pictures*. Metuchen, N. J.: The Scarecrow Press, 1976.

——— and William T. Leonard. *Hollywood Players—The Thirties*. New Rochelle, N. Y.: Arlington House, 1976.

———. *Paramount Pretties*. New Rochelle, N.Y.: Arlington House, 1972.

———. *RKO Girls*. New Rochelle, N. Y.: Arlington House, 1974.

Quigley, Martin, Jr., and Richard Gertner. *Films in America*, 1929–1969. New York: Golden Press, 1970.

Robyns, Gwen. *Princess Grace*. New York: David McKay Co., 1976.

St. Johns, Adela Rogers. *Love, Laughter and Tears*. New York: Doubleday and Co., 1978.

Sarris, Andrew. *The American Cinema*. New York: E. P. Dutton & Co., 1968.

Schickel, Richard. *His Picture in the Papers*. New York: Charterhouse, 1973.

————. *The Men Who Made the Movies*. New York: Atheneum, 1975.

Sklar, Robert. *Movie-Made America*. New York: Random House, 1975.

Smith, John M. and Tim Cawkwell, editors. *The World Encyclopedia of the Film*. New York: Galahad Books, 1972.

Spence, Clark C. *Montana*. New York: W. W. Norton & Co., 1978.

Swindell, Larry. *Screwball: The Life of Carole Lombard*. New York: William Morrow and Co., 1975.

Thomas, Bob. *Joan Crawford*. New York: Simon and Schuster, 1978.

Vidor, King. *A Tree is a Tree*. New York: Harcourt, Brace and Co., 1952.

————. *King Vidor on Film Making*. New York: David McKay Co., 1972.

von Sternberg, Josef. *Fun in a Chinese Laundry*. New York: The Macmillan Co., 1965.

Walsh, Raoul. *Each Man in His Time*. New York: Farrar, Straus and Giroux, 1974.

Wellman, William. *A Time for Insanity*. New York: Hawthorn, 1974.

Willis, Donald C. *The Films of Frank Capra*. Metuchen, N. J.: The Scarecrow Press, 1974.

————. *The Films of Howard Hawks*. Metuchen, N. J.: The Scarecrow Press, 1975.

Wilson, Margery. *Clara Bow: Thumb Prints of the Famous*. Los Angeles: Chimes Press, 1928.

Wilson, Robert, editor. *The Film Criticism of Otis Ferguson*. Philadelphia: Temple University Press, 1971.

Wood, Robin. *Howard Hawks*. Garden City, N. Y.: Doubleday & Co., 1968.

Wood, Tom. *The Bright Side of Billy Wilder, Primarily*. Garden City, N. Y.: Doubleday and Co., 1970.

Yablonsky, Lewis. *George Raft*. New York: McGraw-Hill, 1974.

Zolotow, Maurice. *Billy Wilder in Hollywood.* New York: G. P. Putnam's Sons, 1977.

Zukor, Adolph, with Dale Kramer. *The Public is Never Wrong.* New York: G. P. Putnam's Sons, 1953.

ABOUT THE AUTHOR

HECTOR ARCE covered the Hollywood scene for *Women's Wear Daily*. In addition to *Gary Cooper: An Intimate Biography*, he wrote the best-selling, *The Secret Life of Tyrone Power* and *Groucho: The Biography of Groucho Marx*. He also coauthored *I Remember It Well* with Vincente Minnelli and *The Groucho File* with Groucho Marx. At the time of his death in April, 1980, Mr. Arce was working on another Hollywood biography and his first novel.

WE DELIVER!

And So Do These Bestsellers.

THE PRIVATE LIVES
BEHIND PUBLIC FACES

These biographies tell the personal stories of these well-known figures recounting the triumphs and tragedies of their public and private lives.

Bantam Book Catalog

Here's your up-to-the-minute listing of over 1,400 titles by your favorite authors.

This illustrated, large format catalog gives a description of each title. For your convenience, it is divided into categories in fiction and non-fiction—gothics, science fiction, westerns, mysteries, cookbooks, mysticism and occult, biographies, history, family living, health, psychology, art.

So don't delay—take advantage of this special opportunity to increase your reading pleasure.

Just send us your name and address and 50¢ (to help defray postage and handling costs).